A TRUE-BORN ENGLISHMAN

by M. P. Willcocks

BUNYAN CALLING
MARY QUEEN OF SCOTS
MADAME ROLAND
BETWEEN THE OLD WORLD AND THE NEW
ETC., ETC.

HENRY FIELDING

From a sketch by Hogarth

A TRUE-BORN ENGLISHMAN

Being the Life of
HENRY FIELDING

by M. P. WILLCOCKS

> For Books are not absolutely dead things, but doe contain a potencie of life in them to be as active as that soul was whose progeny they are; nay, they do preserve as in a violl the purest efficacie and extraction of that living intellect that bred them.
>
> *JOHN MILTON*

London
George Allen & Unwin Ltd
40 Museum Street

FIRST PUBLISHED IN 1947
All rights reserved

To.
W. S.

PRINTED IN GREAT BRITAIN
in *11 Point Baskerville Type*
BY C. TINLING & CO., LTD., LIVERPOOL,
LONDON AND PRESCOT

CONTENTS

CHAP.		PAGE
I.	The Harlequin Chamber	7
II.	Excursions and Alarums	12
III.	The Case of Miss Sarah Andrew	20
IV.	Début	29
V.	Fielding and the Beggar's Opera	41
VI.	Grub Street and the Author's Farce	51
VII.	A Young Man with a Cudgel	65
VIII.	The Romance of New Sarum	82
IX.	Fielding and Hogarth	99
X.	Pasquin's Challenge to Folly	108
XI.	The Tragedy of Wit Overthrown	117
XII.	Captain Hercules Vinegar	128
XIII.	Pamela and Shamela	140
XIV.	The Odyssey of Parson Adams	151
XV.	The Heart of Henry Fielding	167
XVI.	The Doves and the Serpents	178
XVII.	Fielding and the Forty-five	186
XVIII.	A Labour of Hercules	197
XIX.	The Domesday Book of Human Nature	210
XX.	The Fool and the Lady	234
XXI.	The Last Fight	248
XXII.	The Journey's End	262

EPILOGUE
THE VERDICT OF THE CENTURIES   274
BIBLIOGRAPHY   280

ILLUSTRATIONS

Henry Fielding	*Frontispiece*
Sharpham House, Somerset	*to face* 16
Sharpham House (*tree*)	17
Sharpham House (*doorway*)	32
East Stour Church and Farm	33
Back of House at East Stour	64
The Dining Room, Cradock House	80
Charlcombe Church	81
Fireplace of ' Tom Jones ' Room	96
Old Boswell Court	97
Frontispiece to " The Jacobites Journal "	112
Modern Bust	113
Fielding Lodge	224
Ryde—*1795*	264
Lisbon—*1793*	265

CHAPTER I

The Harlequin Chamber

IT is hay-making time and the air is full of summer scents and sounds while across the fields lie the long shadows of afternoon. Beside the tree-shaded Abbot's Way there runs a slow-flowing stream. We are approaching the birthplace of Henry Fielding—Sharpham Park, two or three miles to the southwest of Glastonbury, a house which stands below the famous Tor.

Even in the sunshine a ghostly pallor seems to lie over the gabled frontage of the east entrance and the stump of a big acacia tree which once grew beside the front door. Built in the sixteenth century as a country retreat by Abbot Beere, the last of the great building Abbots of Glastonbury, Sharpham carries to this day certain curious signs on its gable; a Tudor rose, a pelican feeding its young, a mitre, a portcullis, and the Virgin and Babe.

Through the deep shadowy porch, its door turning on ornamental hinges and covered with a design in hammered iron, we pass upstairs to the landing and thence by three steps again into the chamber which tradition says was the birthplace of the great humorist. A fine old room it is, filled now with the westering sunshine. Behind the panelling of age-blackened oak is a secret hiding-place known as the ghost's room.

This is the Harlequin Chamber whose little window once looked out across the low roof of the chapel. Cut into the stone wall below this there was to be seen a figure, described either as a Harlequin with crossed legs playing on a viol, or a riddling rebus of a cross and two beer barrels, a play on the Abbot's name, with a hint at his conviviality as well as his religion. For all the world knows that, like the Harry Fielding who was to be, the Benedictines were famous for hospitality.

But now the shape, whatever it was, has been weathered away by the rain and wind of the centuries. Gone too is Abbot Beere's chapel with its mullioned east window, and the great oak staircase, carved in every part, even on the treads, sold for

£1,600 to a museum, but still remembered regretfully by those who live here.

The woods of Sharpham once sheltered four hundred deer on the hill above the Moors. The great bell which used to sound even as far as Walton is still kept in the house. And ancient peace broods here even now : tick-tock, tick-tock, says the eight-day clock beside the stuffed squirrel eating a nut, which stands in the hall.

Here in April 1707 the little Henry Fielding was born in the monkish house which was then owned by his grandfather, Sir Henry Gould, Judge of the King's Bench, whose forebears had acquired the property some time after the Civil Wars. April would seem to be a good month in which to be born, since it saw the arrival of Shakespeare, perhaps on the 23rd, but certainly of Fielding on the 22nd, just a hundred and forty-three years later.

Nor could any place be more suitable than Glastonbury as the birthplace of this most English of all Englishmen. Far back into the past of our race runs the story of the hill and valley that was known to the Britons as Avalon, or Apple-tree Island, from the Welsh apal, an apple ; to the Romans as Avalonia ; and, later, to the Saxons as Glastonbury, perhaps from the Celtic " glas ", blue, the colour of the fen waters below the Tor.

When in 1909 the Abbey ruins were being excavated, and the foundations of the Edgar Chapel discovered, the strange series of automatic writings, known as the Glastonbury Script, were taken down. These describe most vividly the life of old days in Avalon as our forefathers knew it.

Here is the land in the time of the last Saxon Abbot : " an inland valley where the rugged head of the great hill kept solemn watch over the rich-fruited fields and mild water-meads of Avalon. At the calm sweet voice of a bell that called out of the green shadows, promising rest to the tired traveller and mercy for the hunted felon, the mill-wheel ceased to labour, the sickle spared the ripened corn-rows ".

By this time Avalon has become a land of corn and fruit, its waters have receded, its fens are drained. Forgotten now are the Celtic legends which made it the place of immortality to which King Arthur was borne by the three queens ; the valley has been Christianised, and Arthur displaced by Joseph of Arimathea.

The background of Fielding's mind, though he writes scarcely any descriptions of mere scenery, was always country England : his two great characters, Parson Adams and Squire Western, come out of the West ; his Sophia was a girl from a country town, and his Amelia a provincial lady bewildered by city ways. To him the West was Paradise on earth, and when a Jacobite nobleman was banished to Devon for having taken part in the Forty-Five, Fielding thought that such an exile was no hardship. Like the Saxon Abbot of the Glastonbury Script, the author of *Tom Jones* had often " passed the whimpering lambs in their windy pastures at the greening of the year ".

It was the " rich-fruited orchards " of Devon that Fielding remembered when, on his voyage to Lisbon, his ship lay wind-bound in Torbay. Three hogsheads of cider at a cost of £5 ; 10 were bought, one of them for his brother, " dear Jack ", who would certainly enjoy the pure apple juice of the West better than the brewage of turnip sold in London as cider.

The view from the summit of Glastonbury Tor is described in *Tom Jones*. When Squire Allworthy goes out to watch the sunrise from the terrace of his mansion, the scene before his eyes is in part what one may see from the Tor. Here before one is the river that " for several miles meandered through an amazing variety of meadows and woods till it emptied itself into the sea, with a large arm of which, and an island beyond it, the prospect was closed ".

This is the river Brue winding through woods and meadows towards the Bristol Channel. The island is Start in Bridgwater Bay. The right of the valley, says Fielding, is " adorned with several villages, and terminated by one of the towers of an old ruined abbey, grown over with ivy ". The Mendips and Quantocks can be seen from the hill, though they can scarcely be described, save by poetic licence, as a " ridge of wild mountains the tops of which were above the clouds ".

Yet another link exists between Glastonbury and Fielding. At the foot of the Tor, where legend says that the Cup of the Holy Grail was buried, there rises a spring so impregnated with iron that it appears to carry down clotted blood. Stories have always gathered round this Chalice Well ; and one of these brought prosperity to the town. This tale is of an old man, named Matthew Chancellor, who, for thirty years had suffered from asthma, till one night there came to him a dream in which he saw One who pointed to the spring, bidding him drink from it on seven successive Sundays and be cured. This he did, and the asthma vanished.

Rumour carried the news of the miracle till, according to the *Sunday Chronicle* of May 5th, 1751, more than ten thousand people were flocking into the town. Bath was deserted for the time, and the slopes of Wirral Hill became populous as they had never been before, not even in the days when the monks grew their grapes on the eastern side, where to this day the fields are known as the Vineyards.

But Fielding and his brother John being then proprietors of a London Register Office, there appeared in the *London Advertiser* a description of the miraculous " blood-spring " together with an announcement that a regular supply of the waters was being sent up weekly to the Universal Register. Here sufferers could procure it without the trouble of visiting the well.

According to the *Gentleman's Magazine* this was owing to the enterprise of J—e F——g ; who in fact added a personal recommendation : " Having seen," said he, " great Numbers of my Fellow Creatures under two of the most miserable Diseases human Nature can labour under, the Asthma and Evil, return from Glastonbury blessed with the Return of Health, and having myself been relieved from a Disease which baffled the most skilful Physicians", he advised them to seek this new cure. At this time Fielding was holding his court in Bow Street, a terror to highwaymen, cut-throats and thieves. But in all the turmoil of his life he had not forgotten Glastonbury.

The other tradition of the Chalice Well that it is haunted by the apparition of a man without a head, brings one back to Sharpham Park and the fate of the last Abbot of Glastonbury, then an old man of eighty.

Here in the great stone kitchen beneath the Harlequin Chamber Abbot Whyting was seized by the commissioners of Henry VIII and carried off to the Tower. Brought down again to Wells, he was there tried for treason on November 14th, 1539, the charge apparently being that he had been more faithful to the Church than to the State. Sentence of death having been passed, the next day, together with two monks, he was dragged on a hurdle to the top of the Tor and there hanged. His head was placed, according to the pleasant custom of those times, over the gate of the Abbey, while his quarters were borne to Wells, Bath, Bridgwater, and Ilchester.

In the farm to-day they still talk feelingly of the murder and of how the old man refused to plead for mercy. " No doubt ", they say, " he had made his peace with God ".

But the Glastonbury Script, under the signature " Johannes " speaks of how his bones were buried in the Edgar Chapel. " Yee martye was hee ", said Johannes. " They made a martyr's grave. He was not coffined, for they were but bones got by ye faithful from Bathe and Tauntone, and brought in secret. He was placed under ye altare, and they who pulled it downe when Elizabeth was Queene drew hym out. They knew not who he was, our Abbot ye knowe—He who swam in ayre when hee wold not. Whytynge ".

" He who swam in ayre when hee wold not " ; perhaps his eyes in death turned downwards toward his pleasant manor-house of Sharpham by the water mead. On the summit of the Tor where he died there stands the Tower dedicated to St. Michael and once adorned with two bas-reliefs, one of a woman milking a cow, and the other of St. Michael weighing a soul against the devil in a pair of scales.

It is Johannes, whatever he may be, whether earth memory or invention of the sub-conscious, who shall have the last word on Glastonbury and Sharpham. Johannes, who named himself Lapidator, Stone Mason. Of the birthplace of little Henry Fielding he writes in the mysterious script : " . . . Ye must see owre old Manor of Sharpham. There is somewhat for you there : search it diligently and the walls around ".

Then he insists again, " Ego sum Johannes qui ex memoria rei dico . . . . meminisco . . . dixi annorum 1492 ". Of this Lapidator another script says : " He went a-fishing, did Johannes, and tarried oft in lanes to listen to the birds and to watch the shadows lengthening over all the woods of Mere ".

" Ye see the howse in its first condition, and like a falling lace the dremes of later men obscure it ", says the script. This was written of the abbey, but is as true of Sharpham. One is very conscious of the " falling lace " in the Harlequin Chamber, from which the babe was to go forth to watch the ways of men in the eighteenth century and to make his " Bill of Fare " just plain human nature. He would have liked Johannes.

CHAPTER II

Excursions and Alarums

TO the cradle of little Harry Fielding the fairies had brought fine gifts: vitality, energy, a good heart, indomitable courage, a powerful mind, and above all, a tremendous zest for living. One quality only was wanting: Fielding was to see everything in the light of noonday. No poetic vision was his.

The marriage between Sarah Gould, the Judge's only daughter, and the Honourable Edmund Fielding may have been a runaway match. At any rate, in Lady Gould's own words, it was without the consent of her father and mother and " contrary to their good liking ". The highly respectable Goulds wanted no alliance with a wild young officer, even though he was the scion of an aristocratic house. But Sarah went her own way with her lover, as her son in his turn was to do later on with his beloved.

Lieutenant Edmund Fielding came of a long line of soldiers. A Fielding fought in the Wars of the Roses; under Prince Rupert it was a Fielding who fought for Charles I, and was made Earl of Denbigh, while his son was fighting for the Parliament. It has been said that at the end of the seventeenth century there was scarcely an English regiment without a Fielding.

Fierce fighters were they, both in battle and in duel. " In our street ", writes Pepys, " at the Three Tuns Tavern I found a great hubbub ; and what was it but two brothers had fallen out and one killed the other. And who should they be but the two Fieldings ; one whereof, Bazill, was page to my Lady Sandwich ; and he hath killed the other, himself being very drunk, and so is sent to Newgate ".

It was John Fielding, a Canon of Salisbury, brother of the two duellists, who was Harry Fielding's grandfather, through his son Edmund.

Blenheim, Ramilies, Oudenarde and Malplaquet ! The fine-sounding syllables seem to re-echo the English pride in the victories that Marlborough was winning over the French.

Lieutenant Fielding fought at Blenheim under Wade, and was probably absent in France when his eldest son was born at Sharpham.

The name Fielding is said to come from the old English Felden, or Felding, one who labours in the fields. Originally yeomen, the family had risen in life, had assumed the amusing crest of a nuthatch pecking at a fruited hazel bough, and the fine motto *Virtutis Praemium Honoris*. In the seventeenth century, when the head of the house was raised to the peerage, they supplied themselves with a table of descent from the royal line of Hapsburg. It was this imaginary ancestry which Gibbon had in mind when he wrote that magnificent verdict: " the romance of *Tom Jones*, that exquisite picture of human manners, will outlive the palace of the Escurial, and the Imperial Eagle of the House of Austria ".

Henry was of the same breed as his ancestors; a bonny fighter, though not with gun or sword, he counted himself always as a man of good breeding, and exacted from everyone —sometimes amusingly—a recognition of the fact. Yet he followed to the full the English gentleman's habit of being hail-fellow-well-met with people of every class. *Homo sum*, said he, and no human being was ever too high or too low for him.

Yet his friend, Mrs. Hussey, the mantua-maker in the Strand, says : " His manners were so gentlemanly that even with the lower classes with whom he frequently condescended to chat, such as Sir Roger de Coverley's old friends, the Vauxhall watermen, they seldom outstepped the limits of propriety ". A very typical eighteenth century way of putting it.

The Earl of Denbigh, head of the senior branch of the family, spelt his name Feilding, while Henry's line wrote it as Fielding. When the young man was asked one day why this was so, he replied : " I don't know, my Lord, except it be that my branch of the family was the first who knew how to spell ". But as a matter of fact Henry himself often signed his name Ffielding, with the double f, at the end of some of the few letters of his which have come down to us.

His Fielding kinship made him free of the great world in a social sense, but it was from his mother's family that he probably derived the great administrative faculties he was to show when he grappled with the hydra-headed monster of London crime and poverty.

Judge Gould, as he stares out from T. Hardy's mezzotint—a masterpiece of portraiture—is a careful, anxious, irritable man, one who feels himself responsible in a world of fools and knaves The keen eyes, the brows bent in exasperation, the beaked nose that hangs down almost to the wide, apparently toothless mouth, challenge one, even as they had challenged many a criminal, Old as he is, this is no lean and slippered pantaloon ; the quill pen in the fine hand is firmly held.

Of his wife, Lady Gould, we have no portrait, but the documents in the Chancery case which she brought against her reckless son-in-law, Edmund Fielding, prove her to have been a masterful woman who had not lived with a lawyer for nothing. She could fight as well as any Fielding.

The Judge's chief anxiety was, of course, that his daughter and her children should be provided for. Therefore only a few weeks before Henry's birth he left a legacy of £3,000 to Sarah for her sole use, " her husband having nothing to doe with it ".

By this time Edmund Fielding, now a Colonel, had apparently determined to settle down as a country gentleman. Sir Henry Gould then bought the estate of East Stour in Dorset, sending over oxen for ploughing as well as a " Dairye of Cows ". Again the Judge repeats his proviso that all profits and rents should go to Mrs. Fielding, and that her husband " should have nothing to do nor intermeddle therewith ".

Here then, in a farm on the outskirts of a village of thatched cottages, Henry was to pass the next years of his life. Here were born his sisters Sarah, Anne and Beatrice, and his brother Edmund.

The Judge had intended to spend part of his time with his daughter and her children at East Stour, and part, presumably, at Sharpham, with his only son, Davidge Gould. But the old man died in 1710, and it was now Lady Gould's part to watch over Mrs. Fielding and her children, and to protect them from that son-in-law who was probably even more distrusted by the old lady than by her husband.

The house at East Stour was the ancient rectory of solid stone with great oak doors, panelled walls and a large carved fireplace, just beside the church, on the site of the present farm, where the land runs down the hillside into the valley of the Stour. A great locust tree with an elder springing from its trunk stood outside. Orchards and vineyards stretched down towards " the pleasant banks of sweetly winding Stour ", where the willows were reflected in calm waters. Ducks and geese waddled round the pond, and the sound of many rivulets came from the meadows after rain. One Jemmy Tweedle, a wandering fiddler, who is mentioned in *Tom Jones*, was probably a figure well-known to the Fielding children.

It was this village and a neighbouring parish which, according to tradition, gave Fielding the originals of his two parsons, Parson Trulliber and Parson Adams in *Joseph Andrews*. Trulliber is said to have been the boy's first tutor, Parson Oliver of Motcombe, described in the novel as " one of the largest men you should see, and could have acted the part of Sir John Falstaff without stuffing. Add to this that the Rotundity of his Belly was considerably increased by the shortness of his Stature, his Shadow ascending very near as far in height when he lay on his Back, as when he stood on his Legs. His Voice was loud and hoarse and his Accents extremely broad ; to complete the whole he had a stateliness in his Gait when he walked, not unlike that of a Goose, only he stalked slower ". Of Parson Oliver it was related that " he dearly loved a bit of good victuals, and a drop of drink ".

However it may be with Parson Oliver as Trulliber, leaning over his pig-styes in adoration of his porkers, it is certain that the original of Parson Adams was the Rev. William Young, curate at East Stour from 1731-1740, and the friend of Henry Fielding to the end of his days.

Abraham Adams is Don Quixote in English guise, an idealist under whose simplicity there lived all the virtues of a good man, who is the Father in God of so many great figures in English fiction from the *Vicar of Wakefield* onwards. Fielding must have learnt to know him, probably not in boyhood, but when he lived at East Stour for a while in his later years.

However pleasant life in the country may have been for a merry company of children it was dull for a man who had fought under Marlborough, and in 1716, when his son was nine years old, Colonel Fielding is to be found at Prince's Coffee House in St. James's, playing faro, and losing £700 to an army captain and his sister, or " pretended sister ". Evidently there were good reasons why the prudent Sir Henry Gould should mistrust his son-in-law. Finally Colonel Fielding was threatened with a distraint of his goods, although it was then illegal to enforce payment of a gambling debt. How he escaped from this affair is not clear, but six years later we find him charged with owing to Mrs. Cottington, the children's aunt, the sum of £700, the exact amount of his debt to the card-sharpers.

To Lady Gould the whole affair must have been most distressing, especially when, on Mrs. Fielding's death in 1718, she was left the sole buttress between the six " infant children " and their reckless, gambling father.

Two years after his wife's death Edmund Fielding married again, his son Henry being by this time at Eton at a cost of " upwards of £60 a year ", according to his father's statement. And with the appearance of a stepmother on the scene, the battle opened between Lady Gould and her son-in-law. She had now taken a house in New Sarum, or Salisbury, with the idea of having the children to live with her for the sake of their education. Mrs. Cottington appears to have been left in charge of the house at East Stour, pending the removal of the children to Salisbury.

Events follow quickly on the news that the Colonel has married again. This means that he is leaving London to enter into residence at the farm, and a certain Mary Howard appears there with instructions that she is to prepare for the arrival of the bride and bridegroom.

The woman gives herself airs, and demands the household keys from Mrs. Cottington. When these are refused she makes a further request for a horse to carry her to—a Presbyterian meeting of all strange places ! But rumour has evidently been busy : the new wife is declared to be a " Papist ", and of course this upstart housekeeper was going to no Nonconformist meeting, but to mass.

No horse is forthcoming, and no keys. But ten days later comes the Colonel himself, and Mrs. Cottington is forced to yield up the castle she has been defending. She retires to her own room and remains there in ambush in order to watch these people and their treatment of the children. No doubt regular reports were carried to Lady Gould at New Sarum. According to these the new Mrs. Fielding, one Anne Rapha, or Raza, before her marriage, has locked up the Bible, forbidden the teaching of the Protestant catechism, and left the " Romish Prayer Book " lying on the window seat in the hall, that

SHARPHAM HOUSE, SOMERSET
From a print, published in 1826, showing the room in which Fielding was born.

SHARPHAM HOUSE, NEAR GLASTONBURY

favourite place for the storing of books in the eighteenth century, amongst them usually a copy of Baker's *Chronicle*.

What part young Henry played in this conflict we do not know. But both the housekeeper, the cook and the butler declared when giving evidence that " the eldest son in particular carried himself very unhandsomely towards the whole family in general ". It must have been a sordid home for the high-spirited boy, for Mrs. Cottington brings further charges, not connected with religion, but with food. The stepmother is treating the children in a most barbarous, cruel and inhumane manner ; the butter given them is rank, the bread poor, the beer insipid or sour, so that they are forced " to drink water several days together ".

On the other hand, the servants deny all this, declaring that the children were well fed, having two meat dishes at their meals, with fruit and strong beer or ale.

But Lady Gould feared even worse crimes on the part of the Colonel ; she suspected misappropriation of the funds left by her husband in trust for Sarah and her children. It was a fact that the trustees, one of them being Davidge Gould, had allowed Edmund Fielding to receive the rents and profits. The children therefore were in danger, not only of being reared as Papists, but of losing their patrimony.

Lady Gould's house from which she watched and plotted stood on the tree-shaded rampart which was then St. Martin's Church Street, now, alas, a row of ugly cottages. Beyond this rampart ran the road to London, the road which Henry was to follow so many times in the future.

At last the old lady took action, and on February 10th, 1721, a Chancery suit was brought against the Colonel on behalf of her six grandchildren, and in the name of Henry Fielding as plaintiff.

The gist of the charges made in the indictment was that, after using the rents of the estate for his own purposes, Edmund Fielding had " intermarried with one—Rapha, widow, an Italian a Person of the Roman Catholick Profession who has several children of her own and one who kept an eating House in London, and not at all fitt to have the care of (the Children's Education) and has now two Daughters in a Monastery beyond Sea ".

Moreover " he threatens to take (the Children) from School

B

into his own custody although (their) said Grandmother has taken a House in the City of New Sarum with an intent to have (her grand-daughters) under her Inspection and where (three of them) are now at School ".

Worst of all the defendant has " openly commended the Manner of Education of young Persons in Monasteryes ".

This was a clever indictment in those No Popery days. Nor would the " eating House " clause be without effect at a time when class distinctions were almost sacrosanct.

In his reply the Colonel claimed what was probably quite true : that he was in favour with Lady Gould " till he married with his new Wife ". This alone was it which had " Occasioned some Jealosye and Displeasyre in the Lady Gould, though without Just Grounds ".

But the main point in his defence is that actually he has spent more on the children's education than the whole income from the estate. His wife is not Italian ; nor did she ever keep an eating house. And, finally, that he can do more for the children on account of his relationship with his Noble Family than can their grandmother, who is now about seventy years of age.

This last remark is of course the sting in the tail of the Colonel's reply : he is avenging her insult about the eating house. He is an aristocrat ; the Lady is not ; she is old and he is young. No doubt the grandmother was made to smart —for a time, until the case was at last brought before the Chancellor.

But, as appears from the records, Edmund had done more than merely threaten to take away the children from their grandmother. Two of his servants were sent down to Salisbury with instructions to bring them up to London. The girls were now at a boarding-school in the town, probably placed there for safety by Lady Gould. But the school-mistress, one Mary Rookes, refused to give them up, while Lady Gould bolted her doors against the men. There was a lively scene at the siege, for the fellows were only able to deliver their message through the window. And this they did with curses. Or so we are told. But the children remained where they were.

At the same time a threat was held over Henry, then at Eton, that he would be taken away and sent to Westminster School, his father apparently then living in St. James's. But at this rumour the boy " eloped " from school on April 7th, 1721, going down to his grandmother's house at Salisbury. The Colonel was worsted at every turn by his rebellious family.

Counter charges began. After the Colonel had brought a Bill of Complaint against Lady Gould and Mary Rookes, demanding the custody of the children, Lady Gould replied by a Petition that they should not be moved until the suit had been tried. It was becoming clear that something definite should be done.

At last, in May 1722, the case came before the Lord Chancellor. And, prompted no doubt in part by the alleged papistry of that stepmother and the thought of the eating house, the Court declared for Lady Gould. The estate was to revert to the trustees, with a full account of the sums already spent by the Colonel, the children were to continue in their present schools, and even in holiday time they were to reside with their grandmother, " that they may not be under the influence of ye Defendant Fielding's wife, who appears to be a Papist ".

At this point there comes an echo of the affair at Prince's Coffee House when the Colonel had played at faro. For, by way of a parting kick, Mrs. Cottington sued him for the £700 lent to him, which she now desired should be added to the children's estate.

Lady Gould, in spite of her age and social position, had won all along the line. The three women in this affair, a bold triumvirate, Lady Gould, Mrs. Cottington and Mary Rookes, must have spent many a pleasant hour of mutual congratulation.

CHAPTER III

The Case of Miss Sarah Andrew

NOTWITHSTANDING this family quarrel there seems to have been no actual break between Henry and his father's second family. Certainly he was attached all his life to his blind half-brother, John, the " dear Jack " of the letters.

But the Colonel himself, who was made Colonel of the Invalids and died a Lieutenant-General, is rather to be felt than seen in the background of his son's life. Beside the solid flesh and blood figures of Lady Gould and the Judge, the Hon. Edmund Fielding is but a shadow. It is however of course possible that the army officers so vividly painted in *Amelia* may have been studied from his father's friends. One fact we do know, on Henry's own evidence, that the £200 a year which his father should have paid him " anybody might pay that would ". In this careless father we seem to see the faro player of St. James's who gambled away £700 in one night.

There is no record of Henry's life at Eton, though he was reputed to have brought away from it a good store of Greek and Latin. Probably he was not a " colleger ", but an " oppidan ", living in one of the boarding-houses. Of these no registers were kept. But at any rate, according to his father, the boy's fees amounted to £60 or £70 a year, a larger sum than was paid for the young Pitt.

Of his scholarship Fielding says :—

" Tuscan and French are in my head,
    Latin I write, and Greek I————read ".

Since the scholars of the 5th form had to write Greek verse, it has been conjectured from this that he never got above the 5th form, though he stayed on till his 18th or 19th year.

However this may have been, Fielding's pithy, nervous prose speaks for itself. It is the expression of a mind trained in precise and accurate statement.

More important still, from the great classic writers he learnt the stoic courage with which he was to face all the vicissitudes of a stormy life. An " unyielding-spirited man " is the description of an enemy. But it is a true one. Fielding in his middle life was one of those men who always seem to be rowing upstream with the wind in their faces ; and always he rowed steadily, and with unabated courage. Speaking of the classic writers, " these Authors ", he says, " though they instructed me in no Science by which Men may promise themselves to acquire Riches, or worldly Power, taught me, however, the Art of despising the highest Acquisitions of both. They elevate the Mind and steel and harden it against the capricious Invasions of Fortune ".

This man in his own life was to know sorrow, poverty, loss of friends, defamation and scurrillous abuse ; gradually, as time went on, he was also to become more and more deeply acquainted with " the Misery which everywhere surrounds us and invests us ". Yet to the very end he always preserved in the power-house of his mind a source of strength. The key to this power-house was put into his hand by the great writers of Greece and Rome.

In days of poverty and illness we find him reading Cicero's *De Consolatione* ; a splendid copy of *Plato* goes with him on that last voyage to Lisbon. He left a library, whose catalogue has come down to us, that was larger even than Dr. Johnson's, and one hundred and forty volumes of it were in Greek or Latin.

At Eton he must have plunged gaily into his study of *Homer*, *Virgil*, and above all, of *Horace*, whom he seems almost to have known by heart. When Parson Adams is reading *Aeschylus* Fielding shows him as oblivious of every incident of the road.

" Learning ", he writes in his heroic-comic style (" for without thy assistance nothing pure, nothing correct, can Genius produce), do thou guide my Pen. There, in thy favourite field, where the limpid gently rolling Thames washed thy Etonian banks, in early Youth I have worshipped. To thee, at thy birchen Altar, with true Spartan devotion I have sacrificed my Blood ".

That " birchen Altar ", the famous whipping-block of Eton, was a pair of moveable steps kept in a room off the library.

The country books of Fielding's childhood were probably the wonder tales of Guy of Warwick and the Seven Champions of Christendom. One might swear to it also that on the window-seat of the parlour at East Stour there lay Baker's *Chronicles of The Kings of England*, as there used to lie in West Country farms right down to the mid-nineteenth century, the *Apology for the Life of Mr. Bampfylde-Moore-Carew*, commonly called the King of the Beggars; a gentleman with whom Fielding was to have at least one encounter.

The Whole Duty of Man, the book to which Richardson's pure maiden, Pamela, used to have recourse whenever the attacks on her virtue were especially violent, was read aloud to the boys at Eton in Fielding's time. How thorough was the eighteenth century in its training of youth! Posteriors were made to tingle, ears were daily assaulted with moral instructions. It only needed the *Shorter Catechism of Scotland* to finish the good work.

A splendid figure of a fellow Fielding must have been when he left Eton in 1725, and all agog for life and adventure; over six feet in height, broad-shouldered, with " nose a little inclined to the Roman ", with dark eyes and cheeks radiant with health. Evidently his youth had got the better of his stepmother's bad bread and sour beer.

Lady Mary Wortley Montagu, who was his second cousin, tells us it seemed a pity he was not immortal, so well did he love life. No one could possibly have taken greater pleasure than he did in " an excellent sirloin of beef, or a bottle of Burgundy, with a damask rose, or a Cremona fiddle ".

Add to this *joie de vivre* the stoic spirit caught from the great Romans, and there you have Harry Fielding.

In one sense he is another Pepys: in him there is the gusto of the old diarist. Both men were filled with a strong sense of the work they were called upon to do, Pepys in his Navy, Fielding in his magistracy. And each man has left his mark on English history through this devotion to duty.

But there the likeness ends; Pepys was an epicure in taste, a great artist in living who " played his lute through plague and fire ", and whose tricky humour has made him the delight of the centuries. But Fielding was no epicure: he preferred roast beef to kickshaws. He played on no lute, and his humour is the homely criticism of a wise observer, his irony a drink like dry wine and often of fine vintage. Where Pepys was fantastic, Fielding is strong. Perhaps more of a thinker than an artist.

Of the three great satirists of the eighteenth century, Swift,

Pope and Fielding, it is Fielding who is the true humorist. Whenever he has a human being before him he is almost always kind whether this is in a novel or in his Court at Bow Street. He may cry : " *What fools these mortals be !* " but the twinkle in his eye shows little or no contempt. Fielding was a man healthy both in mind and body, and accordingly for him there is more comedy than tragedy in the human scene. There is only one exception to this : in *Jonathan Wild.* But Jonathan himself is not a human being at all : he is a symbol of all the foulness of hypocrisy which lurks behind the masks men wear. And hypocrisy is the one vice for which the author of *Tom Jones* has no mercy.

The case is very different with Swift and Pope ; the satiric spirit in Swift is rooted in horror of himself, in horror at his own body and mind ; in Pope the source of his power is that agony which possessed him at the sense of his own ugliness, of his own twisted body. For Pope was a genius whose love of beauty rose to the height of passionate worship.

Fielding we know was a student of the satirists. At Eton he learnt to admire the Roman Lucian, putting him later beside his two idols, Swift and Cervantes. These three, who " sent their satire laughing into the world ", he counted as his masters.

Curiously, however, he failed to grasp the inner sense of Rabelais, and still less did he appreciate the more cruel mockery of Aristophanes. Of these he says that " their design appears to me very plainly to have been to ridicule all sobriety, modesty, decency, virtue and religion out of the world ".

When a mind like Fielding's cannot pierce below the surface of Rabelais and Aristophanes, we can scarcely be surprised to find how often satire has been seen as pure ribaldry.

If the classics of Eton steeled the character of Fielding, the friendships he made there were invaluable in a worldly sense. His friendship with Lord Lyttelton lasted for a life-time ; Pitt he knew, and among the company at Radway Grange who listened to the reading of *Tom Jones*, according to tradition, was the great statesman. Fox was an acquaintance and the eccentric Charles Hanbury Williams to whom was entrusted the manuscript of Fielding's play *The Good-Natured Man*. With all these fine friends and with the famous wit, Lady Mary Wortley Montagu, as his cousin, the young Etonian was sure of finding a welcome in the great world of his time.

But his first essay in life was made among a much humbler class. In 1725, accompanied by his valet, Joseph Lewis, the young man was in the town of Lyme Regis. He seems to have been at the time in some sort of tutelage at the village of Upton Gray. In Miss Mitford's *Our Village*, when she is writing of her old Nurse Mossy, she describes how Henry Fielding, then on a visit to Overton, near Basingstoke, where Miss Mitford's grandfather was vicar, used to swing the children—Miss Mitford's own mother among them—in the great barn. " He had even swung Mossy herself to her no small edification and delight—only think of being chucked backwards and forwards by the man who wrote about Parson Adams. I used to envy that felicity ". Indeed, who would not ?

Lyme is a very picturesque town, but Fielding was not there to admire the scenery. His intent was to abduct an heiress, an offence which, according to the law, was punishable by death. In fact one Haagen Swendsen was actually executed for stealing Mrs. Rawlins, notwithstanding the excuse he made—that she had married him of her own free will. However, the penalty was not often exacted, and young Henry was prepared to run the risk.

There was living at this time in Lyme a beautiful fifteen-year-old girl, Miss Sarah Andrew, heiress to a great estate. Her family had been successful merchants whose country seat was at Shapwick on Stour, near Blandford. And Solomon Andrew, Sarah's grandfather, had been three times Mayor of Lyme.

The girl's parents were now both dead, and the estate was held in trust for the heiress by her two uncles, Andrew Tucker of Lyme, and Ambrose Rhodes of Modbury. But Tucker wanted her to marry his son John, and Rhodes was plotting to get her for his son Ambrose. Like a bird in the hands of the fowlers was Miss Andrew. And Ambrose it was who won the lady in the end . . . by the interposition of that young rascal, Henry Fielding.

The affair was not as mercenary on the Etonian's part as it looks at first sight, for Sarah was connected with the Fielding family, and no doubt there had been a flirtation between the two young creatures. Henry's uncle and guardian, Davidge Gould, had married the sister of Miss Andrew's mother, and the young lady would no doubt be sometimes visiting her aunt at Sharpham Park, or even at Lady Gould's in Salisbury. Further, it is quite likely that she had been carried off to her uncle at Lyme in order to free her from the attentions of that young detrimental, Henry. However that may have been, here was the young spark on Andrew Tucker's very doorstep, and on mischief bent.

Lyme's main street runs headlong down a steep hill to the beach where Monmouth landed, though the actual sands where his boats came ashore are now below the waves. Many stories are told of how the inhabitants buried their money and plate when the rising threatened. Some of these hoards may still be under the ground.

When the rebellion failed, the gallows were set up on these same sands, but the horses which were drawing the cart filled with Judge Jefferies' victims refused to budge, and so the men to be hanged had to walk to their death.

Here on the beach is the famous cobb, built in the thirteenth century. And in 1662 we find Pepys, with "peirs to build" for the Admiralty, writing to the Mayor of Lyme to send him cobb builders for work in Tangier.

Lyme from the time of Charles II was Puritan and very prim and straitlaced, so that when the ladies were coming down to bathe it was ordered by the corporation that a bell should be rung for all males to leave the beach. In this pious retreat the Sabbath was honoured so much that for long the sands were supposed to be haunted by an old woman who sang :—

" I rue the time —
I sold water for wine,
And combed my hair of a Sunday ".

Such was the retreat which was to be the scene of Fielding's attempt at abduction. No wonder the little town was horrified at his proceedings.

Just below the church, in a winding and somewhat narrow street, there stood in Fielding's time, and still stands, a beautiful Tudor house, with oak-panelled walls, a splendid oak staircase and, so it is said, a subterranean passage to the sea. This was Andrew Tucker's home, which now sheltered Miss Sarah Andrew.

One Sunday, perhaps when she was proceeding to church, the heiress was seized by Henry and his man with, no doubt, in eighteenth century style, a carriage waiting round the corner.

But Tucker's men were able to beat off the assailants. Miss Andrew was borne back into her uncle's house, and there, quite probably, put under lock and key. The following day, which was November 14th, 1725, her angry guardian lodged a complaint before J. Bowdidge, Mayor, and solemnly declared on his oath that he went " in fear of his life or of some bodily hurt to be done to him or to be procured to be done to him by Henry Ffielding, gent, and his servant or companion, both now and for some time past resident in the said borough " of Lyme Regis. Of Joseph Lewis he expresses the special fear that he will " Beat, wound, maim, or kill him ".

Here, in real life, is a familiar figure in the plays of the period—the confidential valet on whom turns many a comic story.

Only Lewis appeared at the court next day; apparently Fielding's contempt for these simple yokels kept him away. But before the mud of Lyme Regis was cleaned from his boots, he stuck up on a wall in his own handwriting this proclamation :

" Nov. 15th 1725
This is to give notice to the world that Andrew Tucker and his son John Tucker are clowns, and cowards.
Witness my hand
Henry Ffielding ".

And all this time we know nothing of what Miss Andrew was feeling or thinking. We do know, however, that Mr. Tucker packed her off to her other guardian in Modbury, South Devon, where soon after, like an obedient girl, she married that guardian's son and so became the ancestress of the Rhodes family of Buckland-tout-saints. Her portrait, which cannot now be traced, used to be kept at Bellairs, near Exeter, and was pointed out as a picture of Fielding's Sophia in *Tom Jones*.

But the original of Sophia was Fielding's wife, a very different lady, being a woman of character as well as of beauty ; a woman who in the world of fiction is the prototype of many good and lovely souls ; all of them simple and kindly women, and, after the old English fashion, gifted with unlimited patience where the sins and follies of men are concerned. This Sophia would never have allowed herself to be sold in marriage as Sarah Andrew did.

Fielding's visit to Lyme was a brawling affair. Nor did it

end with the attempt at abduction. For the Register Book of the town contains this note :—" Henry Fielding of Upton Grey in the county of Southampton, gent, maketh oath that yesterday in the afternoon . . . he was violently assaulted by a servant man of James Daniol——which servant man struck this Examinee two several blows in the face and other parts of his body without any provocation given to him by this examinat ".

Whether this affair had any connection with Miss Andrew's abduction we cannot tell. But the magistrates of Lyme must have been thankful when this young man vanished from their town.

That this was truly a case of first love, and not of mere money greed, is probable. Fielding seems to have been deeply wounded by Sarah's lack of courage. For, as he himself tells us, in the preface to his *Miscellanies*, he translated into burlesque verse part of the Sixth Satire of Juvenal, adding that this was " all the Revenge taken by an injured Lover ".

But the passages this " injured lover " chose for translation satirise the vilest vices of the women of decadent Rome ; an amusing revenge for being jilted by a fifteen-year-old country girl.

The young Fielding flew to verse making in these early love affairs of his. By 1728 he is still connected with Upton Grey, and very tired of it, though he has yet another lady love whom he names Rosalinda. The poem is headed " U—n G—y, alias New Hog's Norton ".

" As the daub'd scene, that on the stage is shown,
Where this side canvas is, and that a town—
Such our half-house erects its mimic head,
This side a house presents, and that a shed.

On the house-side a garden may be seen,
Which docks and nettles keep for ever green.
Weeds on the ground, instead of flowers, we see,
And snails alone adorn the barren tree.
Happy for us had Eve's this garden been ;
She'd found no fruit, and therefore known no sin.

Our conversation does our palace fit,
We've everything but humour, except wit ".

Here is the young man, even in the company of his Rosalinda, dreaming of " the daub'd stage ". In fact he must have been in London sometime in 1727, for his first play was acted there in February 1728, with the encouragement of the great Lady Mary Wortley Montagu. The young swan was turning his back on the duck pond to seek wider waters.

But not before he has written verses to yet another lady whom he addresses this time as " Euthalia ". She may have been of course a country girl, but it is very unlikely, for the atmosphere of the poem is somehow candle-lit, and far more suggestive of the green room at Drury Lane, where the charming Anne Oldfield presided, than of meadows and woods.

The words this time are in praise of a woman's mind, and run thus :—

> " In Locke's or Newton's page her learning glows ;
> Dryden the sweetness of her numbers shows ;
> In all their varied excellence I find
> The various beauties of her perfect mind ".

The verse is boyish, extravagant, and very strange as coming from Henry Fielding who derided all learned women, and whose preface to his sister's story, *David Simple*, is full of apologies because it was written by a woman.

But who is the lady so distinguished ? Is it Anne Oldfield herself, or an unknown ? The verses are passionate enough, but they scarcely fit a famous lady of forty-five, as Anne Oldfield then was. And certainly, however intelligent she may have been, the actress was not learned.

We shall never know who was this " Euthalia " to whom he writes :—

> " Burning with Love, tormented with Despair,
> Unable to forget or ease his Care,
> In vain each practis'd art Alexis tries ———"

CHAPTER IV

Débu̇t

A FEBRUARY night in 1728, just three years after the affair of Miss Sarah Andrew, with " the nimble candle-snuffer " going his rounds in Drury Lane theatre to attend to the lights on the pillars at a performance of Fielding's first play, *Love in Several Masques*. So dimly lit was the auditorium in those days that when Handel was conducting his music the devout were obliged to follow the score with candle in hand.

No young dramatist could have started under more favourable auspices. His cousin, Lady Mary Wortley Montagu, after reading the play in manuscript, attended two out of the three performances, and the darling of the town, Anne Oldfield, was taking the part of the heroine.

Here were the two social orders touched by Harry Fielding in virtue of his birth and his poverty : the beaux, the wits, and the aristocrats of the great world, and the actors and " Playhouse Bards " of Grub Street.

The young man was well aware of his good luck. " I believe I may boast ", he writes, " that none ever appeared so early on the Stage ". No doubt both women, the actress and the great lady, were fascinated by the handsome, brilliant youth. Anne Oldfield he certainly adored. " But the ravishing perfections of this lady ", he says, " are so much the admiration of every eye, and every ear, that they will remain fixed in the memory when these slight scenes shall be forgotten ".

The charm of this actress lingers round her name even yet. Great men admired her for intelligence as well as beauty, and the Abbé Prévost, the creator of Manon Lescaut, learnt English in order to follow her words on the stage. Yet the actors themselves distrusted her woman's wisdom, so that when it was proposed that she should share in the profits of the theatre, the protest was made that their affairs " could never be on a secure foundation if there was more than one sex admitted to the management of them ". But Anne herself was much amused at the quarrels and jealousies of her male colleagues.

She died in her forty-eighth year and, after lying in state in the Jerusalem Chamber, was borne to her grave in Westminster Abbey by statesmen as pall-bearers. The Dean, however, refused her a monument there because twice she had lived " under protection " and left two illegitimate sons. Yet she had attended at Court, and when the Princess of Wales asked if it was true that she was married to General Churchill, her witty reply must have left the lady guessing. " So it is said ", answered Anne, " but we have not yet made it public ".

When she lay shrouded in fine Brussels lace, with Court and Stage in tears, Pope published his famous lines :—

" Odious ! in woollen, t'would a Saint provoke
(Were the last words that poor Narcissa spoke).
No, let a charming chintz and Brussels lace
Wrap my cold limbs and shade my lifeless face ;
One would not sure be frightful when one's dead.
And, Betty, give this cheek a little red ! "

" The short life of beauty ", wrote kind old Colley Cibber in his *Apology*, " is not long enough to form a complete actress. In men the delicacy of person is not so absolutely necessary, nor the decline of it so soon taken notice of ". Like music heard in the distance are the very names of the actresses of a bygone age, each of them with her own peculiar power, lovely or gay, stately or beautiful ; Mrs. Bracegirdle, Mrs. Clive, Mrs. Cibber, Mrs. Siddons.

What a joy it must have been to the young playwright to hear his words echoing through the theatre from Anne's lips. Cibber, the manager himself, was in the cast, with Wilks, the perfect gentleman, always point-device and always word perfect.

" Life runs high ", wrote Cibber of himself. It was true of Fielding too. Both men lived their lives with gusto ; Cibber, afterwards to be Fielding's butt, with the zest of the perfect coxcomb whom no mockery could ever depress because he had such a consummate conceit of himself. In an age when everyone had a passion for explaining himself, Cibber explained himself best of all, though he violated all the rules of grammar in so doing. He shows himself high-hearted, gay, insouciant, unconquerable by fate, bounding up from every rebuff like a rubber ball. He loved to go powdered and scented in satin and diamonds, with the strut of a turkey-cock and the condescending manners of an affable prince. Pope was a fool to turn Cibber into the hero of the *Dunciad*. And if Fielding had not hated him so deeply, what a portrait of old Colley he might have drawn ! It is our misfortune that he did not.

Love in Several Masques would have been advertised with drum and trumpet in the streets. The bills for a tragedy were printed in red on the posts above the steps leading down to the Thames when the river was a highway. The City being still puritanical, the numbers of the theatre-goers were not large. They came from the fashionable quarters, from the great Squares, Cavendish, Hanover, Grosvenor, from the Inns of Court, and St. James's.

Between stage and audience there existed a sort of family feeling ; and since families are sometimes given to rows, so it was in the theatre. Either the fops in the boxes, the critics in the pit, or the footmen upstairs in the shilling gallery would start a catcall and a hiss, the prelude to a shower of half-eaten pippins, nuts and oranges, and for the actresses by way of chivalry, the rinds only. An actor once confessed that the sound of a cracking nut sent the shivers through his frame. Sheridan, when playing Æsop, was hit by an orange so that " it dinted the iron of his false nose into his forehead ".

In a moment the whole place would be a bear-garden and the candlesticks came handy as weapons. The rioters either hated the play or the author or the leading actor. Many times in the future was Fielding to endure this treatment, and bitterly did he protest against the meanness of it all.

The footmen were the worst offenders. Originally admitted only after the fourth act, by way of conciliation they now sat in the upper gallery, and became the pests of every theatre in London. " Dropt ", runs a contemporary notice, " near the Playhouse theatre in the Haymarket, a bundle of Horsewhips designed to belabour the Footmen in the upper Gallery, who almost every night this winter have made such an intolerable Disturbance, that the Players could not be heard ".

Fops found the orange wenches useful in carrying letters to the ladies in the boxes.

" At length 'tis done, the note o'er orange wrapt
    Has reach'd the Box, and lay in Lady's Lap ".

The stage boxes were actually built on the stage, and groups of spectators stood at the back of it, so that the actors often had to force their way to the front of the stage through a crowd; Juliet perhaps in her "banging hoop" or Falstaff carrying before him his fat belly. Behind Juliet lying on the tomb of the Capulets stood groups of Londoners in place of the tombs of her ancestors.

The moment an actor appeared on the stage the audience knew what was to be expected of him, even as children do when the Giant-killer comes into a fairy tale. If he wore a feathered head-dress, then he was cut out to die. A Queen, an Empress, or the heroine of a tragedy was bound to play in black velvet and "diamonds". And if a woman was going mad, she must needs do it in white satin. Stage dresses being costly, kings and queens often bequeathed their state robes to a company of players. To Betterton Charles II gave his coronation finery, and £700 a year was paid to Mrs. Cibber, Colley's daughter-in-law, for stage dress, "not counting the garniture of her head"—a tremendous item of expense.

Stage setting was of course never realistic. And we are told that "laying the cloth is not a more sure indication of dinner than laying the carpet of bloody work at Drury Lane", since actresses who had to swoon never fell on bare boards. And after a battle Falstaff sat, not on a stone or a felled tree-trunk, but on a crimson velvet armchair with gilt claws that was carried on to the stage for him.

Properties were simple. The *Tatler* gives a comic list of these: "One Shower of Snow of the whitest French paper; a Sea consisting of a dozen large Waves; the complexion of a Murderer in a Bandbox". For a forest one was sometimes fobbed off with a palm-tree. The play was the thing; not the historic scene. Yet when Garrick had to cry to the ghost of Banquo, "Never shake thy gory locks at me!" he must have felt a little doubtful, since the apparition wore on its head "a neat Tye-wig".

Great public events were sometimes announced from the stage or the royal box. In this way London heard from the lips of George II the news of the victory of Culloden. And according to an account of the time, this is how his speech began: "Animated with all that majestic grace which he so eminently possessed, he held out the paper and with an ineffable

SHARPHAM HOUSE, NEAR GLASTONBURY.   DOORWAY

EAST STOUR CHURCH AND FARM, TO-DAY

smile of grandeur and beneficence, uttered the exclamation ' Oh ! ' "

In the prologue to *Love in Several Masques* Fielding announces his aim in play-writing. It is satire, with ridicule as its instrument. He intends to use :—

> " Humour, still free from an indecent Flame
> Which, should it raise your mirth, must raise your
>   Shame.
> Indecency's the Bane to Ridicule,
> And only charms the Libertine or Fool.
> Nought shall offend the Fair One's Ear to-day,
> Which they might blush to hear, or blush to say.
> No private Character these Scenes expose,
> Our Bard, at Vice, not at the Vicious throws ".

At the first performance of a new play it was the practice of the Fair Ones to defend their modesty by wearing masks. On such an occasion the fan was not regarded as an adequate defence, though Fielding declares that :—

> " Say whate'er we can,
> Their Modesty's safe behind a Fan ".

The subject of his first play is the hackneyed one of the attempted marriage of a young girl against her will to a wealthy and titled suitor who has the misfortune to be a fool. Sarah Andrew of Lyme Regis was not forgotten. But in the play Fielding's heroine is not like his first love, and actually revolts against the privileges of " imperial Man ". To Sir Positive Trap, her wicked uncle, she protests " I can never like a Fool, I abhor a Fop ", even though he explains that the Fool has three thousand a year and a title. He hopes to see the time " when a man may carry his daughter to market with the same lawful authority as any other of his cattle ". The young dramatist was surely attacking evil with a bludgeon.

But the Fielding who had tried to abduct Sarah Andrew has now learnt some law, for Sir Positive warns the lady's true lover that " she is an Heiress, and you are guilty of Felony and shall be hanged ".

It is Lord Formal, that " empty, gaudy, nameless thing ", who receives the full attack of the playwright's scorn. The idiot has " rid down two Brace of Chairmen, and spent his day with three Milliners, two Perfumers, my Bookseller, and a Fan

c

Shop ". His colour, he moans, is so raised by these exertions that it will need " a fortnight's course of Acids " to bring it back to its delicate hue. And by reading—oh, shade of Harry Fielding who used to sit up half the night over his books—he has so vastly injured the Lustre of his Eyes that he has " perfectly lost the direct Ogle ".

" To be sold to this ! To be put up to auction ! " Helena will not endure it. Neither did Fielding's heroine in *Tom Jones*, who ran away from her father and her home to escape an unwelcome marriage, and so did mightily shock the sticklers for convention. The creator of Sophia Western surely loved a lass with a will of her own.

Contrast is the soul of comedy ; in *Love in Several Masques* the contrast is between the fop and the country squire, between Lord Formal and Sir Positive Trap. At first the fop is not sure what species of animal the country man may be, " unless he be one of those barbarous Insects the polite call Country Squires ". But " the Traps are housewives, cousin. We teach our daughters how to make a Pie instead of a Curtsie, and that good old English Art of clear-starching ". For " the Traps and the Simples are the two ancientest houses in England ".

In one sense all the characters in Fielding's many plays belonged either to the Traps or the Simples ; and certainly his great creation, Squire Western, is the most barbarous of all barbarous insects.

There is of course in this first play the usual mockery of marriage : " Courtship is to Marriage like a fine Avenue to an old falling Mansion, beautiful with a painted Front, but no sooner is the Door shut on us, than we are in an old, shabby, out-of-fashion'd Hall, whose only Ornaments are a set of branching Stag's Horns ".

Here is the right Restoration note ; here we have Wycherley and Congreve once more, yet with a different emphasis. The satirist is uppermost in Fielding, and the miser and the fop are not here for mere amusement : there is a flavour of scorn in it all which is unmistakable. " A lord is the prettiest thing in the world ", and the author's lip curls contemptuously as he writes.

But Fielding can laugh at himself : he has " acquired a perfect Knowledge of the great World without ever seeing it ", and has " discovered Knavery in more forms than ever Proteus had ". And certainly he was thinking of himself when he makes a character say : " My estate is too small, my Father was not a Baronet, and I am—no Fool ".

He was no fool. And this scorn felt by the man of intellect for the millions, " mostly fools ", of his fellow creatures is a characteristic which in part explains the carelessly wrought plays that he flung on the stage for money. His art in these is pure sign-painting. Yet it is sign-painting which does its work. When Fielding, even as a lad, writes down a fool or a knave, he does it in such a way that you can make no mistake about the kind of company you are meeting.

But he was being introduced to life too early ; his cousin, Lady Mary, and kind Anne Oldfield did him poor service when they induced Cibber to put *Love in Several Masques* on the stage.

Fielding knew this to be true ; years later he made Mr. Wilson say in *Joseph Andrews :* " Being a forward youth, I was extremely impatient to be in the World ; for which I thought my Parts, Knowledge and Manhood thoroughly qualified me. And to this early Introduction in Life, without a Guide, I impute all my future Misfortunes ; for besides the obvious Mischiefs which attend this, there is one which hath not been so greatly observed. The first Impression which Mankind receives of you will be very difficult to eradicate ".

This reputation for wildness it is which has pursued Fielding down to our own days. Yet what else but wildness was to be expected from a youth of Fielding's ancestry, a youth who had been plunged into the pleasure-loving London of his century, with no mentor in the background save a gambling, reckless father ?

But the Gould blood also was in him, and as time went on this came to the rescue of the Fielding strain. Harry the gay dog of popular legend, grew into the man of intellect and genius, who used the ugly story of a common receiver of stolen goods to build up an analysis of the roots of evil ; who created those most English of all characters in fiction, Parson Adams and Squire Western ; who gave the world the ideal portrait of a perfect woman, and who ended his life down in the slums of London, grappling with social evil in its most loathsome forms. He killed himself in the doing of it, but he left as his gift to our nation a new sense of social responsibility.

The pompous ass, his first biographer, Arthur Murphy, to whom we are largely indebted for this tradition of dissipation, was only anxious to paint his picture in the most startling colours he could find.

Old Chaucer wrote of his poor Parson that he taught " Christes lore and His Apostles twelve—but first he followed it himselve ". Fielding taught what life is ; but first he lived it himself. He gained his knowledge of what is in man, either good or bad, by living as a man and watching the ways of all manner of men. Books like his could never have been written out of saintliness, or piety, but from actual experience of both good and evil. Much of what he saw in men he hated : three vices especially—cruelty, hypocrisy and meanness. One folly he lashed with fierce scorn—the adulation of the so-called Great Man, an adulation which has brought more misery to the world than any other imbecility.

As life went on he gained his wisdom from all classes : from the players in the theatre, and the country squires down in the West, from the lawyers, his colleagues on the Western Circuit, and the " Nymphs of Drury Lane ", that ill-famed street in which even Letitia Pilkington, the adventuress, dared not live, from the fashionable crowd round Lady Mary Wortley Montagu, and the hack scribblers in Grub Street, from the people on the roads, and his father's friends in the army, the girls with whom he danced at New Sarum, and at last from the thieves, murderers and prostitutes of Bow Street police court.

One quality he valued above all others, the love of free and lavish giving out of the fulness of a kind heart. In this he gloried ; it is the saving grace of Tom Jones as of Tom Jones's maker. In *Joseph Andrews*, out of all the rich company in the stage-coach, it is the post-boy who strips off his greatcoat, his only garment, " swearing (for which he was rebuked by the passengers), that he would rather ride in his shirt all his life than suffer a fellow-creature to lie in so miserable a condition ". The lad, adds Fielding, with a lovely touch of characteristic irony, was afterwards transported for robbing a hen-roost.

Lady Mary Wortley Montagu says of her cousin, among many other things, that there was " a great similitude between his character and that of Sir Richard Steele. He had the advantage both in learning and, in my opinion, genius, they both agreed in wanting money in spite of all their friends, and would have wanted it, if their hereditary lands had been as extensive as their imagination ". She adds of Fielding that " his happy constitution (even when he had, with great pains, half demolished it) made him forget everything when he was before a venison pasty, or over a flask of champagne ".

The lady was never tired of harping on his appetite for the joys of life, but among these he certainly counted the love of work, especially of mental exertion. To her list she should have added, besides the pasty and the champagne, " or before a difficult point in Crown Law, an Ode of Horace, or the true rendering of an obscure Latin text ".

Murphy's evidence is that " disagreeable impressions never continued long upon his mind ; his imagination was fond of seizing every gay prospect ".

Suddenly, after the performance of his first play, the young man left London, and in March was enrolled as a student in the University of Leyden ; not, as was first supposed, in the Faculty of Law, but of Literature, that is of course in classical Literature. And by one of those curious odds and ends of fact that are carried down on the tides of history, we learn that he stayed first at the Casteel von Antwerpen, and, later on, with one Jan Oson.

The reason for this flight is unknown, though in his choice of a foreign University there was nothing unusual. Fielding was a student by nature, and Leyden, founded by William of Orange as a reward for its resistance to the tyranny of Spain, was famed as a centre of learning.

At this period the great Hermann Boerhave, professor of medicine, of botany and chemistry, was lecturing at Leyden. One cannot but regret that the young Englishman learnt nothing from this man of science. Had he done so, he might possibly have escaped the scourge of his century—gout. For Boerhave's diet scheme for this complaint was no alcohol, no acids, very little meat, but milk varied by bread and butter with cooked fruit. And this at a time when the English doctors recommended venison—particularly venison—canary, and a pint daily of red port or old rum, diluted with a quart of water. The gout naturally flourished exceedingly on this regimen. If everything else failed, one tried the famous tar-water. But Fielding, with his burgundy, champagne and roast beef, went on eating and drinking to his own bodily damnation.

Boerhave's knowledge seems to have made but little practical impression on his time, though he was so famous that when a Chinese student directed a letter to him as " the illustrious Boerhave, physician in Europe ", the letter reached its destination.

Holland, the only foreign country except Portugal that was visited by Fielding, left a very unpleasant impression on the young man. In Dutchmen he found no sense of humour : a terrible want in the eyes of a humorist. Always, too, they had " Pay me " on their lips. As for the girls, they were fat and slatternly, and merely stuffed with beef, pudding and plums. Nor did Fielding ever forget the smell of the canals, tree-shaded, sluggish and narrow, which intersected the streets of the town. " Delicious canals " in his satirical term. One thing alone did he admire in Holland : that a man could travel anywhere, and never fear an attack on his money-bags. A vast contrast indeed to England in the days when footpads infested the roads, and highwaymen sometimes worked at their trade in broad daylight.

When he returned to England after a stay of some two years, he brought with him the rough sketch of his play *Don Quixote in England*. Cervantes was one of his masters, and the land of windmills might seem a suitable place to inspire a new incarnation of the Don. But Fielding wanted the English, not the Dutch atmosphere, for his work.

Indeed, though this play was finished in 1733, it never really came to life, although in " Squire Badger " there is the first vague idea which was to be so magnificently fulfilled in Squire Western : here we have the pack of fox hounds, dearer to the Squire than his lady, even when he goes a-courting ; here is Sancho, afterwards to come to life in the inimitable Partridge of *Tom Jones*. But the soul is not in Badger as it is in Western. No Wycherley or Congreve could have created him, and Wycherley and Congreve were still Fielding's models.

Yet how English it all is ! When Landlord Guzzle complains that this foreigner, this Sancho, the Spanish Don's servant, is eating him out of house and home, he feels himself bursting with the sense that he is not as these poor creatures are who come from other countries. " No ", he cries, " I am an Englishman, where no one is above the law ". He would rather have soldiers quartered on him, and so be eaten up by his own country rogues—if indeed it is his fate to be eaten up. It is the tone of the whole century.

Of course in Goodman Guzzle's tavern there needs must be a sirloin of beef at the fire. Says Sancho : " I am so fond of the English roast beef and strong beer that I don't intend ever to set my foot in Spain again ".

As for Squire Badger, " your true arrant English Squire is the first dog-boy in his house. He eats, drinks and lies with his hounds ". And the only jewels in the landlord's house are but " two bobs that my wife wears in her ears, which was given her by Sir Thomas Loveland at the last election ".

Sancho's proverbs, being foreign, are well received by no one in the place, though some of them are quite good, especially " he that's hanged for stealing a horse to-day, has no reason to buy oats for him to-morrow ", and " he who has stood in the pillory ought to know what wood it is made of ".

The play, being Fielding's, must needs have an election scene. Accordingly, up comes the Mayor to the inn to beg Quixote to stand for " parliament man ". And " when we invite a gentleman to stand, we invite him to spend his money for the honour of his party ". But when the rival knight, also seeking election, arrives with six hundred freeholders who will vote for him, Quixote proclaims that " Within these two days not one of them shall be alive " to the horror of all the company of Englishmen. " For very honest gentlemen are all these freeholders ".

All this while Badger is asleep " as fast on the table as if he had been on a feather-bed ", although he had come to woo the Lady Dorothea. Well might Quixote say, when asked why he had come to England: " I was told there was a plenteous stock of monsters there ".

The huntsmen's chorus, sung to the tune of " There was a jovial Beggar ", is a rollicking measure indeed. It is all as English as a plum-pudding. But it is as far away as possible from the spirit of Cervantes.

Fielding felt the humour of *Don Quixote* but not the longing it expresses for something which this world cannot give us. His English Quixote, Parson Adams, is noble, brave, generous and absent-minded ; he believes in the goodwill of all men because he is full of goodwill himself. He has no care for money, and therefore is surprised when money-grubbers lie and cheat to get it. His inner world is not the world of everyman. So far he is Don Quixote.

That is as far as Fielding reached in portraiture. But Adams never actually forgets what is in a vision of what might be. He is born of eighteenth century England. The Spanish Don belongs to no century and no time. He is all of us who dream of the ideal. His windmills were built, not in Spain, but in the kingdom of the mind.

Nor is his Dulcinea a creature of the flesh. She is everyman's desire in womanhood but not for bed and board. She was not in Fielding's mind, nor can she ever be found on earth. She it is, as Hazlitt said, who——

" Still prompts the eternal sigh
For which we wish to live, or dare to die ".

Fielding's mind is no kingdom of romance. Its background is not a dream world, wide as the sky, but the common English scene. In his picture we shall find no peasant singing " the ancient ballad of Roncesvalles " as he drives his mules to plough at break of day. Instead, we have Trulliber feeding his hogs for market and the Parson hunted by the hounds who, his clothes being old, take him for vermin.

CHAPTER V

Fielding and the Beggar's Opera

WHILE Fielding's play was lasting out for a poor three days on the stage, the Town had gone " horn-mad " over Gay's *Beggar's Opera* which, starting on January 29th, was played for sixty-two days, though not consecutively. It earned for the author the comfortable sum of £600 on its first run, and made a fortune for Rich, the manager of the Lincoln's Inn theatre.

If anything could possibly have depressed the spirits of Cibber, Rich's rival at Drury Lane, who had refused the opera, it must have been the sight of the crowds pouring into Lincoln's Inn. What a chance he had flung away in that masterpiece which was making " Rich gay, and Gay rich ! "

The opera, so named from the festival of the beggars at St. Giles's, ran through England, Scotland and Ireland and was played in Dublin by a liliputian troupe of children under the enterprising Madame Violante who had given Peg Woffington her first part. This was to be carried in a basket which was slung from one of the dancer's feet as she walked the tight-rope, with another infant in another basket hanging from the other foot to keep the balance true. In the Beggar's Opera Peg played Polly Peachum when she was a child of ten.

Whether Fielding ever sat in the pit at Rich's theatre to see the performance, we have no means of knowing, though it is highly probable. However this may have been, between Gay's work and Fielding's there is a close link.

For the last heroic years of Fielding's life were to be spent in dealing with the very class that Gay had put on the stage, the rascals of the London underworld. All his powers would then be needed to defeat the craft of men like Peachum, the receivers of stolen goods, the organisers of crime ; to curb the tyranny of the Lockits, the goalers who sweated the last penny out of their prisoners ; to suppress the highwaymen like Macheath and to put an end to the shame of the ride to Tyburn and its glorification of crime and murder.

Nor was this all : the " Newgate pastoral " suggested to Gay by Swift had turned into a jesting mockery of the morals of the ruling class. At the back of it, in the eyes of contemporaries, moved Walpole and his ministers, the masters of bribery and corruption. The rascals of low life are symbols of the rascals of high life. And, lest this should escape the audience, they were told in the opera : " Through the whole Piece you may observe such a Similitude of Manners in high and low life as it is difficult to determine whether (in the fashionable Vices) the fine gentlemen imitate the Gentlemen of the Road ; or the Gentlemen of the Road the fine Gentlemen ".

This idea is the underlying motive of every political play that Fielding was to write ; it is the very pith and marrow of his analysis of evil in *Jonathan Wild*. The wretches who swarm round Newgate are often identical in nature with the sinners who sit in the seats of the mighty, but who do not often die on Tower Hill. " But ", he writes, " without considering Newgate as no other than human nature with its mask off, which some very shameless writers have done, I think we may be excused for suspecting that the splendid palaces of the great are often no other than Newgate with the mask on ; nor do I know anything which can raise an honest man's indignation higher than that the same morals should be in one place attended with all imaginable misery and infamy, and, in the other, with the highest luxury and honour ".

Throughout his life this was Fielding's feeling. As time went on, however, the fiery insolence of his youth gave place to that " Olympian serenity of irony " through which he can look down on evil doers and sometimes enjoy the humour of their rascality, though with a wry smile.

" The same genius ", he writes, " the same endowments, have often composed the Statesman and the prig, for so we call what the vulgar name a thief. The same parts, the same actions, often promote men to the head of superior societies, which raise them to the head of lower ; and where is the essential difference if the one ends on Tower Hill and the other at Tyburn ? Hath the block any preference to the gallows, or the axe to the halter, but was given them by the ill-guided judgment of men ? " The only difference, in fact, is that it is safer to be a king in the over-world than in the under ", for, " there is a crowd oftener in one year at Tyburn than on Tower Hill in a century ".

And as for the " greatness " before which men bow down, it " consists in bringing all manner of mischief on mankind ". To sum up, in an outburst of mockery he exclaims : " 'Tis the inward glory, the secret consciousness of very great and wonderful actions which can alone support the truly GREAT MAN, whether he be a CONQUEROR, a TYRANT, a STATESMAN, or a PRIG (thief).

" For my own part, I confess, I look on this death of hanging to be as proper for a hero as any other ; and I solemnly declare that had Alexander the Great been hanged it would not in the least have diminished my respect for his memory. Provided a hero in his life doth but execute a sufficient quantity of mischiefs ; provided he be but well and heartily cursed by the widow, the orphan, the poor, and the oppressed—I think it avails little of what nature his death be, whether it be by the axe, the halter, or the sword ".

Gay and Fielding were poles apart in character, Gay being easy-going and amiable ; content, with hosts of friends, to live in a cosy nook of some great house, where his clothes and his comforts could be provided as if he were a child. This was assuredly no rôle for a man of Fielding's tough and unbending temperament. Although at first he too looked for some lucrative post under government, and had experienced the bitterness of those who wait on a great man's pleasure, the only office he obtained, when his life was nearly over, was the despised position of a " trading justice ".

Gay, on the other hand, was given a lodging in Whitehall and the profitable sinecure of a lottery commissioner. Even his disasters were blessings in disguise. His money having been lost in the South Sea Bubble, his friends rallied round him. When *Polly*, the sequel to his *Beggar's Opera*, was banned by the Chamberlain on account of its satire, this fact advertised the book so well that it brought him in £1,000. But his affectionate patron, the eccentric Duchess of Queensberry, was banished from the Court for having tried to gain subscribers for it in the Palace.

One wonders whether the lady ever recalled that incident behind the scenes when she found the actors gathered round a table covered with mutton pies, while Peg Woffington held aloft a pot of porter and cried in that squeaking voice of hers : " Down with order ! Let Liberty prevail ! " But of course that would have been a memory of later days, since Peg was only a child of fifteen in 1729, when *Polly* was published.

Yet with a little more of that same Liberty *Polly* might have been as popular as the *Beggar's Opera*.

The tremendous vogue of Gay's masterpiece must have been a glorious example of success to all young and ambitious playwrights. A youth from the wilds of Devon, he was now a man of forty-three, and had started his career under far less favourable auspices than Fielding. The names associated with his boyhood are curiously suitable for this happy, kindly fellow. Born in a house, which still survives in Barnstaple, at the corner of Joy Street, he was educated, not at Eton, but at the local grammar school, which rises now like a tiny mediæval tower among the trees by the parish church. His schoolmaster there was called Luck, a man who had published verse both in Latin and English.

Gay ; Joy ; Luck : was ever a pleasanter promise given to a child ? Nor was the prophecy unfulfilled, if the couplet which they put on his tomb in Westminster Abbey was his true opinion. For it runs :—

> " Life is a Jest, and all Things show it,
> I thought so once, and now I know it ".

Fielding too was a jester, but of a different quality. Beside the wide river of his strong virility, Gay's light-heartedness is like a bubbling brook.

When we consider the exquisite eighteenth century taste for brocades and fine furniture, for prints and chinoiserie, we forget the other side of the picture, its love of the macabre. But at this conventional period, when most things, except women's bosoms, were covered up by the genteel, great importance was attached to the manner of a man's departure from this life and the funeral rites which followed. Theatrical deathbeds were modish, and the long drawn-out burial of Clarissa was quite in accordance with custom.

After a death therefore a respectable family not only tied up its knocker with crape and used crow's quills and black sand for its letter-writing, but sometimes chose stationery printed with a chaste design of skulls and cross-bones. It is this love of the macabre which explains the enjoyment of the Ride to Tyburn and, in part, the popularity of the *Beggar's Opera*.

Nor did Fielding himself altogether escape this passion. His description of the Palace of Death in his *Journey from this World to the Next* is one of the few examples of the grandiose in his writings. " Its structure ", he says, " was of the Gothic order ; vast beyond imagination, the whole pile consisting of black marble. Rows of immense elms form an ampitheatre around it of such height and thickness that no ray of the sun ever perforates this grove " ; and " round it sound for ever the hollow murmur of winds and the very remote sound of roaring waters ". Within sits " the Judge with a square black cap, an Inquisitor General in a robe embroidered with flames of fire ".

But suddenly Fielding, even in this solemn passage, goes on to tell how " one dressed in French fashion " was received by the Emperor Death " with extraordinary courtesy ". Yet the man so ushered in is neither King nor Emperor, but merely " a celebrated French cook ".

That is the spirit of the century : they liked the horrible, the macabre, but they liked comfort very much more, comfort of mind and body. And Hogarth's church scene shows the bewigged worshippers all asleep, the learned divine under the sounding-board solemnly reading his sermon, while the clerk eyes the opulent charms of a pretty girl. And over the alms-box the malicious artist has drawn—a cobweb.

But comfort at whiles becomes boring ; every now and then a man wants something to quicken the heart-beat and set the blood stirring. In Paris he could watch a man broken on the wheel, but in England the crowd loved the spectacle of the Tyburn Tree, and the procession from Newgate, down Snow Hill, along Holborn and the Strand to Tyburn Street, the Oxford Street of to-day, and thence to the place of hanging, near the Marble Arch. When Jack Sheppard was worked off, two hundred thousand people are said to have watched the show.

There were of course other diversions. Every week one could go, either on a Monday or a Thursday, to Hockley-in-the-Hole, where bulls and bears were baited, when sometimes, as a special treat, a beast was maddened by fire-works fastened to its body. The cock-pit brought all classes together, from dukes to chimney-sweeps. And the regular exhibitions included the Madmen in Bedlam, the Lions in the Tower, and the floggings in the Bridewells, where the victims were usually street women too poor to bribe the officials. As Fielding puts it in one of his plays :—

" Smaller misses
For their kisses,
Are in Bridewell banged ".

At these " bangings " an alderman with a hammer presided ; when he considered that the woman had endured enough, he would suddenly knock with this and so end the scene.

Besides these excitements most of the great, and many of the little, gambled furiously, Fox especially. And even " the good Lord Lyttelton ", Fielding's friend, looked forward to a time when his tall oaks might have to go, brought low by a throw of the dice after his son had come into the family estate. The Wheel of Fortune, the lottery wheel worked by Bluecoat Boys, served to provide excitement for humbler citizens. One lady is reported to have asked in church that the prayers of the congregation should be offered up for her success.

But after all it was the Tyburn Tree that provided the finest fillip for jaded nerves. This started even in the prison when, as the condemned sat round their coffins in the chapel, the place echoed with shouts of " Kick off your shoes " ; that is when the cart moved forward beneath the gallows and the moment had come to die. On the last Sunday morning, ladies of fashion were admitted to the prison to see the heroes who were to suffer next morning.

On the Sunday evening the sexton of St. Sepulchre's Church stood under the cells of the condemned in Newgate and chanted in the voice of a crier :—" All you prisoners within, who for your wickedness and sin after many mercies showed you, are now appointed to be executed to death to-morrow in the forenoon. Give ear and understand, that to-morrow morning the great bell of St Sepulchre's parish shall toll for you from six to ten, in order and manner of a passing bell—to the end that all godly people—may be stirred up to hearty prayers to God to bestow His grace and mercy upon you, whilst you yet live ".

A prayer book and an orange were given to each man, and on the steps of the church friends presented nosegays. But questions of precedence arose even here : highwaymen usually went in the first cart, but later on that honour was given to those who had robbed the Mail. The sexton again repeated his exhortation and the procession started. In Hogarth's print, " The Ride to Tyburn," a tall man in black is shown on the cart exhorting a poor wretch to repentance. This was Silas Told, an ex-seaman, who devoted years of his life to work among the outcasts. In his *Journal* Wesley writes : " To-day I buried all that is mortal of honest Silas Told ". At that time the great evangelist was at his work of arousing " the snoring church ", much to the disgust of Henry Fielding.

Loudly did the city chuckle when one of the condemned begged the sheriff to let an umbrella be held over him, " since it was a drizzling day, and he was inclined to take cold ! " Tradition says that the umbrella was granted.

Along the route pedlars sold nuts and oranges, and broadsheets warranted to contain the Last Dying Speech and Confession of the most famous of the men in the carts. A bookseller promised one of these that he would " tip him a coffin as handsome as a man need desire if he would only give him half a dozen more pages of confession ".

When at last the man stood on the cart with the rope round his neck, the hangman lashed the horse till it sprang forward, leaving the wretch to be slowly choked. Fifteen to thirty minutes the process often lasted, even though friends held on to the swaying legs in order to shorten the agony. One victim, after hanging for thirty minutes, was cut down still alive, " to the great admiration of the spectators ".

Strange figures hung round the place of death ; these were the veiled women in black who were buying bodies for the surgeons.

Nothing could possibly be more blood-curdling than such a subject as this. Yet out of it Gay built up his " Newgate Pastoral ". This is the death Macheath prefers to undergo rather than face those Furies, the women whom he has " married ". Says Polly of her highwayman : " Methinks I see him, sweeter and more lovely than the Nosegay in his Hand—What Volleys of Sighs are sent from the Windows of Holborn that so comely a Youth should be brought to Disgrace ".

This is the very sentiment on which Fielding was to seize in after years when he tried to abolish the horror of Tyburn. Take the " heroism " out of this spectacle which corrupted both the malefactor and the crowd, and give the criminal a solemn death. That was what he advocated.

But the show was not ended till 1784, when Fielding had been dead for thirty years.

It is easy to understand the popularity of the *Beggar's Opera*. It was English through and through ; here were no French frogs acting foreign comedies, no Italian eunuchs squawking unfamiliar airs in an unintelligible tongue. And those artificial sopranos of Handel's Italian opera did fairly make the English gorge to rise !

No, the airs adapted by Dr. Pepusch were almost all of them those which had been whistled or sung in Great Britain for generations : " London Ladies ", " Green Sleeves ", " Bonny Dundee ", " An Old Woman clothed in Grey ", " Old Sir Simon "—Squire Western's favourite song—" Lillibulero ", and the " Lumps of Pudding ", with dozens of others. Only the highwayman's chorus was sung to the melody of Handel's *Cara Sposa*, which, anyway, was being played on every harpsichord in England, and the march was taken from his opera *Rinaldo*. Even the chorus went sometimes to the tune of " Let the Waiter bring Clean Glasses ", which surely was English enough.

At this time every man with any pretence to fashion felt himself bound in honour to pursue the virtue of every attractive woman, whether maid, wife or widow. Therefore it was that heads nodded joyfully to the tune of :—

> " Press her, caress her. With Blisses, her Kisses
> Dissolve us in Pleasure and soft Repose ".

And applause naturally followed Macheath's sentiment when he remarked : " I love the Sex. And a man who loves might as well be contented with one Guinea as I with one Woman ".

But the joke is turned against him when his four " wives " appear, each with a child, and the gallant in terror exclaims :—

> " Here, tell the Sheriff's officers I am ready ", for
> " At the Tree I shall suffer with Pleasure since——
> Let me go where I will,
> In all kinds of ill
> I shall find no such Furies as these are ".

It was almost a patriotic duty to applaud such English wit as this. Besides, a joke is all the better for being old. Like wine, its bouquet is only improved by age.

No one in Fielding's days felt ashamed of being sent to prison, where, if you could pay for it, you might eat good dinners, drink good tipple, meet your friends and play cards. Only the debtors had to live on fourpence a day, and the paupers on—nothing. Even in fetters you could play the gentleman. Therefore Lockit says to Macheath that he has : " Fetters of all Prices, from one Guinea to ten. They will fit as easily as a Glove, and the nicest Man in England need not be ashamed to wear them ".

Never were the class barriers higher than in this age, yet crime and debt brought high and low at least under the same roof. And when " Capability Brown " was getting busy with his gardening, the ha-ha was coming into fashion to enclose the estates of gentlemen in place of a wall. But the ha-ha is a sunken bar just where the park ends and the wild begins, and is almost unseen. A certain levelling process had in fact begun. Highwaymen sometimes penetrated into the gambling rooms of the gentry, and all classes could meet at the masquerades. And when, at a wage of thirty shillings a week, the beautiful Lavinia Fenton as Polly Peachum sang :—

> " O ponder well ! Be not severe ;
> So save a wretched Wife !
> For on the Rope that hangs my Dear
> Depends poor Polly's Life ".

she was singing her way into the heart of the Duke of Bolton, who took her, not into " protection ", but as his Duchess.

And many an apprentice must have seen himself as Macheath, and many a London maid as Polly. In fact the opera itself was described at the time as " a glorification of crime ", so that " rapine and violence have increased ever since the first performance ".

But when Peachum sits in front of his registers and turns over the pages in order to plan a decent execution for next session, he is simply Walpole trying to find a scapegoat. Finally the rascally receiver decides that for the guzzling, soaking sot, Tom Tipple, the cart is absolutely necessary, and soon we have the women remarking that " Brother Tom, poor Man, he is among the Otamys at Surgeon's Hall ". The scapegoat in politics had been found.

It was the women who enticed to the gaming tables the men who were to die on the Tree. Says Lockit, " we are more beholden to Women than all the Professions besides ". It was generally believed that the great man's many mistresses had much to do with ministerial corruption.

In the mirror of the *Beggar's Opera* is reflected, not only Fielding's period, but many of his own ideas and prejudices.

CHAPTER VI

Grub Street and the Author's Farce

SWARMING over London, the fierce yellow-eyed kites looked down on Covent Garden. Here was the heart of Vanity Fair. On the famous Piazza walked the beaux, the fine ladies and the women of the town, with sedan chairs standing ready to carry the men to White's Coffee House. It was on a balcony opposite this gaming house that cunning Mrs. Letitia Pilkington used to water her flowers in order to catch the eyes of the gallant gentlemen who attended there.

Coffee houses abounded in Covent Garden, one of them, the Bedford, frequented by Harry Fielding, and taverns where the actors could dine at sixpence or a shilling a head, and drink, when in funds, champagne, punch and the cheaper wines from Lisbon, or the gin that was cheapest of all. When lit up on a fine evening the place hummed like a hive of bees, and round about, as well as in Fleet Street and the Strand, lived the " Hackney writers " in their garrets, the so-called dwellers in Grub Street, four thousand of them, so it was said. Along Thames side were held the masquerade balls started by Heidegger, Master of the Revels to George II, and denounced by the moralists as abodes of vice.

In Soho Square one could visit a drum, a rout, or a hurricane, three different ways of fleeting the time carelessly. In this Vanity Fair three worlds met, of the actors, the hack writers and the fine gentlemen : a Bohemia of fashion and poverty.

Bohemia was lively, but to live in St. James's Square, and to walk in the Mall, according to Dr. Johnson, " comprised nearly all the advantages that wealth can give ". He writes of the Duchess of Leeds in words that paint the Earthly Paradise of the century :—

> " She shall have all that's fine and fair,
> And the best silk and satin shall wear,
> And ride in a coach to take the air,
> And have a house in St. James's Square ".

At night the Mall blazed with flambeaux when the footmen were waiting for their ladies. Smoking was forbidden in this fashionable street for the sake of the ladies' noses. Gay, a London lover if ever there was one, exclaims in his *Trivia* :—

"Oh, bear me to the Paths of fair Pell-Mell,
Smooth are thy Pavements, grateful is thy Smell.
Shops breathe Perfumes, through Sashes Ribbons glow,
The mutual Arms of Ladies and the Beaux".

One year these ribbons bore the motto, " No Jews. Christianity for ever ! " and on pompoms were fastened crucifixes. Anti-semitism, though perhaps not as fierce as anti-popery, was by no means unknown.

Against the duels, fought in St. James's Park, or, further out, in Hyde Park, Fielding wrote in angry scorn at the wickedness and folly of such a custom. Probably he remembered the duel which his great-uncles fought in fratricidal strife.

In the matter of smells, this century was peculiar : lay-stalls, emptied by night-carts, were endured, city churchyards abounded and family vaults in the churches themselves, and yet one James Fair was actually prosecuted for annoying his neighbours by—the scent of coffee-roasting.

In the streets on a windy day the swinging sign-boards rattled overhead. And on a wet one puddles formed between the pebbles that were driven into the ground by way of pavement. Then the fop, delicately walking on red-heeled shoes, must beware of the water which dripped from spouts or fell from the projecting pent-houses. Perils abounded ; from bulls and muzzled bears going to be baited, from the flocks of asses waiting to be milked outside the tall houses. Street cries rent the air, in spring calling sweet smelling flowers, elder-buds, with nettles' tender shoots to cleanse the blood ; in autumn, plums and walnuts with " anny Bakeing Pears ".

In the age of white silk stockings and buckled shoes one had to be always alert in the streets.

" If cloath'd in Black, you tread the busy Town,
Or if distinguish'd by the rev'rend Gown,
Three trades avoid ; oft in the mingling Press
The Barber's Apron soils the sable Dress.
Shun the Perfumer's Touch with cautious Eye,
Nor let the Baker's Step advance too nigh :

The little Chimney-Sweeper skulks along,
And marks with sooty Stains the heedless Throng,
When Small-Coal murmurs in the hoarser Throat,
From smutty Dangers guard thy threaten'd Coat ".

The commonest shops in Fleet Street were the booksellers, with goldsmiths, printers, and one " Face Painter ", with many a sign of the quack medicine vendors. In these were sold " the Anodyne Necklace " for various complaints, " Incomparable Drops for the Palsy ", and, strangest of all, " A true Sympathetic Powder, curing all Green Wounds, and infallibly Tooth-Ache ". The surgeon's sign was a golden ball and acorn, while the quacks themselves were known by their scarlet dress. Fielding was to have many dealings with these when the demon Gout had him in thrall.

Between the fashionable world and the city there ran a deep gulf of difference ; the city was making money and the West End was spending it. And to make money was to live the good life, to be sober, industrious and church-going, though one might of course occasionally visit Vauxhall, Ranelagh, or Marylebone, and take the wife to see an execution at the Tree.

Not to be idle : that was the law. Hogarth's idle apprentice is hanged at Tyburn, but the industrious one sits at city banquets, wearing a wig, and becomes Lord Mayor of London, following the example of Dick Whittington, whose story he learnt from a ballad in his 'prentice days.

Many shop-keepers, mostly dressed in neat drab suits, but some in black velvet, owned a " box ", or country house, at Hoxton, or East Ham, enclosed by a hedge which shut out the world. Islington was a beautiful village, and Highgate and Hampstead were far off.

In the city church-going was the rule, with over forty churches in which prayers were read daily. No press-gang worked within its borders, but the trained bands were part of the defence system. And a city banquet, with the delicious calipash and calipee, of which Fielding speaks, where everyone helped himself from the dish with his own knife and fork, was a feast to satisfy Gargantua.

This was the London into which Fielding plunged on his return from Leyden. Faced with the problem of how to get a living, he had, as he says, to choose between being a hackney coachman or a hackney writer. Naturally he chose the latter, and so joined the company of free-lance writers for the stage or the press. These men, always hungrily seeking a patron, and hoping to make money by a dedication, yet were becoming more and more dependent on the public. The days of the patron were passing, and Dr. Johnson's famous letter to Chesterfield did little more than give the old system a parting kick. But the public was a bad paymaster, as Fielding was to discover during the years when he was following the trade of " Playhouse Bard ". He suffered much from Chaucer's complaint, an empty purse.

Yet he must have enjoyed the struggle since youth and power were his. And, as his first biographer says, life attracted him so powerfully that " like a vortex it drew in all his faculties ". One of these was an overmastering sense of fun. His farce of Tom Thumb, which he calls the *Tragedy of Tragedies*, is the very sky-larking of humour, and had the credit of making Swift laugh, Swift, who only laughed twice in his life, once at the performance of a Merry Andrew, and once when the ghost of Tom Thumb was killed. And as for jingling rhymes, fantastic or absurd, mock-heroic or mere doggerel, Fielding seems to have been able to produce them without pause.

The Grub Street hacks, amongst whom, for his poverty, must be counted Goldsmith, had to depend largely on their invention, even as Defoe had done when he found himself gravelled for lack of matter. One of them boasts : " The last summer I paid a large debt for brandy and tobacco, by a wonderful description of a fiery dragon, and lived for ten days together upon a whale and a mermaid—When winter draws near, I generally conjure up my spirits, and have my apparition ready against the long dark evenings ".

In Fielding's plays and farces, if we except Luckless in the *Author's Farce*, who is certainly autobiographical, all the so-called characters are mere pegs on which to hang a " humour " in the Elizabethan sense. Yet all around him, in theatre, tavern and coffee house ; at hurricane, masquerade or drum, " Human Nature " did most certainly abound. But not until he began to write his novels did he start to create those being so alive with flesh and blood that they seem to walk out of the pages.

Usually this fact is explained by saying that his plays were rattled off in a hurry in order to boil the pot, and that if the two hundred pounds from his father had ever materialised, then Fielding might have become a great dramatist. All this time he was simply learning to write. As he himself confesses, he left off writing for the stage just at the point when he ought to have been beginning.

Yet surely there is another reason. If we consider the characters in his gallery of English portraits, we find that they all spring from the atmosphere of southern England, its fields and woods, its manor houses and villages. They are spacious figures, one and all, who require the freedom of a wide and simple background. These are by nature no walkers in the Mall, no haunters of the Piazza. Even Captain Billy Booth is not safe until he turns his back on the Town.

Murphy's story of the play-writing is that, after a late night, Fielding would rush home to scrawl down a scene for the stage-manager. And next morning it would be sent round to the theatre written on the paper which had wrapped his tobacco. The same kind of tale is told of Handel: that he wrote his scores on scraps because he could not afford music paper. But a waggish commentator in Fielding's case once calculated how much paper he would use for a scene, and therefore how many hours he had spent in smoking before it was finished. It came to hundreds of hours.

In the *Author's Farce*, produced in 1730 at the Little Theatre in the Haymarket, we have a vivid picture of the ways of Grub Street where a young man of fashion is trying to live by his wits.

Harry Luckless cuts a fine figure in a laced coat, but he cannot find the money to pay for a dinner. His landlady clamours for the rent, crying, " Could I have looked for a Poet under lac'd Clothes ? " And when he offers her his unacted play, she answers very sensibly : " I would no more depend on a Benefit Night in an unacted Play, than I would on a Benefit Ticket in an undrawn Lottery ".

He appeals to pity : " I am afraid I shall scarce prevail on my Stomach to dine to-day ". " Oh ", snaps the heartless one, " never fear that. You will never want a Dinner till you have dined at all the Eating-houses round. No one shuts their Doors against you the first time ". Harry Luckless is the forerunner of Dick Swiveller.

But dinnerless, Luckless is still attended by a valet, as was

Fielding on most occasions. This fellow has been going round trying to get a patron for his master. He returns with the news that " his Lordship has such a prodigious deal of Business that he begs to be excused from reading the Play ". But Mr. Keyber, that is, Colley Cibber, " made no Answer at all ".

At this point Luckless becomes Napoleonic. " Jack ", orders he, " Fetch my other Hat hither. Carry it to the Pawnbroker's—and on the way home, call at the Cook's shop. So, one way or other, I find my Head must always provide for my Belly ".

The landlady chimes in : " Well, I am resolved when you are gone away—I'll hang over my Door in great red Letters, ' No lodgings for Poets '.—My Floor is all spoil'd with Ink, my Windows with Verses, and my Door has been almost beat down with Duns ".

Thereupon Witmore arrives in the person of Harry's friend, and not only pays the rent, but bursts out into a diatribe against the times.

" When the theatres are Puppet-Shows, and the Comedians Ballad-singers ; when Fools lead the Town, wou'd a Man think to live by his Wit ? If you must write write Nonsense, write Opera, write Hurlothrumbo, set up an Oratory and preach Nonsense, and you may meet with Encouragement enough—If you would ride in a Coach, deserve to ride in a Cart ".

Here is the young satirist shooting his arrows right and left. The Operas, alas, were those brought over from Italy by Handel, and derided by Fielding because they were foreign ; *Hurlothrumbo* was a concoction of nonsense which no sane mind could understand ; and the preacher was Orator Henley, whose chapel in Lincoln's Inn Fields was attended by a fashionable crowd. This pompous fraud, whenever he got up in his " gilt tub ", as Pope called his pulpit, charged a shilling entrance fee for the service, and so became a rival to the theatres. His " tub " was a gorgeous affair hung with velvet embroidered with *fleurs-de-lys*.

Waving his hands, beringed with diamonds, while " fluent nonsense trickled from his tongue ", Henley compared men to fishes—crabs, eels or pike. And accordingly in a parody of Aristophanes Fielding puts these verses in his mouth :—

"All men are Birds by Nature, Sir,
Tho' they have not Wings to fly ;
On Earth a Soldier's a Creature, Sir,
Much resembling a Kite in the Sky ;

The Physician is a Fowl, Sir,
Whom most men call an Owl, Sir,
Who by his hooting, hooting, hooting
Tells us that Death is nigh.

The Usurer is a Swallow, Sir,
That can swallow Gold by the Jorum,
A Woodcock is Squire Shallow, Sir,
And a Goose is oft of the Quorum.

Young Virgins are scarce as Rails, Sir ;
Plenty as Batts the Nigh-Walkers go,
Soft Italians are Nightingales, Sir ;
And a Cock-Sparrow mimicks a Beau ".

But how Harry Fielding is enjoying himself as he pours out this spate of doggerel ! Naturally it will not be long before he assumes the name of Scriblerus Secundus, after the title of the famous club which Pope founded for the purpose of flaying fools. Next he lets fly at wives and husbands, the cynical young dog, who was afterwards to prove himself the most faithful lover of his wife. The lines occur as an Epilogue to the "Pleasures of the Town ".

"Chang'd by her Lover's earnest Prayers, we're told,
A Cat was to a beauteous Maid of old.
Oh Gemini ! what Wife would have no Tail on !
Puss would be seen where Madam lately sat,
And every Lady Townly be a Cat.

Say, all of you whose Honeymoon is over,
What would you give such Changes to discover,
And waking in the Morn, instead of Bride,
To find poor Pussy purring by your Side,
Say, gentle Husbands, which of you would curse,
And cry, My Wife is altered for the worse ? "

And here is the young man's verdict on life as he has seen it : " what does the Soldier or Physician thrive on but by Slaughter ? The lawyer but by Quarrels ? The Courtier but by Taxes ? The Poet but by Flattery ? I know none that thrive by profiting maintain'd, but the Husbandman and the Merchant—and yet these are represented as mean and mechanical ". This was to break into one of the most cherished ideas of his time.

But the money from his friend once in hand, Mr. Luckless cries : " Jack, call a Coach ; and d'ye hear, get up behind and attend me ". No doubt he went out to dine sumptuously, with a bottle of wine.

To Fielding certain things were sacred because he knew them to be among the great possessions of the human race ; and one of these was Shakespeare and his plays. But in his time producers altered plots and would give a happy ending to a supreme tragedy. Garrick never rested till he had rescued " that noble play, *Hamlet* ", from the disastrous fifth act, and, even worse, given Cordelia a lover. Among the boldest of these offenders were the Cibbers, father and son. Fielding calls them by the name of Marplay, as later, Cibber was to be Ground Ivy, a creeping plant which will smother a great oak.

Says Marplay Junior : " Why, Sir, would you guess that I had altered Shakespeare ? "

" Yes, faith, Sir, no one sooner ".

But the answer produces no effect, and with great complacency Marplay continues : " My Father and I, Sir, are a Couple of poetical Tailors. When a Play is brought us, we consider it as a Tailor does a Coat ; we cut it, Sir, we cut it ".

The scene now shifts to a publisher's office where Dash, Blotpage and Quibble are scribbling away for dear life.

Quibble sings :

> " How unhappy the Fate,
> To live by one's Pate,
> And be forced to write Hackney for Bread !
> An Author's a Joke,
> To all manner of Folk,
> Wherever he pops up his Head, his Head ".

Among these " Jokes " we must not count the cold, proud Addison, nor Steele, the valiant, and certainly not Pope, the idol of the time, so that when he appeared in a crowded assembly of fashionables, they parted right and left to make a way for the sad little cripple.

The song ended, in comes Bookweight, the employer of these damned souls who toil like slaves for him.

" Fie upon it, Gentlemen ! What, not at your Pens ! Do you consider, Mr. Quibble, that it is a fortnight since your Letter to a Friend in the Country was published ? "

" And now, Mr. Dash, have you done that Murder yet ? "

" Yes, Sir, the Murder is done. I am only about a few moral Reflections to place before it ".

" Very well ; then let me have the Ghost finished by this Day se'nnight ".

" What sort of a Ghost would you have this, Sir ? The last was a pale one ".

" Then let this be a bloody one ".

In comes Mr. Index selling Mottoes for the pamphlets at sixpence or threepence each. But Bookweight beats him down. Surely he could get second-hand mottoes from the *Spectator* at twopence each ?

Scarecrow, a very pitiful fellow, is Bookweight's chief translator, and suffers from a complete lack of knowledge of every language but his own.

" Sir ", says he, " I have brought you a Libel against the Ministry ". Aside, Bookweight murmurs : " I have two in the Press already ". What he suggests is a translation of Virgil.

" Translation of Virgil ? " says Scarecrow, and adds truthfully : " I translate him out of Dryden ".

And thereupon Bookweight comes forth with a noble offer : " If you please to take your Seat at my Table, here will be everything necessary provided for you : good Milk-Porridge, very often twice a Day, which is good wholesome Food, and proper for Students ".

Porridge must have been so much poison in the eyes of the eighteenth century which loved roast beef, fat capons, and the favourite goose-pie.

But " Authors and Book-Sellers grow fat " even in the other world to which we are suddenly transported. And here a laureate—a hit at Cibber—is being elected for the Goddess of Nonsense. The scene is on the other side of the Styx, where all the people are damned. Yet not everyone can get admitted to the place. Hell, for instance, is too full of lawyers, so Charon receives orders not to carry over any more. At the brink of the river there now arrives a waggon-load of ghosts from England who were punched on the head at the last election. Also, to judge by the number of other passengers, there must have recently been a plague—or a fresh cargo of physicians come to town from the Universities.

Joke after joke, but most of them are hoary with age.

In this world of the shades according to Fielding they have "just as much Wit as there is in Amsterdam". But that is no wit at all. He never forgot either the smells or the dullards of Amsterdam.

"But what's to be done?" asks Luckless, "if writing don't gain me a Living, shall I turn Lawyer or Parliament Man? No, I'll turn Great Man; that requires no Qualification whatsoever". But the slang name for Walpole was Great Man.

This young man did certainly despise what he calls the Mob, meaning by that, "Persons without Virtue or Sense in all Stations, and many of the highest Rank are often meant by it".

Yet he was to excel, not in the portraiture of great wits, but of quite simple people. For all his learning Parson Adams is no intellectual. And none of Fielding's characters, except the oddities, ever indulges in abstract argument.

Wherever folly raised its head, Fielding pursued it. Cibber defaced masterpieces and broke all the rules of grammar and Henley was a charlatan. From Heidegger, a hideous Swiss adventurer, nothing better than *Hurlothrumbo* was to be expected, since he was a foreigner. But John Rich, manager of Lincoln's Inn theatre, who popularised pantomime, was the prime offender when he brought up machines and monsters from Bartholomew Fair to put them on his stage. Tumblers, rope-dancers, performing dogs drew crowds whilst Shakespeare was being played to empty houses. This degradation must needs appear horrible to a young man who made one of his characters say: "Who would converse with Fools and Fops whilst they might enjoy a Cicero or an Epictetus, a Plato or an Aristotle?"

"I am studying Folly", says Witmore in Fielding's play, "and am come to Town to publish it". And Rich, or Lun as he called himself after a famous Paris actor, was a Prince of Folly.

Many tales were told of this crafty man of business, this vulgar ignoramus, who did not know the difference between 'turbot' and 'turban', and who would say to an actor: "You can't act, and I won't larn you". Yet Rich made a fortune by his theatre, being one of those men who can smell success from afar.

And after all he seems to have been something of an artist with a thin vein of genius. In his skin-tight Harlequin suit, as close-fitting as a seal's fur, he mimed superbly, his masterpiece being "Harlequin Sorcerer", or the hatching of an egg by the heat of the sun. Every movement in this was alive, from the first stirring in the shell to the joyous flight in the sunlight.

"When Lun appears", wrote Garrick, "with matchless
    Art and Whim,
He gives the Power of Speech to every Limb.
Tho' masked and mute, conveys his quick Intent,
And tells in frolic Gesture what he meant".

But Rich himself despised this gift of miming and only longed to be a tragic actor.

Fielding has no compliments for his enemy and addressing Rich as Harlequin, says :—

"Thou shalt make Jests without a Head,
And judge of Plays thou canst not read ;
Whores and Race-horses shall be thine,
Champagne shall be thy only Wine ".

A Big Business magnate spending his wealth in the fashion of the 18th century ! Even for the man's miming Fielding has no admiration ; he only remarks that Rich as Harlequin had " a wonderful and singular power of scratching his Ear with his foot ".

Yet Lun, who lived to be sixty-nine, and spent his thousands mainly in eating and drinking was by no means a bad fellow. He had the honour of starting "The Sublime Society of Beef-Steaks " which lasted for seventy years and whose twenty-four members included Johnson and Hogarth. The steaks were cooked by Rich himself, the port being fetched from a tavern. Fielding, could he have mastered his scorn, might surely have enjoyed himself in this jovial company ? He would, too, have relished Peg Woffington's famous story of how, after nineteen unsuccessful attempts to see the great manager, she found him at last. He was drinking tea with his twenty-seven cats, one of whom was eating toast from his mouth, and another licking out his tea-cup. But Peg got the " Breeches

Part" she wanted at £9 a week and proceeded to create her famous rôle, Sir Harry Wildair.

It is a thousand pities that in Rich's case, as in Cibber's, Fielding's wrath blinded him to the fascinating absurdities of both men. With what zest he would have described Lun's condition when, after marrying his housekeeper who was a Methodist, the poor man " laboured under the Tyranny of a Wife and the Terror of Hell-Fire ". To Harry Fielding a Methodist was always fair game.

At this time Handel was carrying on his struggle not only to make Italian opera popular in England, but also to gain respect for music as a profession. It was looked upon as an amusement no more dignified than playing at ombre or quadrille. And a musician was little better than a mountebank. The elegant Chesterfield advised his son never to play the fiddle when he could get someone else to do it for him.

Fielding took the side against all foreign music. Always the True-born Englishman, he seems to have agreed with the verse :—

" In days of old when Englishmen were Men,
Their Music like themselves was grave and plain,
In Times from Sire to Son deliver'd down :
Now Heidegger and Handel rule our Town ".

And when, in 1728, Handel, for financial reasons mainly, was forced into partnership with Heidegger, Fielding must have felt that he was right in fighting against the flood of foreign singers and foreign music.

But Handel's music won, so that Gay, writing to Swift in Dublin, says : " The reigning amusement of the town, it is entirely Music ; real fiddles, bass violas, and hautboys ; not poetical harps, lyres and reeds ".

The great choruses of the oratorios suit admirably with this virile age of Fielding and Smollett, though probably Handel's generosity and his gifts to the Foundling Hospital had as much to do with his personal popularity as the power of his music. Stories everywhere were told of his vast appetite, his polyglot tongue, his devilish rages, and his generous heart. Again a subject made for Fielding's genius in character-drawing. What would we not give nowadays for biographies of Cibber, Rich and Handel, written by Henry Fielding !

But it is to Dr. Arbuthnot that we owe the truest contemporary appreciation of that colossal figure, the composer of the *Messiah*. " Imprimis ", wrote the doctor " you are charged with having bewitched us for the space of twenty years past. Secondly, you have most insolently dared to give us good musick and harmony, when we desired bad ". That fairly sums up the position at the time when Fielding was watching the spectacle of this great struggle.

The beauty that touched him in literature was the beauty of noble thought, of fine form. Trained like all his generation on the classics, he felt the shaping power of intellect rather than the stimulus of the emotions.

Yet he who counted Shakespeare among our priceless treasures valued beauty in art. In his great novel he goes out of his way to acclaim it. " Reader ", he says, " perhaps thou hast seen the statue of the Venus de Medicis. Perhaps, too, thou hast seen the gallery of beauties at Hampton Court.

" Now, if thou hast seen all these, be not afraid of the rude answer which Lord Rochester once gave to a man who had seen many things. No, if thou hast seen all these without knowing what beauty is, thou hast no eyes ; if without feeling its power, thou hast no heart ".

And as for music, his Sophia, although she played her father's favourite old English tunes to please him, " would never willingly have played anything but Handel ". And Fielding measured all things lovely, both in mind and body, according to the standard set up by his beautiful Sophia.

Always in this century it is the perfection of form that delights us in its art. Form shewn in everything : from its Sheraton and Heppelwhite furniture to the domes and spires of Wren, from Pope's heroic couplets to the perfection of plot in *Tom Jones*.

Among the finest achievements of its art are Pope's *Rape of the Lock*, Fielding's *Tom Jones* and poor Henry Carey's *Sally in our Alley*.

Yet only one of these gains the prize by pure beauty : that is *The Rape of the Lock*, woven by the sylphs out of moonbeam and candlelight, artifice bringing the last touch of perfection to simplicity.

Fielding's novel, altogether apart from its characterisation, stands on sure foundations, like a great building where every smallest detail is meant to serve a definite end ; or like a mosaic in which each fragment dovetails with its neighbours to make a perfect whole.

But *Sally in our Alley* touches our heart only by its pathos, so perfectly expressed in Carey's words and Dr. Arne's notes. The little song is like a stray bird flying in from another century, another way of living.

BACK OF HOUSE AT EAST STOUR, TO-DAY
Fielding's youth spent in a house on this site.

CHAPTER VII

A Young Man with a Cudgel

FIELDING'S plays now came fast and furious : in five years he was to produce seventeen. Certainly it was not the way to write masterpieces, yet they kept his head above water financially, and that was something of a triumph at a time when Rich's popularity as a manager was at its height ; when, as Fielding's friend Ralph, could say in the Prologue to the *Temple Beau* :—

" Only Farce and Show will now go down,
And Harlequin's the Darling of the Town ".

While " Lun " was riding the whirlwind and directing the storm, in Pope's words, the undercurrent of criticism and thought in Fielding's comedies and farces had to make headway against pure brainlessness.

Yet the tide of success was flowing now for Handel as well as for Rich after they became partners in production. It is strange to see great music thus linked in triumph with mean success.

Fielding's *Temple Beau* is a mere sketch of a law student who spends his time, not in study, but in gaiety. When Sir Harry Wilding comes up to see his son, he finds in his chambers no law books, but a copy of Rochester's poems, a few plays and a bill for £40 for a suit of laced clothes. The lad is no better than an extravagant rake. In precisely the same surroundings, the Middle Temple, Fielding was one day to be a law student of a very different calibre.

But something is happening to the young satirist, Henry Fielding. So far he has laughed at folly. But now, though he still laughs, the arrows of his wit are more often aimed at vice.

The Coffee-House Politician has two other titles, *The Justice Caught in His Own Trap*, and *Rape Upon Rape*. It is a curious fact that Fielding will often link two distinct and separate plots together without troubling himself as to structure. Here the Politician is a pure figure of comedy, while the Justice is a type of almost tragic evil. And the link between the two men is the Politician's daughter, Hilaret.

The first play is a skit on the coffee-houses. The hero is a man who knows how to cure every political evil. He lives for politics. His daughter disappears, but he is far more anxious over the invasion of England by the Turks, and the reported death of the Dauphin. Twenty schemes he has in his head to lay before the Government : one a way of paying off the national debt by making a machine which will carry ships on land. By way of a final gibe, he is made to protest, " I never drink anything but coffee, Sir ". He reads forty newspapers every day, and on some days fifty ; and of a Saturday about fourscore. When it is reported that the Dauphin is not dead, he exclaims in delight : " The loss of twenty daughters would not balance the recovery of the Dauphin ".

But Hilaret, his daughter, is now before Justice Squeezum, brought in as making a charge of assault against a man in the street. The Justice has a private room where he examines young girls. And calling Hilaret " my honeysuckle ", he plans to take her " into protection ". But by a clever plot he is himself shewn up to his virago of a wife.

The play is full of pungent comment on " the basket justice ", who " for half a dozen chickens would dispense with one dozen penal statutes ". The day was to come when Fielding himself was to be slandered as " a trading justice " like Squeezum.

The scene is enlivened by sharp arrows of satire : " You are as safe with a justice in England as with a priest abroad ; gravity is the best cloak for sin in all countries ". " I love to see a magistrate drunk ; it is a comely sight. When justice is drunk, she cannot take a bribe ".

But Squeezum is balanced by Justice Worthy, who certainly expresses Fielding's own judgment : " By Heaven ", he says, " it shocks me, that we who boast as wholesome laws as any kingdom upon earth, should by the roguery of some of their executors, lose all their benefit."

Thackeray found that all Fielding's plays were " irretrievably immoral " ; a strange tribute to Victorian propriety. Certainly evil scenes abound in these plays ; vice shows its ugly head, folly its asinine one. But the intention everywhere is as plain as way to parish church.

In both City and West End the coffee-houses flourished

And on these hung the social life of the time, since they were responsible for the separation of the sexes during the greater part of the day. While men of every rank could meet their equals and exchange ideas in an atmosphere which encouraged serious debate, the women were left to card-playing, auctions, and vapid tea-parties where sometimes they drank that " chat-inducing liquor ", green tea, and followed it often by a dram to help digestion. A lady seldom saw her husband till the evening, when he often came home drunk. In society the language between men and women was pure gallantry.

Not until 1750 was a breach made in this wall of separation, when the redoubtable Mrs. Blue-Stocking Montagu started a salon " Where the Fair sex could converse with ingenious and literary gentlemen ". Even so, it was to Madame du Deffand's drawing-room in Paris that Horace Walpole went in search of a freer intellectual atmosphere than any to be found in this country.

A contemporary print shows the interior of a coffee-house. Here is a roaring fire for the supply of constant hot water, with tea and coffee-pots all in a row in front of it. Just plain tables and wooden chairs, with as centre of it all, the pretty bar-maid behind her counter, " to receive the adoration of youth ". A proverb of the time says : " A handsome Bar-Keeper invites more than the Bush ".

According to Steele these " Idols " were the ruin of many youths. " I know in particular ", he writes, " goods are not entered as they ought to be at the Custom-house, nor law-reports perused at the Temple, by reason of one beauty who detains the young merchants too long near 'Change, and another fair one who keeps the students at her house when they should be at study . . . I saw a gentleman turn pale as ashes, because an Idol turned the sugar in a tea-dish for his rival ".

In the coffee-house one read the papers, like the Politician, those small sheets which usually came out two or three times a week, and could have one's letters left at this address.—For all these conveniences one had nothing more to do than to put down " one's penny on the bar ", and to expend another penny on a cup of coffee. When the price was raised to three halfpence, there was vast indignation, though finally, it seems, the price became twopence.

Men of business and men of fashion spent hours of the day in this genial atmosphere of good talk where equality reigned : you might sit next to a peer or a merchant, though gradually the classes sorted themselves out on the principle of birds of a feather. At White's gathered the aristocrats ; at Will's coffee-house, which lived on the reputation of Dryden, men of letters. At Lloyds in Lombard Street auctions were held, and the bidding was ruled by the burning down of a one-inch candle. The founder of the famous Kit-Cat, ominously said to be named from a mutton " pie ", was the publisher Tonson.

At the more free and easy taverns the clubs met, again with the same principle of class equality. And free and easy these taverns must have been when one reads of a man " washing his teeth in a tavern window in Pall Mall ".

In the little play, *The Lottery*, Fielding took a leaf out of Rich's book and put a Wheel of Fortune on the stage—no doubt to show how the cheating could be done.

Fielding's audience was a simple one, or at any rate, he thought so. Only too often did he fling his scenes to the people in pit and boxes as though he were feeding a dog with meaty bones.

But the *Grub Street Opera* of 1731 is like the first shiver of wind among the trees that preludes a storm. It is his first political satire, and in it he hits at the Great Man, Walpole, are far more daring than any in the *Beggar's Opera*. The play concerns the household of a Welsh Squire, one Ap-Shinken, whose general *factotum*, Robin, is accused of " making master brew more beer than he needed and then giving it away to his own family ". He also files the silver, and sells the glasses which he swears have been splintered by the frost.

Everyone in the theatre saw in the person of Robin the Prime Minister, selling patents and commissions in the Army and Navy. In fact, when a pamphlet appeared that attacked Walpole, it bore the title *Robin's Game*. Lady Walpole's passion for thrift is satirised frankly in a dialogue with Susan Cook on the eve of a dinner party.

" This sirloin of beef may stand, only cut off half of it for to-morrow . . . a goose roasted—very well ; take particular care of the giblets, they bear a very good price on the market . . . an apple pie with quinces—why quinces, when you know they are so dear ? "

Nor are the Walpoles the only objectives of this daring

young man. When Ap-Shinken's lady discusses theology with Parson Puzzletext, it is the Queen dabbling in theology. And the Prime Minister's mistress, Miss Skerrett, appears as " Sweetissa ".

But to counteract the general meanness in the atmosphere of the play, Fielding lets himself go in two songs, one in praise of roast beef and the other of tobacco.

" The Roast Beef of Old England ", always linked in men's minds with Fielding, would one day be sung by the audience in his Little Theatre at the Haymarket by way of defiance against the Government.

The lusty strains suit well with this robust century :—

" When mighty roast beef was the Englishman's food,
It ennobled our hearts and enrichèd our blood.
Our soldiers were brave and our courtiers were good.
    Oh, the roast beef of England,
    And old England's roast beef.

———

But since we have learnt from all-conquering France
To eat their ragoûts as well as to dance,
Oh what a fine figure we make in romance.
    Oh, the roast beef of England ".

It was sung to an English air, *The King's Old Courtier.*

Here is the Briton entrenched against the foreigner. John Bull, in fact, to use the title invented for him by Dr. Arbuthnot.

That Fielding smoked tobacco, while most of the rest of the world took snuff, is constantly asserted, generally by his enemies. And certainly in his rhyme in praise of it there is a touch of personal feeling. It is sung to the Freemasons' tune.

" Let the learn'd talk of books,
    The glutton of cooks,
The lover of Celia's soft smack-o,
    No mortal can boast,
    So noble a toast,
As a pipe of accepted tobacco.

———

The Courtiers alone
To this weed are not prone ;
Would you know what 'tis makes 'em so slack-o !
    'Twas because it inclin'd
    To be honest the mind,
And therefore they banish'd tobacco ".

Art thou there, old Truepenny, with thine honesty? 'Twas ever the Fielding virtue.

Echoes of the country sound pleasantly in this *Grub Street Opera*: " Henceforth I will sooner think it possible for butter to come when the witch is in the churn—for hay to dry in the rain—for cheese to be made without milk—for a barn to be free from mice—for a cherry orchard to be free from blackbirds —or for a churchyard to be free from ghosts as for a young man to be free from falsehood ".

The play was badly received. The *Grub Street Journal*, used by Pope when he wanted to attack an enemy, and in which he himself wrote under the pseudonym " Mr Poppy ", actually printed an advertisement inviting the dwellers in the " Street " to come to the theatre in order to hiss. Orator Henley announced in a sermon that the next performance of these " Hedge Actors " would be at Tyburn. It even appears that an attempt was made to arrest the actors in the play. Put on the stage on April 22nd, 1731, the *Grub Street Opera* was quickly abandoned.

By now Fielding had become the storm centre of attack on political corruption. He was also the most successful playwright in London, when in 1731, at the Little Haymarket, there was put on the stage his *Tragedy of Tragedies*, a farce in the mock heroic style on the subject of Tom Thumb, that aimed at " Bombast Greatness " which Fielding believed to be the greatest evil that has ever cursed mankind.

This play held the stage for occasional performances down to 1855, and, although it satirises Walpole as Tom Thumb, it does not " date " as do Fielding's other plays and can be enjoyed as the purest of pure farce. Immoral justices, lotteries, corrupt Prime Ministers, and coffee-house politicians belong to his century, and now seem ghost-like. But " Bombast Greatness " is never out of fashion, and flourishes to-day more vigorously, and with more fatal results, than ever before.

Tom Thumb's begetting is a mystery. But he is humble in origin :—

> " His father was a ploughman plain,
> His mother milk'd the cow;
> And yet the way to get a son,
> This couple knew not how;
> Until such time the good old man
> To learned Merlin goes,

> And there to him in great distress.
> In secret manner shows,
> How in his heart he wished to have
> A child, in time to come,
> To be his heir, though it may be
> No bigger than his thumb ".

And here he is, the Lilliputian, returned from a victorious war, with all his gory honours on his head. Every woman is in love with him, and he is ready to be fooled to the top of his bent.

But the play is more than a satire on " Bombast Greatness " in history ; it is also a parody of the ranting tragedies of Dryden and others : of " Bombast Greatness " in Literature, of such plays as the *Death of Alexander The Great.*

That irony of Fielding's which was to harden into something cold and sharp-edged is here present in *The Tragedy of Tragedies*, but molten and boiling, with little eddies of laughter. Modern tragedy, says he, is often greeted with laughter, why not a tragedy now at which the audience is expected to laugh ?

In the farce King Arthur's wife is one Lolla-Lolla, of course in love with Tom Thumb. So is her daughter Hunca-Munca. Just as the wedding of the two young creatures is about to take place, a tragedy happens and Tom Thumb is swallowed by a cow in the street. And when his ghost rises, the ghost too is slain by a courtier. Not even the ghostly greatness of this hero can survive.

After that an orgy of slaughter ends the scene. All the characters kill one another except the King, who kills himself. Fielding observes that in most modern tragedies the characters "drop" at once on the stage, but he keeps his to the end. And his final holocaust earned such applause that it was " difficult for the actors to escape without a second slaughter ".

On Tom Thumb's return from his victory over the giants, the Queen describes the nation's confidence in its defender :—

> " His arm dispatches all things to our wish,
> And serves up ev'ry foe's head in a dish.
> Void is the mistress of the house of care,
> While the good cook presents the bill of fare :
> Whether the cod, that northern king of fish
> Or duck, or goose, or pig adorn the dish ".

When the King gives Hunca-Munca in marriage to Tom Thumb, the lover sings a triumph song :—

" Whisper, ye winds, that Hunca-Munca's mine !
The dreadful business of the war is o'er,
And beauty, heavenly beauty ! crowns my toils !
I've thrown the bloody garment now aside,
And hymeneal sweets invite my bride.

So, when some chimney-sweeper all the day
Hath thro' dark paths pursued the sooty way,
At night to wash his hands and face he flies,
And in his t'other shirt with his Brickdusta lies ".

In every case the heroic shades off into the vulgar.
The jealous Queen thinks of the hero's lowly birth :—

" Can I bear
To see him from a pudding mount the throne ?
Oh can, oh can ! my Hunca-Munca bear
To take a pudding's offspring to her arms ? "

But the hero is actually a coward and dreads marriage.

" My grandmamma has often said,
Tom Thumb, beware of marriage.

And Noodle, a courtier replies :—

" Sir, I blush
To think a warrior, great in arms as you,
Should be affrighted by his grandmamma ! "

The whole farce in style is a travesty of the play-writing of the day. Habitual play-goers of course would recognise these echoes, now lost to us. So carefully did Fielding work at this side of the farce that the printed edition contains a series of foot-notes by the author himself, giving parallel quotations from popular plays.

Thus, when a character in *The Tragedy* remarks : " Thy voice, like twenty screech-owls, racks my brain ", the foot-note gives us the quotation from the play *Mary Queen Of Scots* : " Screech-owls, dark ravens and amphibious monsters, Are screaming in that voice ".

Again a cry is heard in Tom Thumb :—

" Oh ! Hunca, Hunca, Oh ! "

And the foot-note gives from *The New Sophonisba* :—
  "Oh ! Sophonisba, Sophonisba, Oh ! "

But all these references mean nothing to us now, since the plays so satirised are as dead as Queen Anne.

The courtiers, Noodle, Doodle and Foodle, certainly bring Dickens' list of ministers to the mind.

But the description of how a nation rises to resist when a foe attacks it has no comic descent into bathos like all the other descriptions. Fielding in his wildest mood avoided farce in this direction. He writes most eloquently :—

"So have I seen the bees in clusters swarm,
So have I seen the stars in frosty nights,
So have I seen the sand in windy days,
So have I seen the ghosts on Pluto's shore,
So have I seen the flowers in spring arise,
So have I seen the leaves in autumn fall ".

Fortunately the Parson's blessing at the nuptials of Hunca-Munca and Tom Thumb cannot be fulfilled because of the cow. It runs :—

"Long may they live, and love, and propagate,
Till the whole land be peopled with Tom Thumbs !
So when the Cheshire cheese a maggot breeds,
Another and another still succeeds . . .
Till one continued maggot fills the rotten cheese ".

And if a moral be wanted to explain a farce, here it is. Let us destroy the Great Man, the maggot, lest all the land be maggoty.

If Fielding's audience did not understand, while their roars of laughter filled the theatre, then he might have remarked as he does in the farce :—

"Oh, what is music to the ear that's deaf,
Or a goose-pie to him that has no taste ? "

But the veriest simpleton must surely have seen the thought that underlies the merriment of the *Tragedy of Tragedies*. Is not "Bombast Greatness" that abiding curse of humanity which has recurred again and again through the centuries to bring untold misery to millions ? A *Tragedy of Tragedies* it is truly called.

Tom Thumb pleased all classes in its day : it was acted in a booth at Bartholomew Fair as well as before the wits of the Little Theatre in the Haymarket.

At this point in his career with a great popular success behind him, Fielding, probably feeling that he could do what he liked with the play-goers, chose to put on a play which shocked even an eighteenth-century audience. This was *The Modern Husband*, no " Congreve wit-trap ", but a serious comedy. Lady Mary Wortley Montagu approved of it, apparently because she knew it reflected one side of fashionable life. Even the portrait of the girl of the period, which in the theatre was hissed, she thought was true to life.

But London would have none of it. Not only was it carelessly written, but worse still, it attacked the core of fashionable immorality, by showing a man about town inciting his wife to sell herself to a lover for fifteen hundred pounds. The subtitle, *A Willing Cuckold Sells A Willing Wife*, actually flaunted the subject in the eyes of the public.

This was the very crime which Theophilus Cibber, Colley Cibber's son, had in fact committed, not for a fee from the lover, but in order that he might get damages in court. And certainly Theophilus was not the only " willing cuckold " in London.

The principal scene was hissed, and the play had to be withdrawn, although it was actually performed for six nights. On the last night there were only five ladies in the boxes.

Right up to the close of his career as a playwright Fielding showed all too plainly his contempt for the intelligence of his audiences. And the story told by Murphy of his very late play, *The Wedding Day*, might well have been told of *The Modern Husband*.

According to this, Garrick " told Mr. Fielding he was apprehensive that the audience would make free in a particular passage ; adding that a repulse might so flurry his spirits as to disconcert him for the rest of the night, and therefore begged that it might be omitted. " No, damn'em ", replied the bard, " if the scene is not a good one, let them find that out ".

They did find it out, and Garrick, pursued by hisses, raced off the stage into the green room, where he found Fielding drinking champagne. " He had by this time drunk rather plentifully and cocking his eyes at the actor, with streams of tobacco trickling down from the corners of his mouth, exclaimed : " What's the matter, Garrick ? What are they hissing now ? "

" Why the scene that I begged you to retrench ; I knew it would not do ".

" Oh, damn'em ", said Fielding once more," so they *have* found it out, have they ? "

Told as maliciously as possible by Murphy, this anecdote is very enlightening, and explains why Fielding's social satire was so often unpopular. Not only was it outspoken, it was often contemptuous as well.

The Modern Husband too is more like a novel than a play. And, as Colley Cibber wisely remarks in his *Apology*, there are scenes which we can read quite comfortably, but which would be utterly repellent on the stage.

Still unrepentant, and indeed defiant, Fielding produced his *Covent Garden Tragedy* in 1732, close on that other play which had been damned. Apparently he was so enraged by the reception of *The Modern Husband* that he seems to have been in the temper of a bull in the arena who charges even at the spectators after his hide has been pierced by a hundred darts.

In this new play, which even the genius of Kitty Clive, then Miss Raftor, could not save, Fielding confronts the bucks of the Town with a picture of their own vices. After creating in *The Modern Husband* two of the " vilest characters that ever entered into comedy ", as the *Grub Street Journal* put it, he chose as his scene for the *Covent Garden Tragedy* the back parlour of a notorious house in Covent Garden, and showed in it a well-known bawd, who had stood in the pillory and there been pelted.

The porter of this house he names " Leathersides ", remarking that, as he can read a playbill, he is therefore qualified to write the dramatic criticism in *The Grub Street Journal !* The man was in fact the porter of the infamous Rose Tavern and known as " Leathercoat ", because for a pot of porter he would lie down in the street for a carriage to pass over him. Fielding, like his friend Hogarth, was now making it possible for notorious Londoners to catch a glimpse of their own faces in the mirror of his art.

The riot which followed in the theatre must surely have been expected by him. Lotteries, Prime Ministers, and magistrates were fair game. Who cared if these were shewn up ? But however much the roués might have laughed in secret, yet it was intolerable impertinence when a " Playhouse Bard " dared to let the light of day pierce the dark places where they sought their pleasure.

In a hurry Fielding's adaptation of Molière's *Le Médecin malgré lui* was put into rehearsal and produced as a ballad opera in a single act.

Even in this the play must needs pillory a well-known character of the period. But this time the Town merely laughed when the scene showed up the famous Dr. Misaubin, the quack doctor of St. Martin's Lane.

The address to the physician is in the finest style of Fielding's irony : under its urbane exterior it is scathing indeed.

He writes : " Permit me, therefore, Sir, to prefix to a farce, wherein quacks are so severely exposed, the name of one who will be remembered as an honour to his profession, while there is a single practitioner in town, at whose doors there is a lamp of an evening ".

And, lest the poor man should miss the satire in this, Fielding mischievously adds : " I cannot pass by that Little Pill which has rendered you so great a blessing to mankind ".

No one, not even the quack himself, could mistake the tone of this. Yet before the end of his life, Fielding was to seek the help of several quacks, when the chief doctors of the time could do nothing to cure his gout, his dropsy, and his asthma.

The Old Debauchees, or the *Jesuit Caught*, put on in 1732, soon after the fiasco of the *Covent Garden Tragedy*, took for subject a *cause célèbre* of the day, and in this anti-popery period should have been highly popular.

Father Girard, Director of the Jesuit Seminary at Toulon, in October, 1731, had been brought before the Parliament of Provence and charged with having employed sorcery in order to seduce a girl. He barely escaped being burnt at the stake. This thrilling story was told over and over again in pamphlets and memoirs, as well as in a ballad-opera, *The Wanton Jesuit*.

Fielding provided the most delectable details in his play, getting his " copy " from a contemporary work, " The History of the Devils of Toulon ". Visions are seen, voices are heard, holy water is sprinkled, and the dirty priest is first flung into the horse-pond and then tossed in a blanket to dry him. English humour and French wit were thus pleasantly combined in this bid for popularity. But in characterisation Fielding evidently had Tartuffe in mind when he was at work on the story of Father Girard. At that time he was living under the spell of Molière who, as he says, " Nature's inmost secrets knew ".

The play is " right Fielding " in its jests. England is " that vile heretical country, where every man believes what religion he pleases, and most believe none ". The girl, Beatrice, is made to exclaim : " I have seen enough of a priest to-day, that I really believe I shall spend my life in the company of a layman ".

Fielding's plays at the moment were being written to show up the genius of Kitty Clive. This incomparable actress, whom Dr. Johnson thought the most natural romp he had ever seen, plays the part of the maid, Lappet, in his adaption of Molière's *L'Avare, the Miser*. She it is who frightens the miser by showing to what lengths extravagance can go.

But Lappet does more than this ; she can only be compared with that Figaro who electrified the Parisians in the days of Marie Antoinette by telling a noble that to gain all the privileges of his order he had done nothing, " save give himself the trouble of being born ". Says this English democrat : " Ah, Madam, what a pity it is that a woman of my excellent talents should be confined to so low a sphere as I am ! Had I been born a great lady, what a deal of good should I have done in the world ! "

Half satire, half truth, this saying, especially as it comes from the man who not only chose a footman to be the hero of his first novel, but made him a man of honour.

The list of the dishes at a feast in this play is indeed a revelation in these meagre days : you have at one end of the table a good handsome soup ; at the other a fine Westphalia ham and chickens ; on one side a fillet of veal roasted ; and on the other a turkey, or rather a bustard—" Then, Sir, for the second course a leash of pheasants, a leash of fat poulards, half a dozen partridges, one dozen of quails, two dozen of ortolans . . ."

All the edible birds of the air, in fact, in this rich menu. But the miser wants instead much " soup-meagre ", with " a good large suet pudding, a fine small breast of mutton, a salad, and a dish of artichokes ". But particularly plenty of soup.

Cibber, still ruling at Drury Lane, was now poet laureate. And, although Fielding, like Pope, might ridicule his absurd odes, yet it was necessary to work under a man so influential in the world of the theatre. Accordingly *The Intriguing Chambermaid*, written especially for Kitty Clive, was played at Drury Lane.

In the dedication to this actress, acclaimed by Dr. Johnson as " the finest player I ever saw ", Fielding offers her a splendid tribute which shows how highly he valued, not only genius, but goodness in a woman. It runs : " I cannot help reflecting that the Town hath one great obligation to me, who made the first discovery of your great capacity, and brought you earlier forward on the theatre, than the ignorance of some and the envy of others would have otherwise permitted—But as great a favourite as you at present are with the audience you would be much more so were they acquainted with your private character—did they see you, who can charm them on the stage with personating the foolish and vicious characters of your sex, acting in real life the part of the best Wife, the best Daughter, the best Sister, and the best Friend ".

It is a true charge against Fielding that the good, the kind and generous side of life is seldom expressed in his plays. He certainly gives the impression that the world he knows is inhabited by none but fools and knaves.

There are two reasons for this ; first, that his object is to satirise the evils of his time, and second, that he is, in style and manner, the successor of the Restoration dramatists. It is not until he finds himself in his novels that the true Harry Fielding comes out into the open, where the sun shines alike on the evil and the good, and the wind blows sweetly on high and low.

The completed version of *Don Quixote*, however, acted on March 12th, 1734, is country-born, and like a chapter out of *Joseph Andrews*. If it were only for its great hunting song, "Dusky Night Rides Down the Sky", it is worth preserving. Its jests too are as pointed as ever they were in his farces. Here is the motto of the average elector : " He that serves me best, will serve the town best ; and he that serves the town best, will serve the country best ". And very true is the saying.

This comedy of the open air closes very fittingly the first stage of Fielding's career as a playwright. For now the time was come when he was to go down to New Sarum to live through the idyl of his marriage with his beautiful Charlotte.

The purpose of these early plays is very well put in the Prologue to *The Lottery*, spoken by Cibber :—

> " As Tragedy prescribes to passion rules,
> So Comedy delights to punish fools ;
> And while at nobler game she boldly flies,
> Farce challenges the vulgar as her prize.
> Some follies scarce perceptible appear,
> In that just glass, which shows you as you are,
> But Farce still claims a magnifying right,
> To raise the object larger to the sight,
> And show the insect fools in stronger light ".

No definition of farce could be better than this. And the spectacle of the Great Man as an " insect fool " is surely very pleasing. This Prologue, too, throws a clear light on Fielding's intentions in his play-writing.

During these years as a " Playhouse Bard " the young Fielding—he was but seven and twenty when he went down to New Sarum—had pilloried a cheating publisher, an imbecile " politician ", a rascally magistrate, a " Bombast Hero ", a corrupt minister, a little Great Man, a willing cuckold, a sensualist, a quack, a miser, and a dreamer. Not a bad " bag " for the work of five years !

One of the plainest reasons for the enmity which Fielding undoubtedly aroused in certain quarters was that he had driven humbug and hypocrisy out of too many dark corners to please—humbugs and hypocrites.

Some of the attacks on him were due to mere snobbery. He was an aristocrat and aristocrats must not earn money by honest labour. " I am sorry ", writes one critic, " that any man so well born as this author should be obliged to receive a Benefit Night ". And another says : " I am ignorant of Mr. Fielding as to his person ; I pay deference to his birth : but I cannot think it a title to wit, any more than it is to a fortune ".

That Fielding lost his temper at the stings of the gnats which buzzed round his head is very clear from his reply to the *Grub Street Journal*. " I must tell our Critic ", he writes, (that) " there is a vein of good humour and pleasantry which runs through all the works of this author (himself) and will make him and them amiable to a good-natur'd and sensible reader, when the low, spiteful, false criticisms of a *Grub Street Journal* will be forgotten ".

Pope was, of course, a Catholic, and naturally disgusted by the whole tone of the *Old Debauchees* and especially by its mockery of purgatory and miracles. His organ therefore, the *Grub Street Journal*, attacked the author of the anti-Jesuit play. This it did for three months on end, declaring finally that Fielding's *Covent Garden Tragedy* was no better than an advertisement to bring trade to a brothel.

Yet even so, there were those who valued the plays put forth by Fielding and saw the purpose which lay behind them. These lines addressed to him by an unknown writer, have come down to us:—

> " Long have I seen with sorrow and surprise,
> Unhelp'd, unheeded, thy strong genius rise,
> To form our manners and amend our laws,
> And aid, with artful hand, the public cause.
>
> Proceed, even thus proceed, bless'd youth ! to charm,
> Divert our hearts, and civil rage disarm,
> Till fortune, once not blind to merit, smile
> On thy desert, and recompense the toil :
> Or Walpole, studious still of Britain's fame,
> Protect thy labours, and prescribe the theme,
> On which, in ease and affluence, thou may'st raise
> More noble trophies to thy country's praise.
> When modern crimes, to elder times unknown,
> With worse than Sodom's guilt pollute this town.
>
> Thy equitable Muse asserts her claim,
> To mark the monster with eternal shame,
> Thy brute appears, in the most just decree,
> Triumphant only in his infamy——"

To no Restoration dramatist could this naïve and simple tribute have been written.

And naïve and simple indeed must the man have been who expected help from Walpole for a writer who had written of him as Tom Thumb, the little Great Man, or as the butler Robin who robbed his master in the *Grub Street Opera*.

Yet even as late as 1731, Fielding would seem to have been not entirely without hope of receiving a post under government

[*Reproduced from "The History of Henry Fielding," by Wilbur Cross, by kind permission of the Yale University Press.*

THE DINING ROOM, CRADOCK HOUSE, SALISBURY

[*Grignion, Sculp*

CHARLCOMBE CHURCH, NEAR BATH

From an engraving of a drawing made 1784. Fielding married there to Charlotte Cradock.

which would keep him safe from want. He writes in his usual jesting style when he addresses the Prime Minister in verse :—

> " Great Sir, as on each levee day
> I still attend you—still you say
> I'm busy now, to-morrow come ;
> To-morrow, Sir, you're not at home.
> So says your porter, and dare I
> Give such a man as him the lie ? "

It is difficult to believe that in actual fact Fielding ever hoped to be given any of the many sinecures by means of which the Great Man was in the habit of silencing his critics. His laughter is too loud for any such expectation.

> " I'm not ambitious ", he writes in 1730, " Little matters
> Will serve us great, but humble creatures.
> Suppose a secretary o' this isle,
> Just to be doing with a while,
> Admiral, general, judge, or bishop ;
> Or I can foreign treaties dish up.
> If the good genius of the nation
> Should call me to negotiation,
> Tuscan and French are in my head,
> Latin I write and Greek—I read.
> If you should ask what pleases best
> To get the most and do the least ;
> What fittest for ?—You know, I'm sure
> I'm fittest for—a sinecure ".

It is interesting to speculate what would have been the result of such a sinecure being granted to the creator of *Tom Thumb*. It might have silenced him for a time, but surely not for long. And in the end Walpole was to find means to silence his assailant in quite a different fashion.

F

CHAPTER VIII

The Romance of New Sarum

DOWN in the pleasant old town of Salisbury where in days to come Tom Pinch was to drive Mr. Pecksniff's ancient horse, there lived at this time a widow with two beautiful daughters, Charlotte and Catherine Cradock. The fame of these fair creatures was spread abroad even as far as London, when Harry Price, the harbour-master of Poole, sang their charms in *The London Magazine*, and did it in Latin verse as well as in English.

But a greater man than the harbour-master was to make Charlotte Cradock's name immortal.

No town more suitable for a love idyll than New Sarum, set like a jewel in the Great Plain, with its tall spire and its smooth-flowing waters that reflect the drooping shadows of the willow-trees.

As early as 1730, and probably earlier still, Fielding must have known the Cradocks, Kitty the more sprightly and Charlotte the more beautiful. It is of the Cradocks that he makes Jove say :—

" To form whose lovely minds and faces,
I stript half Heaven of its graces ".

As for Charlotte, she is so beautiful that the preacher in the pulpit forgets his text when his glance falls on her. In all Salisbury, according to Harry, there is none so fair as she.

He is even rude to the *Nymphs of New Sarum* and exclaims :—

" Cease, vain nymphs, with Celia to contend,
And let your envy and your folly end.
With her almighty charms, when yours compare,
When your blind lovers think you half so fair,
Each Sarum ditch, like Helicon shall flow,
And Harnam Hill, like high Parnassus glow,
The humble daisy, trod beneath our feet,
Shall be like lilies fair, like violets sweet ;
Winter's black candles shall outshine the summer's noon
And farthing candles shall eclipse the moon ".

Charlotte, who is Sophia in *Tom Jones* as a girl, and Amelia in his last novel, had a dimple in her right cheek. When she had been dead for years Fielding set down in words a picture of her beauty.

It is a triumph song in which he hails Sophia : " So, bedecked with Beauty, Youth, Sprightliness, Innocence, Modesty, Tenderness, breathing sweetness from her rosy lips, and darting brightness from her sparkling eyes, the lovely Sophia comes ".

The reviewer who advised Arnold Bennett, when he complained of being sick of the eternal love-stories in modern novels, to seek " the love-wisdom in *Tom Jones* ", was making no mistake. Fielding knew all there is in love : worship, reverence, desire, adoration, comradeship, and afterwards long lingering memories of what has been.

In his Charlotte, whether as Celia, Sophia, or Amelia, Harry found a sweetness of temper that diffused a glory over her countenance ; with perfect breeding too, though this was perhaps not quite so easy as with the ladies " who live within what is called the polite circle ".

As if distrusting his own power of finding lovely images for this lady, he quotes from Sir John Suckling :—

> " Her lips were red and one was thin,
> Compared to that was next her chin,
> Some bee had stung it newly ".

The background of this romance is the country where those birds sing " whose sweetest notes not even Handel can excel ". From this we learn that Fielding could distinguish between the vulgarities of Rich and the beauty of the Water Music, or the power of the Hallelujah Chorus.

When Fielding, many years later, reprinted his poems in his collected *Miscellanies*, he omitted the names of the Salisbury Nymphs whose " little foibles " were mentioned in them. To affront them thus in print would be " mean in any man, and scandalous in a gentleman ".

By an odd chance there is preserved in the Public Library at Salisbury a book dated 1742, containing advice for those attending the Assembly balls, as Fielding probably had done many times. The author gives advice to those who wish to be considered well-bred. It is suggested " that no gentleman gives his tickets for the balls to any but gentlewomen—unless he has none of his acquaintance ".

And a most frank but ungallant rule : " That the elder ladies and children be contented with a second bench at the ball, as being past or not come to perfection ".

And further, for gentlemen : " That gentlemen of fashion never appearing in a morning before the ladies in gowns and caps show breeding and respect."

Yet in town " night-caps ", so-called, were regarded as correct wear before noon. Wigs were for going abroad. They showed rank and wealth, though the powder from them got into the soup at dinner, and the wigs themselves had to be flung aside in active exercise. In a cavalry charge a flight of wigs careered behind the riders.

Salisbury's book of etiquette gives a bad name to the town for gossip. " Several men of no character ", it observes, " old women, and young ones of ' questioned ' reputation are great authors of lies in this place ". And nowadays Salisbury folks will confess that its name is an anagram for " Busy Liars ".

Here is the description of how a lady enters the bath : " In the morning the young lady is brought in a close chair dressed in her bathing cloaks——. There the music plays her into the water and the women who attend her present her with a little floating dish, like a basin, in which the lady puts her handkerchief and a nosegay, and of late a snuff-box is added. She then traverses the bath—and having amused herself near an hour, calls for her chair, and returns to her lodgings ".

One could neither bathe, nor be hanged, without a nosegay. The Salisbury balls, held on Tuesdays and Fridays, lasted from six to eleven, hours " not to be exceeded ". But did Mrs. Cradock sit on that second bench as " being past perfection ? " Surely Henry escorted the ladies back to their home ? And, listening to the cathedral chimes at midnight, did he not watch the lighted windows 'till all were dimmed ?

Never, as a husband, would he wish to find, instead of a wife, " poor pussy purring on the pillow by his side ". He paints her portrait as Sophia : a rather tall brunette, with large eyes and black hair that hung below her waist until she cut it off to curl on the neck. Eyebrows full, even, and arched beyond the power of art to imitate. The nose with a little scar on one side, from a carriage accident . . . An oval face, a long

THE ROMANCE OF NEW SARUM 85

neck, skin of a delicate white that with emotion coloured so that " no vermilion could equal it ".

The comfort of Salisbury is perfect : " Our butter cannot be exceeded ", says the little book on etiquette, " the herbage of the neighbourhood being sweet ". Complacently the writer adds " No city in the world can be furnished with better and cleaner cook maids ". A Paradise indeed !

But it is the inns of the city which linger in one's mind : the Old George with Roman coins in its wall, the Plume of Feathers and the gorgeous carving of its porch, the Three Golden Lions. One of them must have been the scene of a ghostly haunting in *Tom Jones*, ascribed to one Doughty, a name well-known in the place.

Salisbury *is* Old England : in the ancient church of St. Thomas is the Doom Picture over the chancel arch, where our Lord sits on a rainbow between the Sun of Righteousness and the Star in the East, while below Angels summon the dead from their graves and demons drag chained mortals towards Hell mouth that is shaped like the open jaws of a dragon.

One is suddenly transported here to the Old Faith, which, as a staunch Protestant Hanoverian, Fielding hated and fought with his pen when the Jacobites crossed the Border in the Forty-five. He saw with the Stuart conquest of England, the coming of the Inquisition and such tortures as are suggested in the Doom Painting.

But Salisbury possesses a memento of the long fight for English liberty. In the cathedral is the tomb of William Longspée, present at the signing of Magna Carta. No city could be more fitting for this wooing of Charlotte Cradock by the man who fought his own battle for the freedom of the stage, only less important than the freedom of the press.

At first apparently the Cradocks had a house in the Cathedral Close, the first on the left as one enters by St. Ann's Gate. Here, as in several old Salisbury houses, are to be found pillars built into the foundations, a reminder of the time when the city stood among the marshes.

The family seems to have moved across St. Ann Street to the Friary Lane where stands to-day the house named after them.

Cradock House was built in 1618 by Matthew and Margaret Bee, with oak-panelled walls, a great hall with flowered ceiling in plaster-work and an immense fireplace with ancient tiles. Over this was a Jacobean mantelpiece showing Joseph and the Lamb, and the Virgin and Babe circling round a York Rose. All the decorations, except a cluster of fruit in an upstair room, are gone, carried away to America. But on a winter day the bare old attics are filled with shadowy light.

This was probably Charlotte's home when Fielding won her as his wife. Now one hears no click of high-heeled shoes, no swaying whisper of a hooped skirt. But Donne's lines, quoted by Fielding about his lady, bring back the flesh and blood reality of a body long since gone to dust :—

> " Her pure and eloquent blood
> Spoke in her cheeks, and so distinctly wrought
> That one might almost say her body thought ".

So Fielding for a time turns his back on Vanity Fair, and his struggle as a " Playhouse Bard ".

> " I hate ", he cries, " the town and all its ways ;
> Ridottos, operas and plays ;
> The ball, the ring, the Mall, the Court ;
> Wherever the Beau Monde resort—
> All coffee-houses and their praters ;
> All courts of justice and debaters ;
> All taverns and the sots within 'em ;
> All bubbles (fools), and the rogues that skin 'em ".

When one day his lady wished for a Lilliputian to play with, her lover would fain become an atomy—

> " Then when my Celia walks abroad,
> I'd be her pocket's little load ;
> Or sit astride, to frighten people,
> Upon her hat's new fashion'd steeple ".

To please her, he would even take the form of her dog, Quadrille. There is no end to his fancies. But when burglaries were talked about, as in *Cranford*, Charlotte left an old man sitting up in the kitchen all night with a blunderbus, but no ammunition, lest, apparently, he should injure himself. Thereupon Venus upbraids Cupid for leaving the lady undefended :—

> " Poor Cupid now begins to whine :
> Mama, it was no fault of mine.
> I in a dimple lay perdue,
> That little guard-room chose by you.

> Thence, by a sigh, I dispossess'd,
> Was blown to Harry Fielding's breast,
> Where I all night was forced to stay,
> Because I could not find my way ".

All foolery and fancy, of course, but the tenderness is unmistakable. And it lasted ; his wife " on whom he doated ", is the evidence of those who knew him best.

And here surely is genuine passion :—

> " Can there on earth, my Celia, be,
> A price I would not pay for thee ?
> Yes, one dear precious tear of thine,
> Should not be shed to make thee mine ! "

How far is this removed from the artificial gallantry of the eighteenth century ! Henry Fielding's " love wisdom " was a true saying.

But across the road in the Friary, just opposite Cradock House is the wonderful old building, Windover House, so called from the Amsterdam and Salisbury merchant who lived there in the seventeenth century. Ages before that it had been the home of the Franciscan Grey Friars of Salisbury. And here in the oldest room of all, the monkish Refectory at the back, tradition declares that Fielding lived as a lodger while he was courting Charlotte Cradock over the way, and that here he wrote *Tom Jones*. But Windover is only one of the many houses in which legend declares that Fielding worked at that great novel. Such places are almost as numerous as the houses in which Queen Elizabeth slept or Charles the First took refuge. And, by the mercy of Providence, or by the genius of mythology, almost all the places so chosen are beautiful and full of ancient memories.

Take, for instance, this Home of the Grey Friars. Here in their chronicles we find them sitting round the kitchen fire drinking their dregs of beer mixed with water and doing it with such gaiety that " he counted himself lucky who could snatch the mug playfully from another ". Fielding would certainly have enjoyed himself among these merry fellows, though perhaps the dregs might not have been to his taste.

In the roof of the Refectory, the thirteenth century timbers are blackened with the smoke that rose from the fire in the middle of the room. Later on were added the great chimney and the ceiling. And here, in the oldest part of the house, with one window that looked over a flower-garden, they say Fielding wrote some of those many thousands of pages of which he speaks. At any rate, an old, old woman who remembered Windover House both as a school and a lodging-house, always declared that she had been told so in her childhood.

But the most delectable part of the story is to come, though with, alas, a grave doubt about it ; perhaps more than a doubt if the truth must be told. For when excavations were going on in this old room, wedged between the hearth-stone and the planking, was found a battered, broken spoon with the initials C.C. engraved on it. No tenant at any time is known from the records as having the initial C. But there was a C.C., a Charlotte Cradock, not far off, either in the house in the Close, or, later on, in the old Stuart place in the Friary.

C.C. Charlotte Cradock ? And did she go to tea in that Refectory with Henry Fielding ? But if she did, why did she bring her spoon with her ?

Delightful vistas of fancy open before the mind. But when that spoon was submitted to an expert on silver marks, he declared that it belonged to a much later period than Fielding's. Yet one handles the spoon tenderly, very tenderly, sighing for the " might have been ". To the romantic mind a new society is needed : a society for the suppression of the expert !

But, anyway, some of these roof timbers came from Savernak, for in 1232 the foresters there were ordered to allow wood for the Grey Friars of Salisbury to be cut. Savernak, a part of the primaeval forest of England, where, even now, in its sunny glades, deer-haunted, we can see what it was like to be a forest-dweller. And from the broken-down walls of Old Sarum on the Plain were taken the stones that built the Friar's chapel. Could any place be more suitable as a shelter for the head that was to create the two hundred English men and women who populate *Tom Jones?*

There are many lovely ghosts, real ones, in this Refectory of the Friars. Here is Friar Stephen who presided when the House ruled over a group of convents. Of him the records say that he " was of such a sweetness, such a geniality, and such an exceeding charity and compassion, that, in so far as he could, he would not allow anyone to be made sad ". It might have been written of Fielding himself. If he did not write in that

Refectory of the Friars, then he ought to have, for there he would have been under the shadow of this Stephen of whom it is also written that "singing in a loud voice, he passed away blissfully". The saying reminds one of the cheerful courage we find in Fielding's *Voyage to Lisbon* towards that " cold tomb " which George Borrow tells us he kissed.

Besides kind Stephen there lived at one time among the Grey Friars of Salisbury one Friar Richard who was famous as a collector of stories " suitable for the pulpit or the hall ". Again, O Shade of Richard, didst thou stand behind the chair of Henry Fielding? But probably the good Friar would scarcely have found the tales in *Tom Jones* fit for the pulpit. Yet one never knows.

A more august figure among the ghosts of this old room is that of Richard II who presided over a meeting of the Chapter here, and on August 15th, 1393, wearing his regalia, ate with the brethren in this Refectory, his Queen beside him. Too early were those days for " writing sorrow on the bosom of the earth ", yet sad stories faced the Chapter on that occasion, one being of Friar Wyke, a Doctor of Divinity, who becoming a leper, had been turned out from Shrewsbury and left to starve, a scandal to the whole Order of Friars, till a Knight, more charitable than the professors of charity, gave him a benefice in a remote village where he might live out the remaining years of his dreadful life.

In the words of one of the unseen writers of the Glastonbury script, dreams, " like a falling lace ", obscure the realities of such old houses as Windover or the Friary.

A mile or two from Bath is the valley of Charlcombe with a tiny church, only eighteen feet wide. The hillside to-day behind this shows green grassy paths running here and there through the bracken. Beyond this the sky hangs like a vast blue curtain across which the white clouds sail. And beside the tower an ancient yew-tree shades the church porch.

Here Fielding was married to his Charlotte. The entry in the registers runs : " 28th November, 1734, Henry Fielding of ye Parish of St. James in Bath, Esq., and Charlotte Cradock of ye same Parish spinster ".

It appears to have been a runaway match : we seem to see the couple riding over from Bath whither they had fled from Salisbury. What story lies behind this marriage we do not know. But Mrs. Cradock evidently forgave the pair, since she left all her money to Charlotte, and the sum of one shilling to her other daughter Catherine, of whom nothing further is known.

In Charlcombe churchyard Henry's sister Sarah, the author of *David Simple*, lies buried. And—it is worth noting—the north door of the church is walled up. This because, according to West Country superstition, it is through the north door of a church that evil spirits enter. So there, in that safe church, did Fielding marry his lady, and on an April day just thirty-four years later was Sarah carried to her grave. Now Charlcombe looks towards Bath over undulating hills as it did in November, 1734.

In those days Twerton-on-Avon was a country village; to-day it is part of the industrial quarter of Bath with factories and gasometers. Here, in a row of newer houses, stands Fielding Lodge : one of the many houses where the great novel is said to have been written. Over the door is a spread eagle sitting in a kind of nest that may represent the turret of a castle. At any rate, we know that in Fielding's time this strange coat-of-arms stood over the door as it does to-day. At Twerton a legend now persists that a Russian nobleman lived here, long before the eighteenth century, and kept a pack of hounds, and that the eagle and turret is his crest. Again how aptly those hounds fall in with the Fielding atmosphere !

To the left of the door as one enters, one finds the very image of that room described by Fielding in his invocation to Fame at the opening of Book XIII of *Tom Jones*. " Comfort me ", says he, " by a solemn assurance, that when the little parlour in which I sit at this instant shall be reduced to a worse furnished box, I shall be read with honour by those who never knew or saw me, and whom I shall neither know nor see ".

Few prayers have ever been answered more nobly than this one. And as we stand here we are almost forced to believe that the words were written in this place.

On the back window of the ground floor, looking across the garden towards Bath in the distance, there is writing traced by a diamond ; merely the names of certain persons who are described as " Churchwardens at Twerton Fair ". The grate, dating from Fielding's time, is as beautiful with its delicate tracery as any Adam ceiling.

But in the house itself they tell you that it was upstairs that Fielding wrote, in a room looking over the fields. For here, when one shuts the door that is deep-set in the wall, and up three steps, not a sound can be heard of what is going on in the house. And when one tries the experiment one finds it is certainly true. The well in the cellar still feeds the pump that, presumably, was used by the Russian nobleman, if not by Fielding, though it ran dry for a time when they were digging the foundations of the row of houses opposite.

Here then, it may be, that Fielding wrote some part of *Tom Jones*, as is maintained by the Rev. Richard Graves, a contemporary, who lived in the district for fifty years and whose word there is no reason to doubt. He adds the further information that in the evening Fielding would walk over to dine with Ralph Allen at Prior Park.

Close to Widcombe Church on the hill above, where Landor prepared a last resting place for himself, is Widcombe Lodge. Here again we are told in which room Fielding wrote when he came down, often with his sister Sarah, to escape from his creditors as a guest of the Lord of the Manor of Widcombe. Of Sarah it is written that the charms of her conversation made her a special favourite among the writers and wits who gathered round Ralph Allen at Prior Park. Here the Fieldings would meet Pope, who finished the *Dunciad* in this house, Lyttelton, and the elder Pitt. By their friends ye may know them, in fact.

At Salisbury there is a curious echo sounding from the time when the cult of Richardson was at its height and the name Clarissa on all men's lips. Here, on the grounds of Milford Manor, is a beautiful old summer-house, square-built, with a cellar full of water beneath it. To this water there is no known out-let or in-let so that it is probably a well. In each of the three walls of the summer-house is set a window and in the fourth is a doorway approached by a flight of stone steps. Around it is utter peace among green lawns. And, cut with a diamond on one window pane, are the words : " Dear Clarissa, *Puellarum omnium formosissima*". Or, in the words of a poetic translator : " She's fairest where thousands are fair ".

Add to these words the tradition, persistent in the town, that Milford Manor was yet another of the places where Fielding wrote his novel, and you get this delectable picture of the creator of Sophia writing about her beneath the invocation to her rival, the white-souled Clarissa. Now Clarissa's purity owed more to heaven than to earth, but Sophia was of homely human nature all compact. It is, at any rate, a lovely juxtaposition. One sighs : if only it were true !

One naturally asks here what are the facts, apart from dreams, that have been established as to the writing of *Tom Jones* ?

In the first place, during 1746 and three-quarters of the year 1747, when he was working at the book, Fielding was paying rates, as discovered by Mr. de Castro, for a house in Old Boswell Court, which stood on part of the site now occupied by the Law Courts in the Strand. Enclosed between tall, four-storeyed houses, with a cobbled yard and fan-lighted doorways, Old Boswell Court had seen many a grim November day. Here was the true birthplace of the great English novel. But in November, 1747, Fielding took a house at Twickenham and there, no doubt, went on with his book. Yet it is perfectly possible that the summers of these years were spent in the country, and especially at Bath, where there was a magnet that drew to it the chief writers of the time in Ralph Allen, the Maecenas of the eighteenth century. Fielding may even have visited Salisbury, though his Charlotte was now dead.

There remains, however, the alleged connection of Fielding with the house of the Salisbury Grey Friars when he was writing *Tom Jones*, and courting Miss Cradock. Fielding was married to her in November, 1734, so that his courting must have been done during the years previous to that month. But *Joseph Andrews* was not published till 1742 when Fielding had been married eight years, and the manuscript of *Tom Jones* was delivered to the publisher in 1749, when Mrs. Fielding had been dead five years. So that neither book could possibly have been written while their author was wooing Charlotte.

But during those years before his marriage Fielding's pen was working with furious activity at the writing of comedies and satires. In April of the year when he married, the play of *Don Quixote in England* was being acted " with great applause " at the Haymarket. And the scene of this is an inn in a country town, as though the play were a sort of foreshadowing of the novel *Joseph Andrews*.

Here is, in fact, the very atmosphere of Salisbury and the Great Plain. And what more fitting room for the writing of this country play could there be than the Refectory of the Grey

Friars, Windover House? It is indeed true that actual facts are often carried down by word of mouth from generation to generation in old country places, as witness the Cornish tale of a golden bowl buried with a giant in a barrow, which was proved to have been true when the barrow was opened for the first time in the nineteenth century.

The reason that the legend speaks of *Tom Jones* and not of *Don Quixote*, or of any play, is perfectly plain : the novel was a national portent. It was supposed to have produced earthquakes on this planet and convulsions in the heavens ; particularly in London and Salisbury. That " Salisbury " should be carefully noted as showing the connection of the town with Fielding in the popular mind. Any old woman who knew that he wrote in his room at Windover House would be sure, later on, to say it was *Tom Jones* that got written there, for that was a portentous work of which she would certainly have heard talk, but of the plays she would know nothing.

The honeymoon must have been a very short one since in January, 1735 Fielding's new play *The Virgin Unmask'd* or *An Old Man Taught Wisdom* was put on at Drury Lane. It had been written to suit the acting of Kitty Clive, more natural than nature itself in the part of a romp, or a pert young minx. In the play the heroine, after interviewing an apothecary, a dancing master, a lawyer, a student, and a singing master, all suitors for her hand, finally runs away with the footman, much to her father's disgust.

This, apparently, often happened so. Mrs. Pilkington, after her unsuccessful attempt at suicide in Rosamund's Pond in St. James's Park, is taken home by a lady who introduces as her husband an ex-footman. This wretch, though he got £15,000 by his marriage, now beats her, according to Letitia.

But what would Fielding have done, when he wanted a farcical situation, without these silly old men and rebellious girls ? Hogarth's benefit ticket for this play took the dancing master for subject.

Fielding's next play, *The Universal Gallant*, was damned from the start, and, although he might say that he put down his want of success to want of judgment, he was merely repeating the mistake he had made in the case of the *Modern Husband*. The audience wanted no more social satire, no revelations of the Town and its vices. The voices of the actors were drowned in hisses. And Fielding protests bitterly, saying : " He must be an inhuman creature indeed who, out of sport and wantonness, prevents a man from getting a livelihood in an honest and inoffensive way, and makes a jest of starving him and his family.

> Can then another's anguish give you joy ?
> Or is it such a triumph to destroy ? "

Fielding's anxieties were heavier, now that he had a wife to support.

But it is interesting to see how low a value he sets on these plays of his—they are but pot-boilers. Very different is his sense of the greatness of his novels. " Do thou teach me ", he cries to Fame in *Tom Jones*, " not only to foresee, but to enjoy, nay, even to feed on future praise ". When we read these words we seem very close to Henry Fielding who so earnestly desires—that he may not all die.

Suddenly in February 1735 the burden of anxiety about money was lifted for a time from Fielding's mind. Charlotte's mother died, leaving a will, dated February 8, 1734, old style, that is, 1735, in favour of her daughter, Mrs. Fielding. " Item, I give to my daughter Catherine one shilling and all the rest and residue of my ready money plate jewels and estate whatsoever and wheresoever—unto my dearly beloved Charlotte Ffeilding, wife of Henry Ffeilding of East Stour in the county of Dorset Esq."

According to Murphy the estate was valued at £1,500. The reason why Catherine was cut off with a shilling is unknown, but in Fielding's *Amelia* there is a daughter, " who had in some way disobeyed her mother ; a little way before the old lady died ". And this daughter was deprived of her inheritance.

When Fielding wrote the lines :—

> " That Kate weds a fool what wonder can be,
> Her husband has married a fool great as he ",

some have thought he was referring to Catherine Cradock, once the vivacious Kitty of New Sarum. From this time we hear no more of her.

No doubt the lynx eyes of the Town noted that Fielding was again in funds, as after a successful play. One of these watchers writes of the change in his dress :—

> "F——g who yesterday appear'd so rough,
> Clad in *Coarse Frieze*, and plaster'd down with *Snuff*,
> See how his *Instant* gaudy *Trappings* shine,
> What Playhouse Bard was ever seen so fine !
> But this, not from his *Humour* flows, you'll say,
> But mere Necessity ; for last Night lay
> In pawn the Velvet which he wears to-day ".

One cannot but think of Charlotte here in lodgings, though perhaps in no attic of Grub Street, nor as yet—notwithstanding the verses—visiting the pawn-shop, after the country plenty, the ease of life, in the gracious old mansion, Cradock House.

But a pleasant time was at hand. After this inheritance no plays appear in Fielding's name in 1735. In all probability the autumn and winter of 1735-6 were spent at East Stour, where no doubt he lived the life of a country squire with his beautiful lady. And, as the registers there show, the Rev. William Young was curate of the parish at this time. All the evidence goes to prove that Parson Adams was created from this country parson.

Even Murphy, the uninspired, rises to eloquence when he recounts the most famous anecdote of Young's absent-mindedness. It was during the time when the curate was an army chaplain in the French wars, that " on a fine summer evening he thought proper to indulge himself in his love of a solitary walk : and accordingly he sallied forth from his tent : the beauties of the hemisphere, and the landscape round him, pressed warmly on his imagination, his heart overflowed with benevolence to all God's creatures, and gratitude to the Supreme Dispenser of that emanation of glory, which covered the face of things ".

This heroic style, " a sort of tumour of dignity ", ends with the meditative Parson suddenly finding himself in the enemy's camp. But the intelligent French officer was so impressed by his innocence that, instead of making him a prisoner, he allowed him to return to the English lines.

Parson Adams in Lady Booby's house, so we are told, was sent to smoke his pipe in her ladyship's kitchen, but we may be quite sure that Parson Young at Fielding's house sat in the hall or the parlour with the other guests. And there the man of flesh and blood came to immortal life, not through the gates of death, but by the genius of his host.

A beautiful engraving of 1813 shows the outside of the old farm, with one gable of the church. Through holes in the high walls of the gardens and orchards Fielding used to shoot rabbits. His massive oak dining-table is preserved at Taunton.

Now we come, in Murphy's account of Fielding, on those famous yellow liveries which, like the scar on Amelia's nose, gave such delight to his enemies, but do now, like the amiable weaknesses of our friends, make him all the dearer to our hearts.

" To East Stour he retired with his wife on whom he doated, with a resolution to bid adieu to all the follies and intemperances to which he had addicted himself in the career of a town life. But unfortunately a kind of family pride here gained an ascendency over him and he began immediately to vie in splendour with the neighbouring country squires. With an estate not much above two hundred pounds a year and his wife's fortune, which did not exceed fifteen hundred pounds, he encumbered himself with a large retinue of servants, all clad in costly yellow liveries. For their master's honour, these people could not descend so low as to be careful of their apparel, but in a month or two were unfit to be seen; the squire's dignity required that they should be new-equipped; and his chief pleasure consisting in society and convivial mirth, his hospitality threw open his doors and in less than three years, entertainments, hounds and horses, entirely devoured a little patrimony".

Probably on the whole a true story; except for the three years. These were certainly not spent at East Stour, but mainly in London, once more as a playwright.

Fielding was open-handed, generous, and free living to the verge of extravagance. He enjoyed living, and spent and gave with both hands. Many a time, it is highly probable, did his rafters ring with hunting-choruses, and sometimes over the prostrate forms of Henry Fielding's guests. Perhaps too over Henry himself.

But it should be remembered when we talk of three-bottle men, that the wines of the period were less intoxicating than ours of to-day. Neither Tom Jones nor Captain Booth, the two characters most attackable in the novels, is described as a drunkard. But the man who wrote "The Dusky Night" in *Don Quixote in England* was certainly attuned to the music of horse and hound. And when the innkeeper in the comedy says of Sancho : " he is as bad as a greyhound in the house ; there is

FIELDING LODGE, NEAR BATH
Fireplace in the "Tom Jones room."

[*By kind permission of Mr. de Castro*

BOSWELL COURT

(From a Sketch taken shortly before its Demolition). On site of modern Law Courts in the Strand. Place of writing of *Tom Jones* in London.

no laying down anything eatable, but, if you turn your back, slap he has it up ", we seem to see that greyhound lying before the fire in the hall at East Stour.

The man who wrote against the cruel treatment of horses in the Strand surely had a dog or two in his country house.

We can fancy the merry company with Parson Young waving his pipe to the tune of " There was a Jovial Beggar ". And the song surely might have been :—

" The dusky night rides down the sky
And ushers in the morn ;
The hounds all join in glorious cry,
The huntsman winds his horn :
And a-hunting we will go.

The wife around her husband throws
Her arms and begs his stay ;
My dear, it rains, and hails, and snows,
You will not hunt to-day.
But a-hunting we will go.

A brushing fox in yonder wood
Secure to find we seek ;
For why, I carried, sound and good,
A cart-load there last week.
And a-hunting we will go.

Away he goes, he flies the rout,
Their steeds all spur and switch ;
Some are thrown in, and some thrown out,
And some thrown in the ditch.
But a-hunting we will go.

At length his strength to faintness worn,
Poor Reynard ceases flight,
Then hungry homeward we return,
To feast away the night ".

With, no doubt, a sirloin at the fire, and the yellow liveries very busy. Perhaps before the dawn crept in at the windows some of the singers were, like Squire Badger, " as fast on the table as if they had been in a feather-bed ".

Other nights there were, no doubt, when Parson Young

turned over the pages of his Aeschylus while Harry Fielding talked, sometimes on a rendering of the text.

Would that there had been a Boswell there! For, according to a contemporary witness, Fielding was a more brilliant talker than any of his contemporaries.

CHAPTER IX

Fielding and Hogarth

THERE is probably nothing more curious in the history of literature and art than the close relationship between Fielding and Hogarth. Though the novelist was a far greater man, greater in the scope of his sympathy, and greater as a thinker, there was a deep likeness between them as men : in their instincts they were almost Siamese twins.

Generous, both, and kindly, yet they were bitter haters of vice and folly. Each lived too, like his century, with zest and gusto, with delight in the flesh and its ways. And both tried all human values by the supreme test of character : the character that a man writes on his face as the years pass. Obvious as this is in Hogarth's case, it is not so clear in the work of Fielding who seldom if ever describes a man's looks. But the lines of character to be seen on Hogarth's faces spring from the very same vices which made Fielding's men and women. One great artist gives the cause, the other the result ; one the secret source, the other the revelation in the open light of day.

They despised all foreigners, hated Italian opera and Italian singers, and vaunted the roast beef of old England against the soup-maigre of the frog-eating Frenchmen. Fielding scorned the dull Dutchmen ; and when Hogarth visited France he openly insulted the Frenchmen he met in the street, and narrowly escaped hanging for his sketches of Calais Gate, getting off with his life only because he amused the Governor by his drawings.

They both pilloried the same contemporaries : the Quack in Hogarth's *Rake's Progress*, and in Fielding's farce, is Dr. Misaubin ; Farinelli, the famous artificial soprano, sings in the *Rake's Progress* while the despised English flautist stands humbly behind him ; Orator Henley, always Fielding's butt, ladles out the punch in the orgy called the Midnight Conversation ; the famous bawd, Mother Needham, in Hogarth, is Mother Punchbowl in Fielding. The Prude in the morning

Scene at Covent Garden in Hogarth is not only the painter's aunt in the flesh, but also Mrs. Bridget Allworthy in *Tom Jones*, " whose conversation was so pure, her looks so sage, and her whole deportment so grave and solemn, that she seemed to deserve the name of saint . . . ." Fielding could not abide a Prude and suffers none to enter his Elysium.

But Fielding was yet more cruel than Hogarth to Bridget: he had the effrontery to give her—in the far past—an illegitimate son. Both Hogarth and his fellow satirist fairly hunted this poor lady.

And here is Bridget Allworthy as she appears in Hogarth :—

> " Yon ancient prude, whose withered features show
> She might be young some forty years ago,
> Her elbows pinioned close upon her hips,
> Her head erect ; her fan upon her lips,
> Her eyebrows arched, her eyes both gone astray
> To watch yon amorous couple in their play,
> With bony and unkerchief'd neck defies
> The rude inclemency of wintry skies,
> And sails with lappet head and mincing airs
> Duly at chink of bells to morning prayers :
> To thrift and parsimony much inclined,
> She yet allows herself that boy behind,
> The shivering urchin, bending as he goes,
> With slipshod heels and dewdrop at his nose,
> His predecessor's coat advanced to wear,
> Which future pages yet are doomed to share,
> Carries her Bible tuck'd beneath his arm,
> And hides his hands to keep his fingers warm ".

The first trace of a connection between Fielding and Hogarth occurs in 1731, when the frontispiece to the *Tragedy of Tragedies* was drawn by the painter. It shows two enormous, big-bosomed women, no doubt Lolla-Lolla, the Queen, and her daughter, disputing over the Lilliputian Tom Thumb at their feet.

Hogarth's own words put him beside Fielding the dramatist. " I wished ", he says " to compose pictures on canvas, similar to representations on the stage . . ." And again : " I have endeavoured to treat my subject as a dramatic writer. My picture is my stage, my men and women my players, who by means of certain actions and gestures are to exhibit a dumb show ".

They appealed to rather different audiences, Fielding to the city and St. James's, Hogarth especially to the illiterate who, being unable to read print, were expected to " read " his warnings in pictures ; warnings against vice and folly, and terrible drawings of the consequences of both. Hogarth always, and Fielding in his plays, were painters of moral sign-posts who made their messages as dramatic as the skull and cross-bones at a level-crossing.

The two men were alike on deeper levels still : neither knew anything of the world of dreams, not even of beauty or strangeness, artists as they were. The curtain which hangs between the visible and invisible worlds to each man seemed as thick as a fortress wall. Hogarth loudly announced his hatred of the " Black Masters ", as he called the great classical painters.

Yet when someone said to him that he was " as good a portrait-painter as Vandyck ", he exclaimed : " And so, by G—d, I am, give me my time and let me choose my subject ". But he chose to paint men's faces when they were convulsed by the passions, by greed, lust, hatred, fury, covetousness, malice, imbecility and pride.

Charles Lamb says of Hogarth's pictures that " they bring us acquainted with the everyday human face . . . and prevent that disgust at common life . . . which an unrestricted passion for ideal forms and beauties is in danger of producing ".

But the faces in his stories are often hideous and sometimes revolting. Surely then we are not looking at the " everyday human face " which is often placid and happy, if not beautiful? Such faces he could also draw, giving us the jolly Shrimp Girl, the beautiful, graceful drummeress in his crowd, just as occasionally Fielding's stage shows, amid the monsters, a merry laughing girl usually played by Kitty Clive, or a Justice Worthy.

But as pictures of life both the print and the play are false in accent. They are warnings, and writ down to " show up " some vice. This is what a man looks like, says Hogarth ; and this is what he says and does, says Fielding, when he is taking the road to the everlasting bonfire. And even a beautiful face Hogarth can make horrible, throwing across the fine contours a veil of evil. So it is with the young harlot in the Quack doctor's room : her life has made her, in Hazlitt's phrase, " docile to vice ".

It is for his usefulness that Fielding praises Hogarth : " I esteem the ingenious Mr. Hogarth ", he wrote in the *Champion* newspaper, " as one of the most useful satyrists any age hath produced—I almost dare to affirm that those two works of his, which he calls the *Rake's* and the *Harlot's Progress*, are calculated more to serve the cause of Virtue, and for the Preservation of Mankind, than all the Folios of Morality which have ever been written ; and a sober Family should be no more without them, than without *The Whole Duty of Man* in their House ".

Hogarth's custom was to memorise the faces seen in a moment of passion, beginning with the men he saw fighting over a quart pot in a Highgate tavern. In his workshop these thumb-nail portraits would be drawn with a touch of exaggeration ; made larger, even as Fielding used farce to heighten his effects. It is coarse work, no doubt, in both cases, but, after all, as somebody once said, " four-ale is a good drink if you don't call it nectar ".

It seems to have been generally believed in the eighteenth century that the surest guide to a man's character is his face. And the actor who remarked of a stranger that he was either a villain, or surely God did not write a legible hand, was of the same mind as Hogarth. Indeed it was always the custom then for the villain to be played by an ugly fellow, and in a black wig, as Charles II once complained, feeling this to be a personal touch.

It is interesting to compare the two " authors " when they are both dealing with the same subject. When Fielding shows in *The Author's Farce* the poverty of the Grub Street writers, he is light-hearted and gay. But Hogarth's version of the same tale is pitiful and tender, and as vivid a picture as was ever painted. It ought to have been set up in every publisher's office.

The poverty-stricken poet sits scribbling for dear life in his garret-window, while his pretty gentle girl-wife is darning his trousers by a meagre fire. You know perfectly well that, however loving she may be, she would not be the slightest help to her husband in fighting the battle of life. Three books and a copy of *The Grub Street Journal* lie on the floor where a cat and kittens sport on the poet's coat. In the doorway stands the bold trollop of a milk-maid, holding out the unpaid milk-score. She is smartly dressed, but you know that the wench has " as little milkiness about her as if she had been suckled on blue ruin and brimstone ". The pathos here is neither exaggerated nor unreal ; it is simply true, and the print is a little masterpiece of homely kindness, without so much as a touch of satire. Nor are the faces in any way distorted by passion.

But Hogarth far surpassed Fielding in painting scenes of horror. Two of these can scarcely be equalled except in the greatest tragic literature. One of them is the picture of the open boat when the idle apprentice is bidden to look towards a shadowy gibbet standing up among the mists of the distant shore. Two sailors hold up before his eyes the cat-o-nine-tails. But their grinning, ribald faces only heighten the effect of that sombre vision of doom. The gibbet seems to bring a message from another world.

The second great scene is among the madmen in Bedlam, where the Rake's half-naked body is being manacled. One poor wretch shrinks from the Cross he has worshipped; another, maddened by the mystery of numbers and figures, has drawn lines of longitude on the wall, and a third, as an astronomer, holds a roll of paper to his eyes as if he were scanning the heavens. A crowned emperor sits, sceptre in hand; the lover's melancholy gleams in one face and in another the glee of a frenzied musician. Two fine ladies, fan in hand, whisper and laugh as they watch the antics of these men in hell.

Of this scene Lamb wrote: " If we seek for something of kindred excellence in poetry, it must be in the scenes of Lear's beginning madness, where the king and the fool, the Tom-o-Bedlam, conspire to produce such a medley of mirth checked by misery, and misery checked by mirth . . ."

Pathos is apt to merge in the maudlin, tragedy in bathos. This often happened in Hogarth's prints, but Fielding usually avoided both pitfalls. It is the everyday truth of everyday characters that makes his novels such masterpieces. We are always in the noon-day light of the temperate zone. But Hogarth's light is often sinister: in the Bedlam print, lit from the fire of hell; in the open boat it strikes icy cold; in the Early Morning at Covent Garden, the very sky threatens.

This last scene reminds one of Peter Breughel's pictures of ice carnivals. And, in fact, in the prints of Beer Street and Gin Lane, Hogarth is supposed to have had in mind Breughel's two studies called *La Grasse Cuisine* and *La Maigre*.

The *Harlot's Progress* starts in the yard of the Bell Inn, Wood Street, Cheapside, where the country girl, Kate Hackabout, has just alighted from the York coach. Her foolish old father, a parson, stands behind her poring over the address of a letter.

Under her broad-brimmed hat Kate's face is the picture of simple innocence, but the vile procuress murmurs kind words, and smooths those rosy cheeks with a smile which any well-disposed person would be glad to wipe from her face. Those two figures, marvellously drawn, tell the whole story, while in the doorway of the inn lounges Colonel Charteris, the well-known rake, who watches with a smile, like a man with a delicate dish set before him. He points the moral of the whole. But to see him there must have given prodigious pleasure to his fellow-roués, and probably even to Charteris himself.

At first shewn as the spoilt mistress of a rich Jew, with her finery, her monkey, and her black boy, Kate Hackabout goes down, until, with John Dalton's wig-box on the tester of her bed, she is arrested and taken to Bridewell by the " harlot-hunting Justice ", Sir John Gonson—again a fine portrait.

In the last print she lies dead, and no one cares, not even her poor child, who gaily winds his " castle-top " in the shadow of her coffin.

John Dalton, highwayman, was hanged at Tyburn on May 12th, 1730, and *The Grub Street Journal* of August 6th records that among the women just taken from the streets was " Kate Hackabout (whose brother was lately hanged at Tyburn), a woman noted in and about the hundreds of Drury ".

The *Harlot's Progress* became appallingly popular and the series was " tasted by all ranks of people ". In the painter's subscription book twelve hundred names were entered for it. And when the third print, with Gonson's portrait, was brought by one of the lords to a meeting of the Treasury Board, and shewn there, each member rushed to a print shop to get a copy.

Theophilus Cibber turned it into a pantomime. It came out as a ballad opera, and fan mounts were engraved with the scenes pictured in miniature. It is said that in Hogarth's house these fans were presented to the maids. But how many girls were saved by this " warning " that the Town thus turned into a mere show with pantomimes and ballad operas ?

If Fielding had written a tragedy for the stage, his plot might well have been that of Hogarth's *Mariage à la Mode*. The first scene in the series, where the gouty Earl and the crafty merchant, each as greedy as the other, and as wicked, are drawing up the marriage settlement, is in fact pure Fielding. The duel scene, where the wife's lover has killed her husband

and is seen escaping through an open window, might have been written by the novelist who filled pages of his *Amelia* with proofs that duelling is a crime. When, too, the Countess commits suicide at the news that her lover has that morning been hanged at Tyburn, we can see the hand of the man who would have ended Tyburn for ever. It almost might have been written in collaboration, this plot of a fashionable marriage.

The turning point in the Rake's progress is his marriage to an aged hag of a woman because she is wealthy. And the topic of crabbed age and youth, usually of a girl and an old man, is one of the main ideas in Fielding's satires.

But Fielding and Hogarth part company when it comes to the treatment of the girl whom the Rake had seduced at Oxford, and deserted when he came into his inheritance from his father. She is shewn weeping when he casts her off, she dogs his footsteps, pays the money for him when he is arrested for debt, and watches with his child by her side, his marriage in the mouldy precincts of an ancient London church. Finally she follows him into the Debtor's prison, and is even found by his side in Bedlam.

To heighten the agony, Hogarth shows the Rake in the prison, with his wife reviling him on one side, and his mistress fainting on the other, until he looks on this picture and on that, and falls raving, plunged into madness by the contrast of what is, and of what might have been.

To the modern mind there is in this print a certain bathos; it is intended to touch the spring of tears, and perhaps did so in the eighteenth century, but we are made of more cynical stuff.

And how different is Fielding's treatment of the seduction theme in *Tom Jones*! There, when poor Jenny is brought before Squire Allworthy as " a fallen girl ", he might have sent her to Bridewell to beat hemp and be turned into a prostitute like poor Kate Hackabout.

Instead, he very sensibly sends her away to another parish where she will not be looked on as a leper, with the words : " Be a good girl to the end of your days ", and not only exhorts in this manner, but adopts the baby whom he supposes to be hers, and provides the money that will put her on her feet again. In all this he is no doubt expressing the mind of Henry Fielding.

But the creator of Squire Allworthy would always, we suspect, have been more merciful to a light-o'-love than to a prude.

The cynical touches in Hogarth's details must have delighted Fielding, such as the miser drawing off the ring from the finger of his dying daughter ; the list of Farinelli's patrons written on a long tail of paper hung from the back of a chair ; the carrier pigeon let loose at Tyburn to fly back to Newgate to tell the Governor that the bell should be rung for the soul of the man just about to be hanged ; the cobweb over the almsbox, and, above all, the *Semper Eadem* over the heads of the Judges in the Court of Common Pleas, all portraits. One is eaten up with self-importance, another is asleep, and the thoughts of the third are far away. So is Justice administered, says Hogarth.

The persons painted in Hogarth's pictures seem to have enjoyed their notoriety. In the satirical Oxford Lecture where dullness rules, Fisher, the Registrar of the University, is actually said to have sat for his portrait.

In quite another way than in his works Fielding resembled Hogarth, who says of himself : " I remember the time when I have gone moping into the city, with scarce a shilling in my pocket ; but as soon as I had received ten guineas there for a plate, I have returned home, put on my sword, and sallied out again with all the confidence of a man who had ten thousand pounds in his pocket ". It might have been Fielding himself.

Garrick's praise of Hogarth is truth itself :—

> " You have the skill to catch the grace,
> And secret meanings of a face ;
> From the quick eyes to snatch the fire
> And limn th'ideas they inspire ;
> To picture passions, and through skin,
> Call forth the living soul within ".

Never was this power more fully shewn than in Hogarth's three great portraits.

The first is of Captain Coram, who built the Foundling Hospital for cast-off babies. Mrs. Pilkington tells us that at this time on the roads out of London were often to be seen the dead bodies of unwanted children. Coram in his portrait is a man you know at first sight : a kindly, great-hearted, generous man, his healthy cheeks shining with the smile that comes of deeds well done. One thinks better of the human race when one looks on Hogarth's Captain Coram. The sea can have made few better men.

The next personality is Simon Fraser, Lord Lovat, executed on Tower Hill as a traitor. The eyes in his square face, as he counts the numbers of the Highland clans on his fingers, show an extraordinary mixture of contradictory qualities. They twinkle almost with an expression of *bonhomie* yet they are savage and leering, cunning and cruel. When Hogarth went down to meet him on the road to London, Simon, his face besmeared with shaving soap, gave the painter a hearty " buss " on the cheek. And Hogarth rewarded him by painting this masterpiece of characterisation.

But the third portrait, of Wilkes in his moment of triumph when he was acquitted in Westminster Hall, is the most masterly of all. Here is a satyr indeed, leering, squinting with his eyes, above a grossly sensual, savage mouth : the whole a complex mixture of snake and wolf. And this effect, apart from the squint, which was Nature's gift to the man, was accomplished by Hogarth with a mere twist of the muscles of the face.

Yet Wilkes had been Hogarth's friend, nor did he seem in any way to resent this masterly caricature of himself, simply remarking that Hogarth possessed " the easy talent of gibbeting in colours ". And that is a very true word.

In this picture he certainly had obeyed Swift, who told him:—

> " You should try your graving tools
> On this odious set of fools ;
> Draw the beasts as I describe them,
> From their features, while I gibe them ".

> " Draw them so that we may trace
> All the soul in every face ".

Hogarth, for all his pity, was a good hater. Yet his friends loved him, especially Garrick who wrote to General Churchill : " He is a great and original genius ".

But it is Fielding, so like him in many ways, who gives us the real truth about Hogarth's pictures. In *Joseph Andrews* he says : " It hath been thought a vast commendation of a painter to say his figures seem to breathe but surely it is a greater and nobler applause, that they appear to think ".

As from a thinker to a thinker, no finer praise than this could possibly come.

CHAPTER X

Pasquin's Challenge to Folly

FULL of electric energy and ready to attack every abuse, Fielding returned to London some time in 1735, there to open the Little Theatre in the Haymarket as a stronghold of satire directed against Walpole and all his deeds. His partner was James Ralph, free-lance writer of Grub Street, an American who had come over with Franklin, and behind him were the leaders of the Opposition, the party of freedom. Among these were George Lyttelton, respected everywhere as a man of honour, the Duke of Bedford in the House of Lords, and the "terrible Cornet of Horse", William Pitt, who, as Walpole was soon to discover, utterly refused to be muzzled. With them was Chesterfield, afterwards to speak as Fielding's defender in the House.

As Fielding himself says, he was "supported by the greatest wits and finest gentlemen of the age". Always he had regarded "greatness in mean hands as a subject for burlesque". And soon the burlesque of *Pasquin* was ready for the stage. In thus joining battle he had apparently no misgivings as to what might be the outcome of it all. Pride in his countrymen's love of liberty possessed him to the exclusion of all fear of consequences. No one in England, he declares, is afraid of *lettres de cachet*, of the Inquisition, or indeed of any of the other "damned engines of tyranny".

Yet there still existed in England one of those "damned engines" that he had forgotten.

The Little Theatre stood next door to the present Haymarket, as is proved by a print of 1821, discovered by Miss Godden, which shows it in process of demolition. From here Fielding's comedians, under the name of "the Great Mogul's Company", were to issue forth like an attacking army against stupidity and ignorance everywhere, but especially in high places.

He was too great a man to be the mere mouthpiece of a party: his target was Brainlessness; on the stage, in literature, law, religion, medicine and politics. Seldom has there been a more purposeful, a more determined assault on ignorance than this.

When Shakespeare had in mind the destructive force in intellect and wit, he created Falstaff. This most subtle attack Fielding could not emulate. Nor would his century have understood it if he had. The mob, that is those without sense, must be given its lesson by a show which no blockhead could fail to understand : every scene in his play must be as easily read as a wall-painting by Hogarth.

The announcement of the new play runs thus :—

" By the Great Mogul's Company of English Comedians, Newly-Imported. At the New Theatre in the Haymarket, this Day, March 5, will be presented

PASQUIN,

A Dramatic Satyr on the Times. Being a Rehearsal of two Plays, viz : A Comedy call'd *The Election* ; and a Tragedy, call'd *The Life and Death of Common Sense* . . .

N.B. Mr. Pasquin, intending to lay about him with great Impartiality, hopes the Town will all attend, and very civilly give their Neighbours what they find belongs to 'em.

N.B. The Cloaks are old, but the Jokes entirely new ".

The play was fire to the tow of public opinion, and became as popular as the *Beggar's Opera*. By May the Company was advertising the sixtieth performance as a Benefit for the Author. And the publication of a fourpenny pamphlet, *A Key to Pasquin*, seems to be a sign that the satire was reaching a class that came neither from Pall-Mall nor St. James's.

Mrs. Delany in writing to Swift, remarks : " When I went out of town last autumn the reigning madness was Farinelli. I find it now turned on *Pasquin*, a dramatic satire of the times ".

Pope belonged to the Opposition party, and according to the *Grub Street Journal*, he attended a performance, though this was at once denied. But in one of Hogarth's rare prints, showing the stage of the Little Theatre when Common Sense is being overthrown, a deformed figure is seen leaving one of the stage boxes, and saying—what must have delighted Fielding —" There is no white-washing this stuff ! "

Nowadays we have lost the useful 18th century word " pasquinade ", meaning a satire on some form of folly. The name Pasquin was given in old Roman days to a statue to which citizens were invited to affix their criticisms of current evils. Over against this Pasquin was another statue, Marforio, to whose marble the replies were fastened.

Rich did in fact answer the challenge of Fielding's *Pasquin*, in a play called *Marforio* in which he introduced " the Great Mogul " as a character. But this was a failure, only lasting one night.

Pasquin is in two parts, *The Election*, intended for the simple-minded, and *The Life and Death of Common Sense* for those of more intelligence. The form used, that of a rehearsal, allowed free comments by the author, put into the mouths of the two " poets ", Fustian, the tragic, and Trapwit, the comic.

Very simple is the jesting in the first part. The Mayor and Aldermen sit round a table talking over the Candidates for Parliament, Sir Harry Foxchase and Squire Tankard for the County Party, and Lord Place and Colonel Promise for the Court. As there isn't a pin to choose between them, the Aldermen are simply bribed by both sides.

" Is this wit, Mr. Trapwit ? " enquires the tragic poet. " Yes, Sir ", replies the comedian, " it is wit ; and such wit as will run over the kingdom ".

It was suggested by an admirer of the farce that it should be played throughout England before the next election. For the problem is put, which must have occurred to many minds : " How can a man vote against his conscience who has no conscience at all ? "

Mrs. Mayoress longs for the excitements of the town, to see rope-dancing, and performing dogs, and all the follies of the stage.

As for the morals of the lady, when her daughter asks the innocent question :

" But must I go into keeping, Mama ? " her mother replies : " Child, you must do what's in the fashion ".

Miss : " But I've heard that's a naughty thing ".

Mrs. Mayoress : " That can't be if your betters do it ; people are punished for doing naughty things ; but people of quality are never punished ; therefore they never do naughty things ".

At this Q.E.D. no doubt the house roared. And thereupon

a Bill is proposed to extirpate all trade out of the nation, " Such as the *canaille* practise ", leaving several which people of fashion may pursue, such as gaming, intriguing, voting and running in debt.

Mr. Pasquin is indeed laying about him, and with zest. Then Cibber gets his turn.

Says the second voter : " I'm a devilish lover of sack ! "

Lord Place : " Sack, say you ? Odso, you shall be poet laureate ".

2nd Voter : " Poet ! No, my Lord, I am no poet. I can't make verses ".

Lord Place : " No matter for that—you'll be able to make odes ".

Cibber was a great maker of odes, as all the readers in the theatre must have known. And here, as a specimen, is his *Ode to The New Year* :—

> " This is a day, in days of yore,
> Our fathers never saw before ;
> This is a day, 'tis ten to one,
> Our sons will never see again.
> Then sing the day,
> And sing the song,
> And thus be merry
> All day long ".

This, so Fielding once remarked, " is the Cream and Quintessence of all the Odes I have seen for several years past ".

But how Cibber-like is that conclusive : " Thus be merry, all day long ". It was his principle from youth to age, and manfully did he live up to it.

Hitting right and left, Mr. Pasquin aims now at a notoriously effeminate fop and politician, Lord " Fanny " Hervey whom Pope called " a mere white curd of asses' milk ". When Miss Stitch, the tailor's daughter, breaks her fan, she cries : I have torn my fan ! . . . Oh, my poor dear Fan ! " Every one of the fashionable crowd would take this jest.

Sir Harry Foxchase wins the day, but the Mayor cooks the returns, so that there may be a disputed election, which will enable Mrs. Mayoress and her daughter to . . . see Rich as Harlequin, and attend a Masquerade.

The Life and Death of Common Sense starts in the mock-heroic style that recalls *The Tragedy of Tragedies* of Tom Thumb. The prelude is like the opening of Julius Caesar, when ghosts did squeak and gibber in the streets of Rome. Similar portents of horror shew in Fielding's farce that events quite out of nature are to be expected :—

> " The Temple shook, strange prodigies appeared ;
> A cat in boots did dance a rigadoon,
> While a huge dog played on the violin ".

This is of course to out-do the absurdities of Rich's stage. When Fielding's spirits are on top of the bough, his lightning flashes in all directions.

The drama about to be unfolded is nothing less than a plot against Queen Common Sense, made by Law, by Physic, and by Firebrand, the priest of the Sun. These three powers, which should be the supporters of society, are now in open rebellion, and presently will be found fighting on the side of Ignorance.

Not yet a lawyer, but always a man deeply interested in justice, Fielding drops the mock-heroic style altogether as soon as he comes to the heart of his subject.

Into the mouth of Physic he puts his Criticism of Law as practised in England.

" My Lord ", says Physic to Law : " There goes a rumour through the Court that you are descended from a family related to the Queen (that is, to Queen Common Sense) ; Reason is said to have been the mighty founder of your House ".

" Perhaps so ", says Law, " but we have raised ourselves so high,

> And shook this founder from us off so far,
> We hardly deign to own from whence we came ".

In *The Coffee-House Politician*, Fielding gives an instance of injustice. " Golden sands ", he writes, " too often clog the wheels of justice and obstruct her course ; the very riches which were the greatest evidence of villainy, have too often declared the guilty innocent ".

And when Queen Common Sense appears with two Maids of Honour, she brings forward shameful abuses that ought to have been remedied at once.

[Reproduced from "The History of Henry Fielding" by Wilbur Cross, by kind permission of the Yale University Press.

FRONTISPIECE TO "THE JACOBITE'S JOURNAL"

[Photography by Neville Rodber of Taunton.

THE MODERN BUST IN THE SHIRE HALL, TAUNTON

"Two men", she says, "it seems, have lately been at law
  For an estate, which both of them have lost,
  And their attorneys now divide between them".
"Madam", Law replies, "these things will happen in
    the law".
"Will they, my Lord? Then better we had none;
  But I have heard a sweet bird sing,
  That men unable to discharge their debts
  At a short warning, being sued for them,
  Have, with both power and will their debts to pay,
  Lain all their lives in prison for their costs".
"That", replies Law, "may perhaps be some poor
    person's case,
  Too mean to entertain your royal ear".
"My Lord, while I am Queen I shall not think
  One man too mean, or poor to be redressed".

This is the authentic voice of Fielding's heart, the man who was to hold no porter's quarrel too low for him to judge.

And when the Queen complains of laws so large in number " that the great age of old Methusalem would scarce suffice to read " them, she touches a subject which makes laymen still wonder to see how far from Reason, that mighty Founder, Law has travelled.

When Queen Ignorance lands, with "a vast power from Italy and France, of singers, fiddlers, tumblers, and rope dancers", Firebrand proclaims her praises :—

  "This Queen of Ignorance ...
    Is the most gentle, and most pious queen,
    So fearful of the gods, that she believes
    Whate'er their priests affirm".

In retort Queen Common Sense exclaims :—

  "But know, I never will adore a priest,
    Who wears pride's face beneath religion's mask,
    And makes a pick-lock of his piety
    To steal away the liberty of mankind".

What shades of fighters for this liberty come to the mind at the echo of these words! As long as there is hypocrisy and tyranny in religion, injustice in the law, and ignorance and humbug in the practice of medicine, the satire of *Pasquin* can never be out-moded.

As for Physic, his accusation against Common Sense is that :—

> "She has averred, ay, in the public court,
> That water gruel is the best physician".

At this time Fielding's gout had not yet begun to trouble him. When it did, he forgot his defence of water gruel, and went from doctor to doctor and from quack to quack in quest of help.

Hereupon, Queen Common Sense, after meditating on the state of Europe, and, naturally enough, finding herself unable "thoroughly to comprehend it", falls into a quiet nap.

At last comes action, when Queen Ignorance raises her standard at Rich's theatre in Covent Garden. The two queens and their respective followers confront each other.

Queen Common Sense demands :—

> "And can my subjects then complain of wrong?
> Base and ungrateful! What is their complaint?"

Queen Ignorance :—

> "They say you do impose a tax of thought
> Upon their minds, which they are too weak to bear".

Queen Common Sense :—

> "Wouldst thou from thinking then absolve mankind?"

Queen Ignorance :—

> "I would, for thinking only makes men wretched;
> And happiness is still the lot of fools".

Queen Common Sense, having been stabbed in the fight, yet "rises to soft music" as a ghost and frightens Ignorance away. Though Common Sense may be conquered, yet her spirit still haunts the minds of men.

Fielding sums up his challenge :—

> "Religion, law and physic, were design'd
> By heaven the greatest blessings on mankind,
> But priests, and lawyers and physicians made
> These general goods to each a private trade,
> With each they rob, with each they fill their purses,
> And turn our benefits into our curses".

Having thus shown the sordid meanness of too many average

men, Fielding bids us, in his Epilogue, look upwards to the hills, to the great men of England. He asks :—

" Can the whole world in science match our soil ?
Have they a Locke, a Newton, or a Boyle ?
Or dare the greatest genius of their stage
With Shakespeare, or immortal Ben, engage ?
Content with Nature's bounty, do not crave
The little which to other lands she gave ;
Nor like the cock a barley-corn prefer
To all the jewels which you owe to her ".

Here in Fielding's *Pasquin* is that hatred of injustice which lies deep in the national character, with—a rarer quality in Englishmen—respect for intellect. This forgotten farce is in fact a key to unlock the mind of its author. And the sudden drop in the style of the Epilogue to the simile of the cock and the barley-corn gives just that return to the homely earth after a flight which is " pure Fielding ".

Naturally the contemporary press cracked jokes over this popular show. The *Prompter* offered a reward to anyone who would hand over to a Justice of the Peace " a lean, ragged, uncurried creature called Common Sense ", who had been driven out of the London theatres. One " Verax " replied that he had found her straying, but would keep her till the theatres were more ready to receive her. And it was suggested that " Verax " must be no other than Mr. F—d—g.

A cartoon, " The Judgment of the Queen of Common Sense ", shows the Queen standing on a stage-platform and giving to Fielding with one hand a purse from which drop gold coins, while with the other she hands Rich a halter. In his Harlequin dress he is surrounded by a group of humbugs, a priest, a lawyer, a doctor, and a tumbler standing upside down. Two players, possibly Kitty Clive and Quin, support Fielding, while Shakespeare leans from his writing table towards the author of *Pasquin*. The ghost of Hamlet's father rises from a trap-door to enjoy the scene, the cock beside him in fighting form.

Fielding is here accredited with having made a fortune by his farce. But in this year, which made him the most popular playwright of the moment, catastrophe was not far off. And his Charlotte, after the pleasant Manor House of East Stour was soon to become familiar with those humble London lodgings which are so vividly described in *Amelia*.

But the mere fact that *Pasquin's* defence of intellect, clear and outspoken as it is, should have gained the plaudits of the Town throws a light which cannot be ignored on the character of Fielding and his period. The Church was " snoring ", as even its defenders confessed ; the Ministry was not only corrupt but tyrannical ; the administration of the Law a degrading spectacle ; yet even so, thought was not dead, but only sleeping. And Fielding was the man to arouse it.

CHAPTER XI

The Tragedy of Wit Overthrown

THROUGHOUT the summer of 1736 Fielding's Little Theatre in Haymarket remained open, putting on plays twice a week. Among these was a skit entitled the *Deposing and Death of Queen Gin*, wherein she drinks so great a quantity of this spirit that she dies of it. A companion picture to Hogarth's famous Gin Lane, it is actually a satire on Walpole who had passed a bill exacting a £50 licence for selling gin. The act was aimed at a terrible social evil, yet the spectacle of a three-bottle man supporting such a measure was naturally provocative of ribald mirth.

Fielding was soon ready with his audacious play, " The Historical Register for 1736 ". By a bold stroke it is dedicated to no nobleman, but simply to the Public, who are told that this dedication is just an introduction intended to give the nation a great opinion of the Ministry.

The audacity of this Prologue is pointed by the anecdote of how two gentlemen walking together, suddenly catch sight of a street sign with the figure of an ass on it.

" Bob, Bob, look yonder ", cries one to his friend, " some insolent rascal has hung out your picture ! " The short-sighted victim, calling for the innkeeper, threatens a prosecution. But the fellow calls out to the mob that the figure of the ass is an exact picture of the gentleman, and no caricature.

But Bob was the slang name for Walpole. The wit is rude and school-boyish. It has, however, the merit of being easily understood by persons of low intelligence. Fielding had, in fact, the curious habit of hitting right and left in his satires, first in a blow aimed at the simple, and second at the intelligent. He never believed that one stone could kill two entirely different birds.

The dedication then turns to the subject of political corruption. " If ", he says, " a general corruption be once introduced, and those who would be the guardians and bulwarks of our liberty once find—an interest in giving it up, no great capacity will be required to destroy it ; on the contrary, the meanest, lowest, dirtiest fellow—will be able to root out the liberties of the bravest people ".

Thereupon he boldly declares his purpose. " If Nature hath given me any talents at ridiculing vice and imposture, I shall not be indolent, nor afraid of exerting them, while the liberty of press and stage persist, that is to say, while we have any liberty left among us ".

Among the guardians of English liberty by whose vigilance its cause has been defended from century to century, Fielding should certainly find a place, even though he worked by jest and satire rather than with the noble reasoning of a Milton.

The form of the *Register*, like *Pasquin*, is a rehearsal where the actors assemble as politicians to discuss foreign affairs. Unfortunately none of them know anything about the subject, except " that little gentleman who says nothing ". He knows all ! It is not difficult to find a name for this little man.

The next topic is : Money : how to get it ? The answer is of course by taxing. But by taxing what ? Learning. No, better lay it on ignorance, learning being the property of very few, and these nearly all poor.

An auction follows. And here the satire is barbed. The Auctioneer's name is Mr. Hen, a parody of the name Christopher Cock, a famous dealer in rare furniture and china in the Piazza of Covent Garden. Here, too, is Orator Henley, for once out of his " tub ", who challenges the world to show curios as rare as these now offered for sale. And rare they are indeed.

Lot I is a most curious remnant of Political Honesty. You can use both sides alike. Turn it as often as you will and it makes a very good cloak. " I assure you several great men have made their birthday suits out of it ".

Lot II. A most delicate piece of patriotism. A courtier remarks. " I wouldn't wear it for a thousand pounds. A suit only proper for the country ".

Lot III. Three grains of modesty. " Never changes colour on any account. Half a crown for all this modesty ! Serves mighty well to blush behind a fan ". But no one bids.

Lot IV. One bottle of courage.

Lots V & VI. All the wit of Mr. Hugh Pantomime, and

THE TRAGEDY OF WIT OVERTHROWN

Mr. William Goosequill, composer of political papers in defence of a Ministry. (Three hundred folio volumes).

Lot VII. A very clear conscience worn by a judge and a bishop. " Whoever has it will never be poor ". Bid, one shilling.

Lot VIII. Interest at Court. One thousand bid.

Lot IX. All the cardinal virtues. Bid, eighteen pence. But the gentleman who bought it brings it back in disgust. What he wanted was : " A Cardinal's Virtue ", a very handy implement.

Finally comes a job lot. " Here's temperance, chastity, a deal of wit, and a little common sense ". But for this there is not one single offer.

Excellent fooling surely ? One can hear volley after volley of laughter. " But, it is all in Corsica, Sir, all in Corsica ! "

The first Patriot cries : " Gentlemen, I think this our island of Corsica is in an ill state : I do not say we are actually at war, for that we are not ; but however we are threatened with it daily, and may not the apprehension of a war—be worse than the evil itself ? "

The country was then straining after war but held in leash by the Prime Minister. This long peace it was that made England prosperous in trade during the Walpole administration. But Fielding, having no mind to economic values, saw it as mere inertia.

Of course he must have a bribery scene. One Quidam suddenly enters with four Patriots. Throwing gold pieces on the table, he asks : " Can Corsica be poor while there is *this* in it ? " The Patriots snatch up the money and fill their pockets while Quidam fiddles a merry jig. As they dance the money pours out of the holes in their pockets, and the fiddler picks it all up again.

But who is this Quidam ? Is it not the devil ? " Indeed, it is so plain who is meant by this Quidam, that he who maketh any wrong application thereof might as well mistake the name of —Old Nick for old Bob ".

Fielding's sign-posts are very clearly painted.

Next Cibber must have his turn. Here he appears as Ground Ivy, the ivy that saps the strength of great oaks. And when Apollo sits casting the parts in Shakespeare's *King John*, Cibber protests that it will not do ; it must be altered. " Shakespeare was a pretty fellow, and said some things which only want a little of my licking to do well ".

The *Register* was bold, but the playlet next written, *Eurydice Hiss'd*, went far beyond it. The sub-title alone was a defiance of discretion, being " a word to the wise, giving an account of the Rise, Progress, Greatness and Downfall of Mr. Pillage . . . with the dreadful Consequence and Catastrophe of the Whole ".

There is no doubt that Fielding expected the fall of Walpole almost at once. But Leviathan lingered on at the Ministry years after Fielding had been banished from the stage.

The first version of *Eurydice*, brought out at Drury Lane in 1737, had been a failure. The reason for this is not clear, since nobody can have minded whether Eurydice went to the devil or not. But the cat-calls started with the footmen, who invaded the boxes and created an uproar. In the free fight which followed, Eurydice was left in hell, since Orpheus never reached the end of the rescue act.

In *Eurydice Hiss'd* Pillage is seen holding a levee where he suggests the plot of a farce. But when his courtiers turn on him and hiss, he confesses that he has failed, and in trying to drown his misery, gets very drunk. The sight of a drunken Prime Minister bewailing his sin and then falling into a stupor was not hissed; which is very significant indeed.

Suddenly with a mad plunge, Fielding shifts his scene into hell, his favourite locality whenever his sense of fun gets hold of him.

" What a delicious place this hell is ! " exclaims an actor.

" Sir, it is the only place a fine gentleman ought to be in ! And as for the devil, ' the old gentleman ', my dear, you have seen him five hundred times already. The moment I saw him here I remembered to have seen him shuffle cards at White's and George's, to have met him often on the Exchange . . . and never missed him in or about Westminster Hall ".

And here once more Fielding returns to the crimes of the Law. But as for Signor Quaverivo, the opera singer, Charon has been ordered not to take him over the Styx, since he is " neither man nor woman ", being but an artificial soprano, a Farinelli.

Suddenly, surrounded by his friends, Honestus appears. He is, of course, the man of brains whose subject is neglected genius, especially the genius of Butler, author of *Hudibras*, a poem illustrated by Hogarth in a series of satirical prints.

" Who would not rather ", asks Honestus, " wish a
    Butler's fame,
Distressed and poor in everything but merit,
Than be a blundering laureat to a Court ? "

In order apparently that it might reach a wider public, the *Register* was hastily published, with the additional remark that the politicians in the farce were only a set of blundering blockheads, " too low even for a conversation at an alehouse ". This naturally made matters no better.

Fielding had no idea that a blow was soon to fall on him which would end his career in the theatre. He speaks hopefully of starting a subscription to beautify and enlarge the Little Haymarket and to procure a better company of actors. He intends to use his talents to the full " at ridiculing vice and imposture ". Like a man exulting in his strength, he takes the people into his confidence.

In a letter to Lord Chesterfield in 1733, Fielding puts his purpose clearly. " The freedom of the stage ", he writes, " is, perhaps, as well worth contending for as that of the press. It is the opinion of a man well known to your lordship that examples work quicker and stronger in the minds of men than precepts ... The most ridiculous exhibitions of luxury and avarice may make little effect on the sensualist, or the miser ; but I fancy a lively representative of the calamities brought on a country by general corruption might have a sensible and useful effect on the spectators ".

True enough, since to be shewn one's own failings is an unpleasant experience, but to condemn the doings of others, particularly of those who govern us, is a pleasure indeed.

Always Fielding plays the part of the intelligence, or as his age would say, the wit, which disintegrates whatever is false.

" There are ", he observes, " among us those who seem so sensible of the danger of wit and humour that they are resolved to have nothing to do with them ; and indeed they are in the right on't, for wit, like hunger, will be with great difficulty restrained from falling on, where there is great plenty and variety of food ".

No words could better describe the part played by this " very adventurous author ", as Fielding calls himself. But, although there might be no inquisition in England, what he had overlooked was nothing less than the power of the Government itself. One thing which they dreaded above all others was movement, agitation and consequent upheaval. The creatures of a stagnant pool naturally hate the idea of a current of fresh water.

The immediate cause of Fielding's fall was the mysterious affair of the Golden Rump. Suddenly in the paper *Common Sense*, behind which were Lyttelton and Chesterfield, there appeared not only an attack on Walpole but even on the King and Queen. This was " the Vision of the Golden Rump, described as an image with a head of wood, and a backside of gold ". And presently in the streets one could buy, price one shilling, a caricature of the Rump.

Whether Fielding took any part in all this is unknown. But, according to the story told at the time, a two-act farce was sent to Giffard for his theatre in Goodman's Fields. This he promptly carried to Walpole, who showed the worst passages to the King, and read extracts from it to the House of Commons.

On the other hand, there were many who believed that the Prime Minister himself had engaged Giffard to write this bit of treason.

Within a month the Licensing Bill was prepared. This set up a censorship of stage plays, derived from an Act of Queen Elizabeth—against the " Common players of Interludes ", under the pretext of protecting morals. By this, all plays, before they could be acted must be licensed by the Lord Chamberlain under a penalty of £50.

In Cibber's words, Fielding had " set fire to his stage by writing up an act of Parliament to demolish it ".

Lord Chesterfield, whatever his morals may have been, was always on the side of liberty and against oppression. He it was who led the applause in the theatre when the popular actress, George Ann Bellamy, slapped the face of an insolent fop for kissing her neck as she passed him on the stage. Actresses were then considered fair game for the beaux of the fashionable world.

And now in the House it was Chesterfield who came forward to fight against the Licensing Act.

His line of defence strikes a modern as curious. But Fielding understood it well : the Bill was an encroachment on the rights of property—the one thing held sacred by the Englishmen of the time.

"Wit, my Lords", said Chesterfield, "is a sort of property ; it is the property of those who have it, and too often the only property they have, to depend on ".

Here at last we have a defence, not only of Fielding, but of all the dwellers in Grub Street.

"As the stage", he continued, "has always been a proper channel for wit and humour, therefore, my Lords, when I speak against this Bill, I must think I plead the cause of the British stage and of every gentleman of taste in the kingdom ".

It was all in vain : the forces of fear and inertia were too strong. Nor is this surprising, since, seated before Chesterfield were some of the very gentlemen who had been scourged by that same "wit" which my Lord was defending.

The Licensing Bill passed on June 6th, 1737. All the theatres were to be closed except Drury Lane and Covent Garden, the two patent theatres. The managers of these now held everything in their own hands. They could also bring down their actors' salaries, and raise the price of seats.

But you can drive a coach and four through most acts of Parliament. And this Giffard did by giving "concerts" at his theatre, which were actually plays with incidental music between the acts. Since he had brought the manuscript of the Golden Rump to Walpole, or was perchance its author, no notice was taken of this evasion of the law. It is even said that £1,000 was the reward for his "loyalty".

Fielding was too proud to adopt any such trick. Since political satire was banned on the stage, he refused to sink back into a mere purveyor of amusement for the brainless genteel.

Yet he was by no means silenced. Always there remained the press in which he could "lay about him", even though he was not on the staff of Lyttelton's paper *Common Sense*.

That his hand in the press was well known is proved by the story of a reader who was heard exclaiming in a coffee-house : "Art thou thereabouts, my boy ?—Ha, Ha ! old Truepenny ! —Well-said, well-done, old Boy ". The man had one of Fielding's articles before him.

The spirit of Fielding still reigned in his Little Theatre long after his plays had faded into silence. For when in the autumn of 1738 a company of French players had been licensed to play in it, the audience revolted. Still the English people even now held fast to their privilege of saying what they thought.

The interruptions were so violent that at last two justices were brought into the pit and one of these announced that the play was being acted by the King's command. He was told that an audience in this country always held to the custom of expressing its dislike of a play.

Although grenadiers with fixed bayonets stood on the stage, and a company of the Guards outside the theatre, the objectors were not to be intimidated. The magistrate who tried to read the Riot Act found his candlestick suddenly snatched from his hand. Thereupon a voice from the gallery started to sing Fielding's song, " The Roast Beef of Old England ". The whole audience joined in, ending with cheers.

But in our eyes to-day the manager of the Little Haymarket theatre had made a far greater venture than *The Political Register* when he put on the stage a tragedy of common life. This was *The Fatal Curiosity*, by George Lillo, a jeweller in the Moorfields, who had already scored a success in 1731 with the play *George Barnwell*, the story of a London apprentice and how he came to be hanged at Tyburn. Never before had any dramatist " ventured to introduce the character of a merchant or his apprentice into a tragedy ", in an age when everything was held to be " low " which did not concern the doings of the Beau Monde.

Those who went to the first performance of *Barnwell* brought with them copies of an old ballad on the subject which had been hawked about the streets. They intended to mock the play by shouting the rough rhymes of this. But so moved were they by the passion of the scenes that their laughter was soon changed to tears.

Then on May 27th, 1736, Fielding published the advertisement of *The Fatal Curiosity* : " Guilt its Own Punishment. Never acted before. By Pasquin's Company of Comedians. Being a true Story in Common Life and the Incidents extremely affecting ".

The plot belongs to that class of legend which crops up again and again, and is confined to no country in particular. *The Fatal Curiosity* tells of the return of a sailor, ship-wrecked from an East Indiaman and kept by the Moors, who is so changed in looks that his parents fail to recognise him as their son. Believing him to be a stranger, they murder him for his casket of jewels. The tragedy that follows is one of remorse, when the guilty couple discover what they have done.

The scene is fixed in Cornwall, at Penryn, where to this day stories are told of East Indiamen flung on these rocky coasts. A grassy mound is said to be the place where once there stood the fatal farm.

Lillo's plays are more than merely curious : they are the shadows of things to come in literature. And these " things to come " are not only the hosts of humble people who crowd the pages of Fielding's novels—Parson Adams, Partridge, honest Joseph and his Fanny, Mrs. Whitefield of the Bell Inn, Gloucester—but all the " low " characters in fiction and drama throughout the nineteenth and twentieth centuries, to say nothing of the centuries to come. A statue put up to George Lillo would not be amiss.

The play of humble life has made its way very slowly on the stage. Only *Arden of Faversham* remains from the Elizabethan drama, and that is crude indeed. Yet when one stands in the garret of the old house where the actual murder of Arden took place and looks on the walls where the plaster has fallen in patches, and on the cupboard where the assassin hid, one feels again a quiver of horror at murder done in such a homely scene. *Arden* was drawn, rough as it is, from " the vast authentic book of nature ".

So is *The Fatal Curiosity*. Lillo knew how to show the agony of a tortured conscience, which bears the torment of the damned in this world, and expects to endure it in the next. The scene where old Wilmot hesitates to commit the murder and his wife spurs him on, of course recalls *Macbeth*.

Then, when the father knows what he has done, he cries, a distraught :—

> " Compute the sands that bound the spacious ocean.
> And swell their number with a single grain ;
> Increase the noise of thunder with thy voice . . .
> Add water to the sea, and fire to Etna,
> But name not thy faint sorrow with the anguish
> Of a curst wretch who only hopes for this ".
> ———stabbing himself . . . .
> " To change the scene but not relieve his pain ".

Behind the grandiloquence, so foreign to the terse language of to-day, the words do give a sense of the endlessness of eternal torment.

Tom Davies, actor, bookseller, author, and friend of Dr. Johnson, played the part of young Wilmot, the son, and has left an account of the efforts made to secure a success for Lillo's play. It is a charming picture. He says : " Mr. Fielding, who had a just sense of our author's merit, and who had often in his humorous pieces laughed at those ridiculous and absurd criticks who could not possibly understand the merit of *Barnwell*, because the subject was low, treated Lillo with great politeness and friendship. He took upon himself the management of the play and the instruction of the actors . . . Fielding was not content merely to revise *The Fatal Curiosity*, and to instruct the actors how to do justice to their parts. He warmly recommended the play to his friends and to the public. Besides all this he presented the author with a well-written prologue ".

This Prologue begins on a lofty note :

"The Tragic Muse has long forgot to please,
With Shakespeare's nature or with Fletcher's ease :
No passion mov'd, thro' five long acts you sit,
Charm'd with the poet's language or his wit.
Fine things are said, no matter whence they fall ;
Each single character must speak them all.

But from this modern fashionable way
To-night our author begs your leave to stray.
No fustian hero rages here to-night,
No armies fall to fix a tyrant's right :
From lower life we draw our scenes' distress.
—Let not your equals move your pity less !
Virtue distrest in humble state support ;
Nor think she never lives without the Court ".

Clearly Davies is conscious of a slight feeling of surprise at Fielding's friendship with a tradesman. None the less, he sees the beauty of it.

With the passing of the Licensing Bill the curtain fell on Fielding's career as a " Playhouse Bard ". Yet old Bob had surely done him the greatest possible service when he flung him off the stage, and so opened a way for the true expression of his genius.

The plays, from *Love in Several Masques* to *The Political Register*, have a value of their own. Without them, we cannot realise the full stature of Henry Fielding. In them, more plainly than in his novels, there is written down the character of the man who hated and scorned the vice and folly he saw all round him in the contemporary scene. So true is this that he actually seems to have found it sometimes a relief to plunge into hell, there to find a society no worse than what he encountered on earth.

Dr. Johnson once said contemptuously of another man's writing : " Sir, a man might write such stuff for ever, if he would abandon his mind to it ".

He might have been referring to Fielding's plays : in the literary sense they certainly are " such stuff ", yet the mind which produced them belonged to Henry Fielding. And that is worth studying in all its phases.

The sensibility and critical power which possessed him in his youth Fielding was to express in action one day among the lowest and most helpless outcasts of an ill-organised society. In the novels we feel the great heart which, like the sun, shone on all alike. In the plays, amidst all the jesting, we feel the secret of his satirical power, that hatred of hypocrisy which came so finely to flower in *Jonathan Wild*.

This is a many-sided man.

CHAPTER XII

Captain Hercules Vinegar

FIELDING was a man of sudden decisions: only a few weeks after his first play he appears in Leyden as a student; in less than six months after the closing of his theatre by the Licensing Act, he is entered as a law-student of the Middle Temple. Murphy tells us that " disagreeable impressions never continued long upon his mind ", the reason no doubt being that he turned his back on his troubles and steered his course suddenly in another direction. It has been argued that he might have continued as a writer of farces, if he left politics alone. But could a Fielding humbly present his work for the approval of a censorship he had resisted? It was not in him to do it.

It must have been a difficult decision for a man of thirty to start on a new career, now that he had a wife and family. His first child, Charlotte, born in 1736, was, like himself, an April baby. When the next child, Harriet, was born we do not know. But there is a spice of reckless audacity about this man: he is resolute and determined, fully aware of his own powers, and by difficulties never subdued; " on the contrary ", says his first biographer, " they only roused him to struggle through them with a peculiar spirit and magnanimity ".

The man's energy made him a human dynamo. In fact he must have been, for a delicate lady accustomed to the pleasant, easy-going society of New Sarum, often gey ill to live wi' ; not because he failed in affection, but simply because his wife would be bound to feel, not only the ups and downs of their finances, but that she was being drawn at the tail of a whirlwind.

There appears to have been about this time, not the three years' residence at East Stour spoken of by Murphy, but a coming and going in summer up and down to the farm. In the *Journey from this World to the Next* he writes of " the change to a little, pleasant country house, where there was nothing grand or superfluous ", adding " I began to share the tranquillity that visibly appeared in everything round me. I set myself to do works of fancy and to raise little flower-gardens, with many such innocent rural amusements . . ."

Not for long would a Fielding be satisfied with these diversions, which do in fact rather suggest a woman's activities and tastes.

Local tradition in Salisbury will have it that Mrs. Fielding passed the winter of 1737-38 in Salisbury, either in the house in the Close, or in the large mansion at the foot of Milford Hill. The old red-brick house is gone, but the mantelpiece was used in the new one. There may be truth in the story, since she was apparently in delicate health during these years.

Several changes had been taking place at East Stour. First, the property was divided into six parts to be shared by Fielding with his sisters. Next in 1738 Fielding sold his share for £260 and the farm finally fell into the hands of Herbert Walter, probably the " Peter Pounce " of *Joseph Andrews*.

This money no doubt was badly needed during the time that Fielding was reading for the law, although by the will of his uncle, George Fielding, he had been left a legacy of £50 a year.

On November 1st, 1737, Fielding paid down his fee of £4, was entered as a student of the Middle Temple, and so started on two and a half years of close and exacting study.

He had the good wishes of many friends. One of these hoped he would be Lord Chancellor, and put his wish into a line of verse, which ran : " May Furry Honours Crown the Muse-lost Bard ! " The barrister's gown came all right, but not the Chancellorship.

Murphy gives a picture of Fielding as a student : " His application while a student in the Temple was remarkably intense ; and though it happened that the early taste he had taken of pleasure would occasionally return upon him . . . yet . . . nothing could suppress the thirst he had for knowledge, and the delight he felt in reading ; and this prevailed in him to such a degree, that he has been frequently known to his intimates, to retire late at night from a tavern to his chambers and there read and make extracts from the most abstruse authors, for several hours before he went to bed. So powerful were the vigours of his constitution and the activity of his mind ".

Two pages in Fielding's hand-writing have survived from this period. They consist of two lists, one of the crimes known as High Treason and the other of slighter offences against the Crown.

What his resources were at this time we do not know. But in July, 1739, a year before he was called to the Bar, he is writing up to London to Nourse, his book-seller, to find him a house near the Temple. " I must have one large eating Parlour in it, for the rest shall not be very nice. Rent upwards of £40 p.an. : and as much cheaper as may be. I will take a lease for seven years ". He is no garret-dweller, although he apologises to Mr. Nourse for having failed to pay his bill, " which I shall certainly do on my coming to town ".

The " large eating Parlour " is very characteristic : no one more hospitable than Fielding, who, even during the last months of his life in Lisbon wrote home to his brother to send him out a " conversible man to be my companion in an evening . . . who will drink a moderate glass in an evening or will at least sit with me till one when I do ".

On June 20th, 1740, he was called to the Bar, chambers being at once assigned to him at No. 4 Pump Court, " up three pair of stairs ", worn and narrow stairs, " for the term of his natural life ", though as a matter of fact he vacated them in five months' time. The panelled rooms faced Brick Court and from the staircase one could look out on Pump Court and its sundial, with the motto " Shadows we are, and like shadows depart ".

With what high hopes he must have put on his barrister's gown in these chambers ! But one fact he had overlooked, that prudent attorneys would be unlikely to risk giving briefs to a man with a reputation for pasquinades against the Government and riotous farces which attacked all the pillars of the State—Law, Religion and Physic.

There is an extraordinary blank at this point of Fielding's life as it has come down to us. Not a single legal anecdote of him has survived of those years when he travelled the Western Circuit, from Winchester to Salisbury and Dorchester, thence to Taunton and Exeter, to Launceston and Bodmin, or attended the trials in Westminster Hall. In July 1740 he was certainly at the Dorset Assizes. Yet he had many friends among the lawyers, for when his *Miscellanies* were published by a subscription which brought in £700, more than half the subscribers were men of the law. They had forgotten, or forgiven the attacks made on their profession in *The Life and Death of Queen Commonsense.*

Yet a legend there is of these days, and a very picturesque one, which seems to have some foundation since it explains an incident in *Tom Jones.* Riding west one evening Fielding was overtaken by a heavy rain-storm and taking refuge in a cave, found in it a company of gypsies. And there, the story goes, he spent the night, joining with his hosts in a carouse.

But in their journey towards London, Fielding makes Tom Jones and Partridge spend an evening in the same way, except that instead of carousing, Tom discusses gypsy laws and customs with the king of the gypsies, and—unfortunately—one rascally fellow offers his wife to Partridge for a consideration.

This passage in the novel aroused the wrath of the actual " king ", of the West Country gypsies, Bampfylde-Moore-Carew, commonly called King of the Beggars. Carew, the runaway son of the famous Carew family of squires, had read the novel, and the 2nd edition of his *Apology For His Life*—everybody wrote ' Apologies ' in those days—contained a furious attack on Fielding : apparently because the reputation of the gypsies had been smirched by the incident of Partridge and the wife.

The venom of the Beggar King against Fielding and his novel fills many pages of Carew's *Apology*, a book that fifty years ago was often to be found in the window-seat of many a West Country farm, along with the seed catalogues.

The style of this diatribe is sufficiently amusing to be honoured by a quotation. " Among the spectators of Mr. Carew ", who had been begging as was his custom, " was the house-keeper of Madam Mohun, in the parish of Flete, who . . . led him to her mistress's house, where she seated him before a good fire, gave him two large glasses of brandy with loaf sugar in it . . . . Here could we hope our work would last to future ages, we would immediately immortalize this good woman ; however, we at least hope and presage that she will be honoured in our writings, when Mrs. Honour, Black George, and the other fine characters of one who stiles himself an author of the first-rate, will be forgotten or read only by some plodding school-boy, when he fetches a pound of cheese from some petty chandler's shop ",

Having thus sentenced Tom Jones and his friends to oblivion, Carew falls to explaining how, by pretending to be a shipwrecked sailor, he made nine or ten pounds.

After this diversion he returns again to Fielding : " For the celebrated writer of the Life of Mr. Jones, who assures us that he (and indeed seems to insinuate that only he) has been admitted behind the scenes of the great Theatre of Nature and professes his book to be written for the instruction of youth . . . after having informed his readers with one of the heroes of his History defrauding his friend and generous benefactor of 500 pounds, which he knew was all he had in the world, adds that though his readers may look upon such a man with the utmost abhorrence yet he (who knows better than any of them, being no less than Nature's Privy Counsellor) can censure the action without any absolute detestation of the person, for though the man is a villain, it is Nature for all that, and perhaps she may not have designed him to play an ill part in all her dramas, since it is often the same person who represents the villain and the hero ".

A trifle incoherent is this passage, but very clear in purpose, and, whether Mr. Carew wrote it himself, or employed " a ghost ", it certainly expresses the gist of much contemporary criticism on the morality of *Tom Jones*.

Finally, the King of the Beggars draws an elaborate comparison, " after the manner of Plutarch ", between Mr. Bampfylde-Moore-Carew and Mr. Thomas Jones, greatly to the detriment of the latter.

Before the close of his legal studies Fielding had plunged into political journalism, either for ready money, or because he could not keep away from politics when he saw how badly things were going in the Spanish War. Walpole still remained in power, though now tottering to his end.

Under such circumstances a new venture was started, and the first number of the *Champion Journal* appeared in November 1739. Fielding not only wrote in it, but according to Boswell, owned two-sixteenths of the shares. The paper, published three times a week, was not allowed to pass through the post on account of its principles.

Once more in his country's time of humiliation is Fielding seen playing the part of Pasquin under the title of " The Celebrated Captain Hercules Vinegar Bottle ", a cudgel-player at a bear garden, and the Champion of Virtue, Honour and Patriotism.

Several members of the Vinegar family supported him ; his wife, Mrs. Joan, did the ladies' column. Criticism of books and plays was left to Mr. Nol Vinegar who had spent a whole year in studying one word in Horace. Politics were to be handled by the Captain's father, a gentleman who " seldom opens his mouth, unless to take in his food, or puff out the smoke of his tobacco ".

The papers signed C. & L. are generally believed to have been Fielding's. And it is worth noting that the term " Vinegar Bottle " is still used in the West to describe a sharp-tempered person, generally a woman.

The most pointed criticism of the conduct of the war appeared when the *Champion* published two lists, the first showing the names of the ships taken by the Spaniards, and the second, those taken by the English. In this there was the word N O N E, printed in capitals. Captain Vinegar had lost none of the power of sarcasm shewn by him in *Pasquin*.

On a day of solemn fast, ordained to secure a blessing on the Fleet, the *Champion* came out with the tale of how all ancient nations, when faced with calamity, used to demand a victim to appease the wrath of the gods.

Everyone knew who the English victim should be ; especially when there was suggested another prayer in the Litany. This was : " From the Prime Minister, good Lord deliver us ".

But Hercules Vinegar had many targets besides the Prime Minister. The debtors' prisons he declared to be a " prototype of hell ". He inveighs against cruelty to horses in the Strand ; against the fashionable sport of " roasting ", or making fun of some simple awkward fellow. The Grammar Schools fall beneath his lash, when he suggests that the masters of them should be made drunk in order that the boys may see what a man looks like in that condition. Nor are the parsons left alone : he who truly follows his Master is put over against the churchman who " rejoices like a devil " at the tortures of hell for sinners. And as for their speech, some of their words and phrases convey no more meaning than the sounds made by the brute creation.

" Would that mine enemy had published a book " is a very wise prayer. In Fielding's case it was most truly answered when, in 1740, Colley Cibber came out with an *Apology* for his life.

Fielding, of course, promptly fell on the book with all the weapons in his armoury of satire. Cibber is called to the Bar to answer for his grammar. " You stand indicted here . . . for that you, not having the fear of Grammar before your eyes . . . in and upon the English language an assault did make, and then and there, with a certain weapon called a goose-quill, value one farthing, which you in your left hand then held, several broad wounds but of no depth at all, on the said English language did make ".

Cibber's *Apology* is a most entertaining Autobiography, or character sketch. But again and again the writer of it tangles himself up in sentences which are like labyrinths. They require to be read many times before the meaning emerges. None the less, the real Colley Cibber somehow gets written down, his vivacity, his conceit, his complacency, his intense enjoyment of himself and all his vices. He lays claim, of course, to all the virtues, except Chastity, but his folly pleases him far more than his wisdom. A crafty fool, an arrant rogue, is Cibber, but his *Apology* is almost a masterpiece.

The dedication to " a certain gentleman " is refreshingly naïve, when he speaks of himself as possessing " a heart that has just sense enough to mix respect with intimacy and never is more delighted than when your rural hours of leisure admit me, with all my laughing spirits to be my idle self, and in the whole day's possession of you— 'Tis then I taste you—then life runs high—I desire, I possess you ".

" Life runs high " : 'tis Cibber to the life. How he must have loved playing Fondlewife to the young actresses ! And how kind he was to Mrs. Pilkington, giving her wise advice, introducing her to the generous Great, and releasing her from the Marshalsea by paying her debts, and thoughtfully doing this in small coins only, lest she should be robbed. He sold her poems for her, wept at the pathos of her poem—*Sorrow*, and kept alive the courage of the little adventuress when she almost despaired. A coxcomb he was, vain as a peacock, and often, no doubt, sometimes as mischievous as a monkey. And what a subject for Fielding's genius !

One is glad to know that this gay old boy lived to be nearly ninety, and passed out as easily as he had lived. When his valet went in to him at seven in the morning, the man was told : " I will shave at eight ". But by that hour his master had gone where they neither shave nor eat.

Surely few can withstand the charm of that passage in the *Apology* where Cibber describes how he stood as a waiter behind the chair of the great Sarah Churchill at a banquet, longing to hear some fine sentiment fall from those august lips, and heard instead the words " Some wine and water ! "

Again, he played the Chaplain in *The Orphan,* and was afterwards clapped on the shoulder by a great man who exclaimed : " If he doesn't make a good actor, I'll be damned ! " And Cibber adds : " I make it a question whether Alexander himself, or Charles XII of Sweden, at the head of their first victorious armies—felt such joy ".

Here is surely a superb touch of nature, in the lad who had the audacity at the age of twenty-two to marry on a capital of £20.

Cibber was a character made by Nature herself to arouse the creative power of Fielding, and no style could have suited the subject better than his favourite mock-heroic attitude.

But here we touch on the strange fact that Fielding as a creator of character never drew his living personalities from the world of the theatre. Fops, beaux, rakes, and coxcombs, the whole tribe of Vanity Fair, belonged, in his mind, to the footlights ; they carried with them the smell of candle-fumes. The true spiritual home of the creator of Parson Adams was not in Covent Garden or the Mall. And therefore all those stage figures of his in the plays seem to be blown away by a wind which carries them off into limbo in a flutter of silks and satins, of wigs and fans. But the countrymen remain.

Cibber was of that world, and of no other. He won his laureateship for a political play, the *Non-Juror,* where a Jacobite acts the part of a Tartuffe. His way of living was more garish than a night at Vauxhall. Fielding would have none of him.

Yet Cibber was no fool. And his analysis of the English character has never been surpassed. It is truth itself. " To have seen " he writes, " all England of one mind is to have lived at a very particular juncture. Happy nation ! Who are never divided among themselves but when they have least to complain of. Our greatest grievance since that time seems to have been that we cannot all govern ".

Cibber appears to have modelled his deportment on Charles II, who was, he says, " regarded as a deity ", which was exactly what the poet laureate desired for himself. " Even his indolent amusement of playing with his dogs ", he adds, " and feeding his ducks in St. James's Park, (which I have seen him do), made the common people adore him ".

It almost appears that the old fop enjoyed the jests at his expense. At any rate, his philosophy is perfect.

" If ", he argues, " I can please myself with my own follies, have I not a plentiful provision for life ? Let them call me any fool but an uncheerful one ".

His reply to Fielding's attack is not undignified, although he calls him " a broken wit ", and broken he certainly was by the Licensing Act. " This enterprising person ", says Cibber ', found it necessary to give the public some pieces of an extraordinary kind, the poetry of which he conceived ought to be so strong that the greatest dunce of an actor could not spoil it. He knew, too, that as he was in haste to get money it would take less time to be intrepidly abusive than decently entertaining ; that to draw the mob after him, he must rake the channel and pelt their superiors . . . upon this principle he produced several frank and free farces, that seemed to knock all distinctions of mankind on the head. Religion, laws, government, priests, judges and ministers, were all laid flat at the feet of this Herculean satirist . . . that spared neither friend nor foe, who to make his poetical fame immortal . . . set fire to his stage by writing of an act of Parliament to demolish it ".

In essentials this is a true enough picture. But Cibber could afford to write calmly of Fielding since his own position as the manager of Drury Lane, one of the two patent theatres, was assured.

Some sixty or seventy articles in the *Champion* appear to be Fielding's. And on May 24th, 1740, he slyly inserts a glimpse of himself. As usual, Charon is busy ferrying souls across the river. But when these embark on the farther shore, all baggage must be left behind. Then, " a tall man came next, who stripp'd off an old grey coat with great readiness, but as he was stepping into the Boat, Mercury demanded half his Chin, which he utterly refused to comply with, insisting on it that it was all his own ".

This length of chin, these nutcracker jaws, are familiar to us all to-day in the drawing Hogarth made after his friend's death. And that " old grey coat " must have been well known everywhere in the regions of Vanity Fair.

Cibber, too, with his laurel on, is sent to Hades in the vision. As they were crossing, all naked and unashamed, " an elderly gentleman with a piece of wither'd laurel on his head slipped unnoticed with the laurel on—it was so small that it escaped the notice of the clear-eyed Mercury ".

It is a gentle and a witty hit. Perhaps Fielding remembered what he had written in the *Champion* in praise of good nature : " This makes us gentle without fear, humble without hopes, and charitable without ostentation ". Only occasionally, and when goaded beyond endurance, did Fielding forget this.

In February 1741 Walpole was openly attacked in the House by the Opposition leaders in what was known as " the Motion ".

This failed, and a cartoon appeared showing the leaders of the revolt walking in a funeral procession towards the family vault of the " reformers ". In this, Fielding carries the standard of the *Champion*, second only to the famous *Craftsman* in the line of newspapers. Old Sarah Churchill, a bent and aged figure, totters behind the bier, while Walpole shakes with laughter at the sight of his enemies' defeat.

But the war was still going disastrously, although Admiral Vernon had taken Porto Bello. Nearly all the summer of 1740 the fleet lay inactive in Torbay, because of " contrary winds ".

Fielding thereupon brought out a pamphlet in verse, supposed to be a fragment from Homer. This " Vernoniad " shows how Satan sends down Mammon to the earth that he may bribe the winds to ruin England. It is clear who this Mammon is since he covers his palace walls with " ill-got Pictures ", and on his return to hell gives a " three weeks' Feast ". At Houghton, Walpole's palace in Norfolk, every spring he entertained a house-party. This lasted exactly three weeks and the place was famous for its collection of pictures.

In the address to Mammon Fielding cries :—

" Submissive men yield to thy sway,
The world's thy puppet-show, and human things
Dance, or hang by as thou dost touch the strings ".

There are signs that Murphy was not far wrong when he described this time in Fielding's life as being burdened by "severities of want and pain ". For in a pamphlet called *True Greatness* he describes " a great tatter'd Bard " who fears to walk in the open streets for fear of arrest by bailiffs. Hungry and thirsty too he is,

"As down Cheapside he meditates the Song ".

But in that " Song ", and in nothing else, there is comfort and hope. For the subject of it is the contrast between the false greatness and the true. And Fielding knew that his was real greatness. Poor and struggling as he was, with personal sorrows and dread of illness and death for wife and children, encompassed by enemies, there was yet peace at the very heart of this man. It is not generally present in genius, this sense of the power within, but Fielding possessed it : partly the worker's delight in his work, the thing he has made, and partly the sense that real value, eternal value, lives in the mind, and not in anything that the world calls great.

Always haunted as he is by this sense of contrast, Fielding was to express it in his two supreme masterpieces : the false greatness in *Jonathan Wild*, the true in *Parson Adams*. And the power to show it came from years of suffering and struggle in the world. " True Greatness ", he then learnt, " lives but in the Noble Mind ".

In June 1741 the death of Lieutenant-General Edmund Fielding was briefly announced in the *London Magazine* as that of an officer " who had served in the late wars against France with much Bravery and Reputation ".

In that same month Captain Hercules Vinegar ceased to wield his cudgel against abuses. The fall of Walpole was at hand. Curiously enough, Fielding withdrew from all political activity at this moment. He was even accused of helping the Government by writing in Walpole's *Gazetteer*. The charge is incredible. But in a vision Fielding accounts for his withdrawal. Having fallen asleep over " a large quarto book ", Cibber's *Apology*, that is, he sees the Opposition for which he had fought so valiantly all assembled in a waggon drawn by horses so ill-matched that disaster threatens the whole affair.

On February 2nd, 1742, the Great Man, or Quidam, or Mr. Pillage, or Mammon, fell from power. And from that moment, Fielding left political journalism behind him, until the Jacobite Risings again called him to the service of England.

In Richardson's *Familiar Letters* he quotes a sort of proverb : " He, they say, who is not handsome by Twenty, strong by Thirty, wise by Forty, will never be either handsome, strong, wise, or rich ".

Fielding was now thirty-five, and as his novels were soon to prove, wise beyond the wisdom of many of the wisest men. He was certainly handsome at twenty, and strong by thirty, but never rich, except in the real wealth of life, in character, in genius, and in the immortality that arises from both.

CHAPTER XIII

Pamela and Shamela

IN the *Champion* of November 6th, 1740, there appeared the following advertisement: "*Pamela*: In a series of Familiar Letters. Now first published in order to cultivate the Principles of Virtue and Religion in the Minds of both Sexes;" a description very much to the taste of the period, however sanctimonious it may appear in ours.

The name of the author was not given, but by January of the next year, when a second edition came out, the *Gentleman's Magazine* reported that it was "judged in Town as great a sign of Want of Curiosity not to have read *Pamela*, as not to have seen the French and Italian dancers".

One fine lady at a party would hold up the book to show another that she had in hand the novel everyone was reading. It was recommended from the pulpit by the Vicar of St. Saviour's, Southwark; Pope is said to have declared that it "would do more good than many volumes of Sermons"; and at Slough, where the blacksmith read it aloud to the villagers, the church bells were rung when Pamela at last "got" him, and became the virtuous Mrs. B——.

It was finally translated by the Abbé Prévost, and a Frenchman reports that "tout le monde le lit", yet, contrary to the English verdict, "personne n'en parle avantageusement".

The novel had every possible advantage in its favour: the great world was bored by the interminable romances of Mlle. de Scudéry and her clan; the little world, as shewn by the villagers of Slough, was delighted to read a tale where the high and the low met to break down the class barrier. Here was a servant who married her master; a much bigger feat than the familiar tale of the great lady and the footman. The English middle-class, to whom the book was chiefly addressed, were here presented with a girl of low birth, exquisite beauty, and peerless virtue who gained the position of the Squire's wife. And everybody, too, after the Vicar's sermon was assured that the book was absolutely " safe ", and beneficial indeed to the pure virgin.

Nor was this all, for *Pamela* was written by a genius, the fat, fussy, old-maidish father of many children, Samuel Richardson, the printer of Salisbury Court, who by some miracle of instinct was able to follow the very windings of a girl's heart. To say that he learnt all this by writing love-letters for the country girls of Derbyshire is to say nothing. Richardson's genius, like all genius, still remains a mystery.

A story which had been told to him twenty years earlier of a maid who resisted her master's attempts at seduction and who came near to drowning herself from misery and despair, rose into life in the printer's imagination.

The book was real because the heroine was real. The other characters gain a look of life from Pamela. They talk and act like real human beings. For the first time the readers of a novel were able to feel the people in the story. They were made to laugh, to cry—particularly to cry. To this day, notwithstanding the long-winded style, one is held, made to go on reading *Pamela* as if by a spell ; and even against one's better judgment, just as in *Clarissa Harlowe* one is ashamed of being moved by so morbid a tragedy.

Yet one feels all through that Pamela was not really what Richardson makes her seem. At the age of fifteen she is a complete mistress of all the arts by which husbands are caught. When Mr. B—— is trying to trap her, actually she is trapping him into " Wilt thou have this woman ? " It is really a comedy of diamond cut diamond, and the female it is who shows all the subtlety in an extremely funny situation. Only of course Richardson never sees the comedy. And that in itself is entertaining.

Pamela quotes *Hamlet*, and talks about writing in the present tense ; very learned she is. All this is put down to the fact that she has been educated by Mr. B's mother above her station, which is that of a private waiting-maid. But if she wrote Greek, it would make no difference : she is real.

No one should blame her for this craftiness. Caught in a web by her pursuer, what weapon has she, except the cunning by which through the ages women have held their own against the power and strength and audacity of the male ?

According to Austin Dobson, the rake, Mr. B—, came out of

a play book. More true is it to say that, as a reformed penitent, he came out of a copy book.

Nowadays any writer who had to deal with such a position would treat it as a comedy played by Mr. B— the simpleton, and Pamela, the minx, using the word minx, not in condemnation, but as a woman says the word—with a humorous twinkle in her eye.

But Richardson saw his story in quite another light : Pamela's success comes from her purity and piety. She is held up as an example to all young virgins who are obliged to live in a world inhabited by lusting males. The dancing of rigadoons and minuets, she herself reflects, has made her unfit to live with her milkmaid companions. Far better for her character would it have been if she had learnt only to wash, scour, brew and bake. When she blistered her hand in scouring a pewter plate, she piously reflected that a Bishop once put his fingers into a lighted candle to show his faith by martyrdom.

She loves dress, as indeed did Richardson himself, who never loses a chance of describing his heroine's russet frocks in her humble days ; her silks, her laces and her diamonds when, as the Squire's lawfully wedded wife, she worships beside him in the parish church.

The pretty little creature says in one of those letters which she writes incessantly : " I bought of a Pedlar, two pretty enough round ear'd Caps, a little Straw Hat, and a Pair of knit Mittins, turn'd up with white Calicoe . . . and two yards of black Ribbon for my Shift Sleeves, and to serve as a Necklace ; and when I had 'em all come home, I went and look'd upon them once in Two Hours for two Days together ".

Did Richardson smile when he wrote this exquisite touch ? One doubts it.

Squire B—— owns two country houses, one in Bedfordshire, with a good housekeeper, and one in Lincolnshire, with a bad one. In both counties he is a Justice of the Peace, therefore Pamela cannot appeal to the Law for protection. Since the good house-keeper in Bedfordshire refuses to help him in his plans of seduction, he despatches Pamela to his Lincolnshire Manor House, where Mrs. Jewkes presides. She is a bawd out of Drury Lane in morals, and a real Hogarth study.

With a few strokes of his pen Richardson can create atmosphere; the large, lonely mansion in the midst of lofty elms and dreary pines does really give one a shiver. Honest Robin, the man-servant, almost apologises for bringing Mr B's victim to this abode of darkness. " I never saw an execution but once ", he says, " and then the hangman asked the poor creature's pardon—and pleaded his duty, and then calmly tucked up the criminal ! " He feels himself like the hangman.

She appeals for help to Williams, the curate of the parish, and to a certain Squire, Sir Simon Darnford, whose view of the affair is simply that " Our neighbour has a mind to his mother's waiting-maid !—He hurts no family by this ".

And Pamela comments : " Poor people's honesty is to go for nothing ! " No doubt the blacksmith's audience in Slough did thrill to hear such a sentiment.

The Psalm which Pamela writes during her captivity is based on the 137th——

> " When sad I sat in B—n Hall,
> All guarded round about,
> And thought of ev'ry absent friend,
> The tears for grief burst out——
>
> Remember, Lord, this Mrs. Jewkes
> When, with a mighty sound,
> She cries, " Down with her chastity,
> Down to the very ground ".

Solemnly no doubt did Richardson's first readers enjoy this. So may we, but not as they did.

Escape is planned, and very thrilling is the attempt. But Richardson, even though he works us up by the tenseness of the situation, cannot avoid throwing a ridiculous light over it.

Pamela succeeds in getting out of the garden, and into the field beyond. But then " I looked, and saw the bull, as I thought between me and the door, and another bull coming towards me the other way : well, thought I, here is double witchcraft to be sure ! Here is the spirit of my master in one bull, and Mrs. Jewkes in the other ".

But when she retreats, and looks back, she finds that they were " only two poor cows ! "

Thoughts of suicide come, but from the edge of the pond she throws her petticoat and handkerchief into it, instead of herself. Her prayer had been to have a decent funeral and to be saved from " the dreadful stake and the highway interment ". And,

"Oh, not to be the subject of their ballads and elegies!"

It is too great an honour for her to drive in "the chariot" with the Squire. Yet, as she watches him leave the house, she asks herself: "Why can't I hate him?" And when she is being sent away from Lincolnshire she is loath to leave the house. Her heart was so "lumpish".

The experienced reader knows what this means. "For", she writes, "I know not *how* it came, nor *when* it began, but crept, crept it has, like a thief upon me ... and before I knew what was the matter, it looked like love".

It was love!

He falls ill and feverish and is blooded. She returns and is married, thus taking advantage of his weakness. After marriage she hears a fellow-servant exclaim: "They are a charming pair!"

In a general orgy of good will, Gaffer Andrews, the humble father, arrives and is fitted with a suit of Mr B's clothes in order that he may attend church. The lumber is cleared out of the family chapel, and the knot is tied.

Pamela prepares for her future: no ladies will call on her of course, and therefore there will be no card-games for winter evenings. Instead, her pursuits will be: "Family economy, accounts, the poor, jellies, sweetmeats, marmalades—Music, reading, scribbling", and drives with Him in the chariot.

But Mr. B—— will insist on discussing "What your bashful modesty will not permit you to hint ... babies".

In a conclusion possible only to a writer entirely devoid of humour, Richardson makes Pamela say to her Mr. B——: "Oh, Sir, I have seen God's *Salvation!*—I am sure, if anybody ever had reason I have to say, with the Blessed Virgin, *My Soul doth Magnify the Lord; for he hath regarded the low estate of his handmaiden—and exalted one of low degree*".

This solemnity it was that made *Pamela*: or *Virtue Rewarded* fair game for a satirist.

But almost all the great literary lights of the time looked on *Pamela*, and still more on *Clarissa*, as immortal works—as they are—but also as examples of holiness expressed in living forms. Dr. Johnson thought that Richardson "taught the passions to move at the command of virtue". Alfred de Musset that *Clarissa Harlowe* was "le premier roman du monde" and

Diderot put Richardson's works on the shelf with Moses, Homer and Euripides.

Pamela in a literary sense was like the driftweed which showed Columbus that he was approaching a new continent. A new spirit was coming, the spirit of sentiment, and a new form of art —the analytical novel.

Wise men and fools piped to the new tune played by Richardson. The ever chatty Mrs. Pilkington tells us that over *Clarissa* Cibber " did almost rave ", and when she remarked that Clarissa was fated to die, he cried : " G—d d—n him if she should, and that he would no longer believe Providence or Eternal Wisdom or Goodness governed the world, if merit and innocence, and beauty were to be so destroyed ".

Clarissa Harlowe, trapped by a villain and fighting against dishonour, is a picture of inexorable fate as Richardson tells her story. Yet one thinks all the time what a pity it was when she reached London that she did not appeal for protection to Mr. Justice Fielding at his court in Bow Street. He would have made short work of Lovelace and his plots.

But, as has been beautifully said, " When we read we forget to criticise. The dragon comes to devour the maiden with all the flash and glitter and whirl of wings. Some time elapses before we suspect that he is merely a stage dragon ".

By the publication of a spurious sequel to *Pamela*, called *Pamela's Conduct in High Life*, Richardson was forced to produce a further book, telling the world how Pamela reformed her husband's parish, adopted his illegitimate child and gave courses of lectures to young ladies on how to avoid being seduced.

Actually this so-called novel was a treatise in which Richardson told the world his opinions on every subject, from wet nursing to politics, education and the morality of the stage.

It was at first believed that the famous *Pamela* was the work of Colley Cibber, whom all the wits combined to deride.

Certainly this was the impression of that unknown writer who produced one of the wittiest, grossest burlesques in the English language in the famous parody called *Shamela*. In the sub-title of this, according to the custom of the time, there is explained the purpose of the skit.

This runs : " In which the many notorious Falsehoods and Misrepresentations of a Book called

PAMELA

are exposed and refuted ; and all the matchless Arts of that young Politician set in a true and just Light. Together with a full account of all that passed between her and Parson Arthur Williams, whose Character is represented in a manner somewhat different from that which he bears in *Pamela*.
Necessary to be had in all Families.
By
Mr. Conny Keyber ".

Now Colley Cibber was named Keyber in Fielding's *Author's Farce*, when Harry Luckless submits to him the manuscript of a play. " Conny " is not a rabbit, as we at first imagine, but the dupe of a sharper : that is, Mr. Conny Keyber is Colley Cibber, dupe of Pamela, called " the young Politician ".

Another reading of this " Conny " is that it stands for Dr. Conyers Middleton, who had dedicated his life of Cicero to Lord Hervey in a fulsome address wherein his Lordship is praised for his temperance in diet. This interpretation is suggested by the dedication in *Shamela*, which congratulates Mr. Keyber on his frugality, " in spite of all the luscious Temptations of Puddings and Custards ".

The satire opens with a letter from a town parson, one Parson Tickletext, who writes to his friend, Parson Oliver, in the country. The latter has apparently heard nothing of the sensation created in London by the publication of *Pamela*.

" Herewith ", says Tickletext, " I transmit to you a Copy of sweet, dear, pretty Pamela—The Pulpit as well as the Coffee-house, hath resounded with its Praise, and it is expected shortly that his Lordship (the Bishop of London) will recommend it in a (Pastoral Letter) to our whole Body . . . This Book is the Soul of Religion, Good-breeding, Discretion, Good-Nature, Wit, Fancy, Fine Thought and Morality. As soon as you have read this yourself five or six times over (which may possibly happen within a week), I desire you would give it to my little God-Daughter, as a Present from me. This being the only Education we intend henceforth to give our Daughters. And pray let your Servant-Maids read it over, or read it to them ".

Good fooling of course, but in his reply Parson Oliver speaks out : " The Instruction which it conveys to Servant-Maids is, I think, very plainly this, to look out for their Masters as sharp as they can. The Consequences of which will be, besides Neglect of their Business ... that if the Master is not a Fool, they will be debauched by him ; that if he is a Fool, they will marry him. Neither of which, I apprehend, my good Friend, we desire should be the Case of our Sons ".

As it happens, he has in his possession the true Story of Pamela, and in order that this little Jade may not impose on the world he will now produce it, from a bundle of real letters.

Her father was a drummer in a Scotch regiment and became an informer after the Gin Act ; her mother was an orange woman at the Playhouse. Pamela is a schemer, Mr. B—— an idiot, and as for the grand folks, they simply don't exist.

Thereupon he proceeds to tell the story, keeping all the incidents and persons as they are in the novel, but with the light of the real facts thrown over them.

The housekeepers remain in the two Manor Houses. But Parson Williams, no innocent, but a scoundrel, is the key to the whole. Pamela has already had by him what she calls a " bantling ", unknown of course to her Master.

The ambition of " the young Politician " grows as her power increases over the idiot, Mr. Booby, who bears his real name and is no longer Mr. B——. When it is suggested that the Squire is really captured, she answers sharply : " No, Mrs. Jervis, nothing under a regular taking into keeping, a settled Settlement for me and all my Heirs, all my whole lifetime shall do the Business——"

Later on, hope rising, she writes : " For my own Part, I am convinced he will marry me, and faith, so he shall. O ! Bless me ! I shall be Mrs. Booby, and be Mistress of a Great Estate, and have a dozen Coaches and Six ".

At a tender moment, she swoons ; Lavender water and Hartshorn are used for a full half-hour. " O what a silly Fellow is a bashful young Lover ! "

Whoever the author of *Shamela* may have been, he certainly enjoyed the writing of it.

Sent off to the Lincolnshire house, Shamela there finds her old friend Nanny Jewkes as housekeeper. This woman had helped her in the affair of " the bantling " the year before, and the two women, under the tutelage of Parson Williams, live in the atmosphere of a house of ill-fame.

Williams is a rare hypocrite. As to Shamela's " fall ", he

remarks that " the omission of the Service was Sin, yet as I have told you, it was a venial one, of which I have truly repented, as I hope you have, and also that you have continued the wholesome office of reading good Books ".

Among these were *The Whole Duty of Man*, but with *The Duty to One's Neighbour* torn out, *Venus in the Cloister;* and *God's Dealings with Mr. Whitefield.* This last had been sent to her by her mother, " Mrs. Henrietta Maria Honora Andrews, from her Lodgings at the Fan and Pepper Box in Drury Lane ", where, if marriage with the Squire should fail, Shamela plans " to keep a House ".

Reproved for lightness of tone, she writes to her mother : " Marry come up, good Madam, the Mother had never looked into the Oven for her Daughter, if she had not been there herself ".

Being taken into keeping is no longer her aim. She would not be mistress to the greatest king . . . . " I value my Vartue more than I do anything my Master can give me ; and so we talked a full Hour and a half about my Vartue ".

This " Vartue " is now a commodity. " I thought once of making a little Fortune by my Person. I now intend to make a great one by my Vartue ".

To lure her master she practises all her Airs before the glass, and then sits down to read a chapter in *The Whole Duty of Man.*

Once married, she makes a practice of demanding a hundred pounds from her husband every day. If he refuses, she throws a fit, and then he fetches the money.

From the Chariot they watch Parson Williams hunting a hare. " Like the Parson's impudence to pursue a few Hares which I am desirous to preserve ", cries Booby.

" No, no ", thinks Pamela, " I am the Hare for whom poor Parson Williams is persecuted, and Jealousy is the Motive ".

Riding in the chariot by her side, Williams proceeds to instruct her in theology. He " told me the Flesh and the Spirit were two distinct Matters, which had not the least relation to each other. That all immaterial substances . . . such as Love, Desire, and so forth were guided by the Spirit. But fine Houses, large Estates, Coaches and dainty Entertainments were the Product of the Flesh. Therefore, says he, my Dear, you have two Husbands, one the object of your Love, and to satisfy your Desire ; the other the Object of your Necessity, and to furnish you with those other Conveniences . . . as then the Spirit is preferable to the Flesh so am I preferable to your other Husband, to whom I am antecedent in Time likewise ".

Finally, a book is to be written about her. " But they say my Name is to be altered, Mr. Williams says the first Syllabub hath too comical a Sound, so it is to be changed into Pamela ".

Pamela's round-ear'd cap and bodices became the fashion, and not far from Richardson's house there was opened an exhibition of her in waxwork, for which tickets were sold at sixpence each. The novel ran into four editions in 1740, after the Vicar's sermon on it.

Shamela was published anonymously, but Richardson believed that Fielding was the author of it. And since Fielding's sisters were frequent visitors at the novelist's house, he may have had the information from them. At any rate, this was Richardson's conviction to the day of his death. In a letter to Lady Bradshaigh, he declares his opinion that *Pamela*, which Fielding had abused in *Shamela*, first taught the rogue " how to write to please ". And a letter wherein *Shamela* is mentioned, is endorsed " Written by Mr. H. Fielding ", in the trembling hand of Richardson's old age.

The style of the burlesque is certainly Fielding's, his " hath " for " has " ; his " lady " rather than " wife ", as in his plays. And, as in his first novel, Malapropisms abound, such as " sect " for " sex ", " Statute of Lamentations " for " Statute of Limitations ". Parson " Oliver " recalls the Parson of that name in Fielding's boyhood. In fact, as one reads *Shamela*, one feels all through : " Aut Diabolus, aut Henricus Fielding ".

Whoever wrote *Shamela* had certainly no idea that he was attacking the printer of Salisbury Court. But that Fielding should attack Cibber, after the latter's criticisms of him as " a broken wit " in the *Apology*, was very probable. The sentimentality, the sickly morality of *Pamela* is mainly the target aimed at by the author of the skit. And any folly, sentimental or otherwise, Fielding would naturally lay down at Cibber's door, Cibber who had actually sentimentalised the Restoration dramatists in his *Love's Last Shift*.

The two men, Cibber and Fielding, are queer contrasts : the actor walking like a strutting fowl, a complacent admirer of himself, and Hercules Vinegar, that long, lean, hatchet-faced, cudgel-player with his scorn of every affectation.

Certainly *Shamela* was to *Pamela*, just what the farce of Tom Thumb, *The tragedy of Tragedies*, had been to the heroic drama. And this makes the authorship of the burlesque more suggestive of Fielding than any other fact.

The spirit of Fielding is surely present in *Shamela* : in his view the actual truth should be the aim of every writer. The great crime in his eyes was deception. But in order not to deceive, one must first see clearly, for all writing from the standpoint of a preconceived theory is false. *Pamela* is sentimental, and therefore not true.

Even in its grossness *Shamela* suggests the Fielding who defied the conventionality of the age when he attacked the vices of the fops in *The Covent Garden Tragedy* and *The Modern Husband*.

His irony, like all satire, is most effective when it is quiet, contained and ruthless. But like a man struggling in a torrent, he was apt to be carried off his feet ; then he lets himself go, and puts on the stage, or in print, what everybody knows is true, but will not face. The cudgel is not a subtle weapon, though Fielding often used it. Yet the rapier in his hand was a far more deadly weapon, especially when he used it on hypocrisy.

Richardson, at any rate, never forgave Fielding for, as he supposed, having coarsely derided him in *Shamela*. This life-long hatred of the author of *Tom Jones* was not entirely due to jealousy of a rival novelist, but to something much deeper, since the prattler of pretty things is always mortally offended with the man who drags ugly truths into the light of day.

Shamela, whoever was the author of it, is refreshing after the cloying sweetness of Richardson's character-drawing. A slice off a brown loaf tastes delicious after a long diet of marzipan.

And if the skit came from Fielding, how pleasant it is to meet him in *déshabillé* when, the lofty periods of his Augustan prose forgotten, he sits down beside one and tells a gossiping tale.

CHAPTER XIV

The Odyssey of Parson Adams

IT was a bright moonlit winter evening at seven o'clock when Pamela's chaste brother Joseph, in Fielding's first novel, shut the door of Lady Booby's London house behind him, and set his face to the West. Great moment as it was for Joseph Andrews, it was a far greater one for his creator whose genius was now coming to the birth, and with it the English novel of country life.

Behind Joseph, the footman, were the hot rooms, as the novel tells, where he had handled his mistress's tea-kettle; had stood behind her chair, and been the unwilling and astonished recipient of her favours. Wisely had the young man been christened Joseph.

Behind Fielding now were the candle-lit fumes of the theatre, the bitter satires on a corrupt society, and the attempt to wrest a livelihood from the practice of the Law, notwithstanding Wycherley's wise saying that " Apollo and Littleton seldom meet in the same brain ". In front of him now was the full expression of his own powers in the medium best suited to them.

Joseph Andrews, like almost all great novels, is the expression of a central idea, whose motif, as in a symphony, recurs again and again in one form after another. It may, of course, be read merely as a " rogue " story, a novel of the road ; *Gil Blas* in another mood. Its atmosphere is picaresque, its style mock-heroic, with sudden sly turns of irony. This " comic-epic " of Homer Fielding supposes to have been long lost. He now restores it to the world in the form of the Adventures of Joseph Andrews, and of his Friend Mr. Abraham Adams.

In Fielding's view the proper subject of satire is not villainy, which we should abhor, nor great qualities, which should be admired ; nor poverty, ugliness and deformity : these deserve our pity. Always the object of attack should be affectation, the spirit that is rooted in vanity, either as the hypocrisy which conceals vice, or as the pretence of fine character in order to gain admiration.

Men, almost all men, wear masks, but behind the mask is the real man. Tear this away, and you will find him. Character after character is unmasked in *Joseph Andrews*: squires, parsons, doctors, clergymen, a publisher, innkeepers, coachmen, tavern wenches, postilions and prudes, those creatures in human form more loathed by Fielding than misers.

So far for the background, in the foreground is Parson Adams, an ill-dressed, uncouth, poverty-stricken, absent-minded old curate, whose cassock, torn years ago in climbing over a stile, is still ragged, much to his wife's discredit, and hangs down below his coat. Every possible humiliation befalls him, every moment he grows more absurd, and every moment we like him the better for it. He is no saint : he believes a schoolmaster to be the greatest of all men, and himself the greatest of all school-masters. He preaches a calm bearing under all misfortunes and yet cries out in agony when he thinks his little Dick has been drowned.

A scholar, Parson Adams judges men by the standard of the great heroes of classical days. His favourite master is Æschylus ; he can translate French, Italian and Spanish, and is well read in Oriental languages. Yet in knowledge of the world he is a mere babe. Because his heart is good, he never guesses that such passions as envy, malice and greed are all about him wherever he goes. He takes the actual world for the ideal, because the ideal is in his own nature.

Fielding, going about like a man testing for gold, finds in this uncouth figure the pure gold of compassion, generosity and purity of heart. And all this in the manner of a jest, so that there is no shadow of sanctimoniousness in the whole picture.

The English have always admired this type of unworldly simplicity, perhaps because it is so rare among us. Adams re-appears of course three times in Thackeray, as Colonel Newcome, as Dobbin, even at times as Colonel Esmond.

But the Parson smoking his pipe in Sir Thomas Booby's kitchen and drinking his cyderand, is no Victorian gentleman, and no fool, though many people took him to be so. By a miracle of genius, Fielding shows him to be like St. Francis himself, far above all the assaults of the rich and the insolent.

My Lady Poverty has given him the mastery of this world. "He that is down need fear no fall". But when he threw himself, again like St. Francis, on the goodwill of others, as a brother may in one great family, his plea was refused with curses. St. Francis would have found Parson Trulliber a hard nut to crack.

We are all desperately lonely at times. Only once now and again, in a flash of love or hatred, do we really fuse with one another. But in Parson Adams, a mere ghostly form, a being made by words, we do actually seem to come close to another soul, so kind, so simple is he. Amazed he is at wrong-doing, but never as if he were of another flesh and blood from the sinner. It is impossible that he should look down contemptuously on another man.

In a sense, here is the stoic idea that nothing from outside can injure the spirit of a man : neither torture, nor mockery. Adams goes through grotesque experiences enough : he is tied to a bed-post, hunted by hounds, drenched in pig's blood, "roasted", or made the butt of a set of ill-bred Squires. Still he retains his human dignity intact.

On another plane Fielding had endured humiliations; called "a broken wit", lampooned again and again, saddled with the name of rake and spendthrift, he had waited vainly on great men's favours. Yet he remains a man of mastery. And, like his queer old curate, whatever is human in the common man he understands. He cannot take us up to the heights, or down to the depths, like Shakespeare. But—man of the world as he is—he never forgets the reality behind the show. And his scorn of false greatness burns like a fire, his scorn of these tyrants and conquerors who tear their greatness out of the hearts of the lowly.

Two writers have tried their hands at creating ideal characters. Dostoievsky's Alyosha, young and Christ-like, is altogether lovely. But he is of heaven, not of earth. And Richardson's Grandison is an epitome of all the moral virtues. His limbs never grew in a woman's body; his bones are "articulated" like those of a skeleton.

But nobody was ever more of this earth than Parson Adams, and no one ever made us feel before how rare and beautiful simple goodness can be.

The humour of the story is started by making Joseph a brother to Pamela; he is a companion picture to that holy maiden. Just as she refuses to be ravished by her master, so Joseph will not be seduced by his mistress, Lady Booby. Joseph, who has been in the country a bird-scarer, a kennel boy, a stable lad and a jockey, is now an Adonis of a footman, among his " parti-coloured brethren ", the gentlemen's gentlemen.

Luscious is the description of his beauty; his nut-brown hair in wanton ringlets, his eyes full of sweetness and of fire, his teeth even and white. A delicious morsel indeed for a lascivious old woman. She is in love with him, and so is Mrs. Slipslop, her waiting-woman, the original Malaprop, with " incense " for " essence " and " sect " for " sex ". It is the scene of *Pamela* turned upside down.

But Joseph has been the Parson's pupil, and his father spent sixpence a week on his schooling, so that he has read *The Whole Duty of Man*. Also, as he is Pamela's brother, he has learnt to keep himself pure for his lovely country-maid, Fanny, away in Somerset, where the estates of the Booby clan are situated.

Being turned out of the London house for rejecting his lady's love, Joseph shuts her door behind him, and so ends all attempts on Fielding's part to write a satire on *Pamela*. We hear nothing more of this until the end of the story when everything has to be rounded off.

The tale is to be a merry adventure. We are to have no fear of ridicule, and no scorn of anything except shams. An epitaph on the clan of the Andrews gives the tone of the whole :

" Stay, traveller, for underneath this pew,
Lies fast asleep that merry man Andrew.

Be merry while thou canst, for surely thou
Shalt shortly be as sad as he is now."

" The words ", remarks Fielding, " are almost out of the stone with antiquity ". And probably the persons called " Merry Andrews " are kin to this sleeper.

We are going to be in very low company, for in Abraham Adams we meet a man whose stipend, at the age of fifty, was but £23 a year, as a country curate, on which he was not able to cut much of a figure, " as he lived in a dear country, and was somewhat encumbered with a wife and six children ".

Fielding flaunts his parson's poverty in the faces of those many people who went about labelling everything as " low " which was not aristocratic.

" Be it known ", he writes, " that the human species are divided into two sorts of people, to wit, high people and low people . . . Now the world being thus divided . . . a fierce contention arose between them ; nor would those of one party . . . be seen publicly to speak to those of the other, though they often held a very good correspondence in private ".

On the road Joseph meets robbers, who leave him stark naked and wounded in a ditch. Along comes the stage coach full of passengers. When the postilion hears groans from the side of the road, a halt is made, and the position is made a test for all the characters present. It is the parable of the Good Samaritan played in eighteenth century England.

The coachman, because they are late, is for going on and leaving Joseph ; so is the lady because the man is naked; so is the elderly gentleman who fears they are going to be robbed. The lawyer alone is for taking the man up " lest, if he died, they might be called to some account for his murder ". The coachman wants a shilling from someone for the poor wretch's fare.

No one will cover the naked man with a great-coat, though the coachman is sitting on two. Only the postilion strips off his, swearing—for which he was rebuked by the passengers— " that he would ride in his shirt all his life rather than suffer a fellow-creature to lie in so miserable a condition ".

The lad, adds Fielding, with that sly sarcasm of his, " hath been since transported for robbing a hen-roost ".

The postilion is the fellow of that poor pedlar who, having but six and six in his pocket, gives it all to Parson Adams so that he may pay his debt at the inn. Very certainly Fielding is on the side of the low.

Joseph is at last carried to the Dragon Inn kept by the Towwouses, the husband with kind instincts, but under the thumb of a money-grubbing wife. When Joseph longs for a cup of tea, she " can't be slopping all day ". She refuses to give him a clean shirt, but changes her tune when she knows he has rich friends. The wench of the inn, a girl of no virtue at all—in Pamela's sense—is the only one who helps the wounded man.

Then Abraham Adams arrives on his way up to London whither he is going to sell three volumes of sermons, hoping to gain much wealth by the deal. No notion has he, poor man, that the market is overstocked with these.

When Barnabas, the Vicar of the parish, comes to prepare Joseph for the other world, he is followed by a publisher—a strange fowl to be found on a country road. The long arm of coincidence never stood in Fielding's way when he thought it would be useful.

It appears now that unless the sermons are by Mr. Whitefield, Mr. Wesley, or a Bishop, the man of business won't touch them. But sermons by such great men sell like farces! The Parson is horrified by such a comparison, and then discovers that . . . he has left his manuscript at home! The two men, Joseph and Adams, determine to " ride and tie ", travelling down to Somerset, using the horse the Parson has borrowed from his clerk, an animal with the unfortunate habit of kneeling down suddenly *en route*, leaving his rider, if he is lucky, standing upright over him.

The Parson walks on, forgetting that the horse's corn is not paid for. Joseph, with only sixpence in his pocket, is left to deal with the matter. But the Tow-wouses are adamant. Meanwhile on strides Abraham, wading up to the waist at a point where the water is across the road because he never looked over the hedge to find the footpath. He sits down to wait, and is soon lost in reading his Æschylus.

Again the convenient arm of coincidence, when Mrs. Slipslop, on her way to Lady Booby's estate in Somerset, arrives at the inn and pays the reckoning for the horse's keep. But that unlucky animal, by his trick of suddenly falling on his knees, has made a gash in Joseph's leg. When the landlady of the next inn stoops to chafe it, her husband takes the worst view of the affair. In the fight that follows, when Adams tries to interfere to save Joseph, he gets a pan of pig's blood emptied over his head.

Later on, when a woman's shrieks are heard coming from a wood, Adams with his cudgel flies to the rescue. In the fight he gives the man what seems to be a death-blow. But the fellow recovers and the woman is found to be no other than the beautiful milkmaid, Fanny, the beloved of Joseph Andrews. At this point a company of boys out " bird-batting " arrive on the scene, and promptly hale off to the nearest magistrate poor Fanny and the Parson.

"Bird-batting", says Fielding, "if you are ignorant of it (as perhaps if thou hast never travelled beyond Kensington, Islington, Hackney, or the Borough, thou mayst be), I will inform thee, is performed by holding a long clapnet before a lantern, and at the same time beating the bushes", so that the birds make for the light and are caught. It was practised in country places down to our own days.

The scene before the Justice that follows is a riotous farce. No one can decide in what language the Parson's Greek book is written, but a mittimus is made out in the name of Mr. Æschylus. Then suddenly Adams is recognised by one of the Squires who vouches for him and the J.P. instantly changes, saying : " I know how to behave myself to a gentleman as well as another. Nobody can say I have committed a gentleman since I have been in the Commission ".

Again by the light of the moon, Fanny and the Parson set out, but in the next inn all eyes are on beautiful Fanny who is "not one of those slender young women who seem rather to be intended to hang up in the hall of an anatomist than for any other purpose ". On the contrary, she was so plump that she seemed bursting through her tight stays. Her fair complexion, when not touched by the sun, attained a whiteness " which the finest Italian paint would be unable to reach ".

A crisis is reached when a voice is heard singing like a lark in the next room. At the sound Fanny faints, the Parson, distraught, flings his Æschylus on the fire, and Joseph rushes into the room. Soon it is a case of " O Joseph, you have won me ! I will be yours for ever ! " But the Parson insists that the banns shall be called and the licence drawn up before the lovers are made happy.

Again the reckoning is the trouble. Seven shillings is owing, and the Parson has but sixpence-halfpenny in his pocket. But at the news of a rich parson in the parish, Adams capers round the room and sets off to find him. This is Trulliber, whom tradition associates with Fielding's first tutor, Parson Oliver of Motcombe by East Stour. To him goes Adams to borrow the needful.

At first he is taken for a pig-dealer, and after falling down in the sty with the cry of " Nil habeo cum porcis ", he begs a loan from Mr. Trulliber. Seven shillings for the reckoning at the inn, and also seven shillings more. " Which, peradventure

I shall return to you; but if not, I am convinced you will joyfully embrace such an opportunity of laying up treasure in a better place than any this world affords".

Abraham has now to learn how it happens that a man may starve in the midst of plenty. Trulliber, who knows "where to lay up his little treasure as well as another", cries that the Parson is no better than a beggar, and not a clergyman at all.

"But suppose I am not a clergyman", rejoins Adams, "I am nevertheless thy brother".

From Trulliber he gets nothing, while the pedlar pays, giving his all. And, as the Parson had sixpence in his pocket, and the pedlar six and sixpence, all is well. With his usual caper Adams pays up.

In one of the characteristic introductions to the Books into which the story is divided, Fielding tells us that his aim is to "hold the glass to thousands in their closets, that they may contemplate their deformity and endeavour to reduce it, and thus by suffering private mortification may avoid public shame".

As to the truth of his portraits, "I question not but several of my readers will know the lawyer in the stage-coach the moment they hear his voice. It is likewise odds but the wit and the prude will meet with some of their acquaintances as well as all the rest of my characters . . . I declare here, once for all, I describe not men, but manners; not an individual, but a species. Are not the characters then taken from life? To which I answer in the affirmative, nay, I believe I might aver that I have writ little more than I have seen. The lawyer is not only alive, but hath been so these 4,000 years . . . He hath not indeed confined himself to one profession, one religion, or one country; but when the first mean selfish creature appeared on the human stage who made self the centre of the whole creation, would give himself no pain, incur no danger, advance no money, to assist or preserve his fellow-creatures, then was our lawyer born".

As the travellers proceed in the dark night, to their great terror they see lights moving about. These they take to be ghostly. Worse still is it when a voice comes out of the darkness which says that he had "killed a dozen since that day fortnight".

This scene is one of the very few instances where Fielding introduces "atmosphere". Usually he is of the same mind as the stage manager who put out a palm tree and expected his audience to see a gloomy forest. Only once are we given the descriptive touch which shows the Parson smoking his pipe in the gallery of an inn.

But the lights were carried by sheep-stealers, not ghosts. Yet Adams was heard to mutter that " he was convinced of the truth of apparitions for all that ".

At the cottage where they shelter for the night, since Fanny looks white and faint, she is sent to bed, while the master of the house recounts to Joseph and the Parson the story of his life.

Never quite autobiographic, this digression assuredly recalls at certain points, the past experiences of Fielding himself. Here, in Mr. Wilson's story, is his too early introduction to the world, his wildness and the reputation it earned for him, though " doing nothing " was certainly never Fielding's way of passing the time, but a refusal to fight a duel is quite likely to have actually happened to him. No doubt, too, he had learnt, like Wilson, that the Town Harlots are but " painted Palaces, inhabited by Disease and Death ". Certainly he never gained a wife at a cost of £3,000 in damages, though he probably did join a club where the members talked philosophy, but acted very much like other people. And, like Wilson again, in the playhouses he had been able to study vanity in its natural home.

Adams here interposes that he only wishes he had with him his sermon on vanity, " for I am confident you would admire it ". The good man is so ignorant of the vain world, however, that he does not know the meaning of the word " coquette ".

When Wilson comes to his poverty, and his attempts to pay for his food and lodging by play-writing, he is Fielding once more. " Many a morning ", says he bitterly, " have I waited hours in the cold parlours of men of quality, where after seeing the lowest rascals in lace and embroidery . . . admitted, I have been sometimes told that my Lord could not possibly see me this morning ". And, when he tried to get work by " hackney writing ", he found " that Plato himself did not hold poets in greater abhorrence than these men of business ", the publishers. Here is a reflection of that distressful period when, after being called to the Bar, Fielding was given no briefs ; when men laughed at him, saying that they were afraid he would turn their deeds into plays. The reputation of poet " was my bane ", says Wilson. Is not this Fielding face to face with the men of the Law?

But in Wilson's story a little idyll follows. After a happy marriage the husband and wife walk in their garden beside the filbert hedge and talk together as though they were living in the golden age; Fielding is surely recalling his good days with Charlotte at East Stour.

In Wilson's story we have the gay world of the time and what Harry had learnt from it. This picture is indeed the background which he carried in his mind when he painted his three innocents, the Parson, the footman and the milkmaid.

While the travellers, after discussing a cold fowl, are resting in a valley, the peaceful scene changes when the hounds dash forward in pursuit of a hare. The Parson is asleep until the pack, mistaking his cassock for a hare skin, apply their teeth to his wig. Instead of calling off the hounds, the Squire swears 'tis " the largest jack-hare he ever saw ".

Joseph runs to the Parson's aid, but the leading hound has a firm hold of the cassock. The cudgel brings Jowler and Rockwood to the ground, while Thunder and Plunder and Wonder and Blunder measure their lengths, till the bitch Fairmaid bites Joseph in the leg.

The hunting Squire is awake in Fielding and in glowing terms he sings the praises of the mighty hound Ringwood: " Ringwood, the best hound that ever pursued a hare, who never threw his tongue but where the scent was undoubtedly true; good at trailing, and sure in a highway; no babbler, no over-runner; respected by the whole pack, who whenever he opened, they knew the game was at hand ". That Ringwood was an old friend we cannot doubt.

Adams uses his crab-tree till the Squire and his party come upon the scene, whereupon all eyes are fixed on Fanny's beauty. And that was dangerous in a time when in every wood there lurked the ravishers of maidens. But the huntsman has the last word: he " wondered that his master would encourage the dogs to hunt Christians; that was the surest way to spoil them, to make them follow vermin instead of sticking to a hare ".

The Parson and his friends are invited to dinner with the Squire, who has already fixed his desires on the beautiful Fanny. It offers too an opportunity for the " roasting " or badgering of Adams, one of the most popular amusements of the time, and one against which Fielding was never tired of inveighing.

Accordingly the Parson's chair is pulled away as he is saying grace; the soup is overturned into his breeches; jests are made at the poverty of his cassock, to which one wag has fastened a cracker.

An extempore " poem " is chanted :—

" Did ever mortal such a parson view?
His cassock old, his wig not over-new,
Well might the hounds have him for fox mistaken,
In smell more like to that than rusty bacon ? "

The Parson's speech is calm, but frank. Its tone may be judged from the remark : " I am your guest, and by the laws of hospitality entitled to your protection ".

This produces no effect on these fellows who finally lure him on to preach a sermon. A throne for him is prepared made of a plank set across a tub of water, with two stools on each side, all covered with a blanket. A man sat on each stool and when the Parson got up between them, they rose suddenly, so that he was soused in the water.

It is the Parson who keeps his dignity, for, says Fielding, " I defy the wisest man in the world to turn a true good action into ridicule ".

After this they leave the house, of course taking Fanny with them. But the Squire lusts after her, and sends two of his servants to bring her back. These beauties force their way into the inn where the travellers have taken refuge and a fight follows in which Joseph and Adams are beaten. Fanny is carried off, while the two men are left, each tied to the leg of a bed.

In the nick of time arrives Mr. Peter Pounce in his chariot with outriders. Fanny is saved and the men are untied from their posts. Pounce is Lady Booby's steward, traditionally said to be studied from a certain Salisbury attorney, one Peter Walter, whom Fielding knew well.

The conversation between Pounce and the Parson, as they ride along side by side in the chariot, is the finest bit of satire in the whole book.

The Parson having defined charity as " a generous disposition to relieve the distressed ", Pounce is mightily pleased. He likes the " disposition " as long as he is not asked to turn it into a deed.

L

"But, alas! Mr. Adams", says he, "who are meant by the distressed? Believe me, the distresses of mankind are mostly imaginary, and it would be rather folly than goodness to relieve them".

"Sure, Sir", replies Adams, "hunger and thirst, cold and nakedness and other distresses which attend the poor can never be said to be imaginary evils".

"How can any man complain of hunger", rejoins Pounce, "in a country where such excellent salads are to be gathered in almost every field? Or of thirst, where every river and stream produces such delicious potations? And as for cold and nakedness, they are evils introduced by luxury and custom. A man naturally wants clothes no more than a horse or any other animal . . ."

The Parson is so disgusted, especially by Pounce's references to people in torn cassocks, that he opens the chariot door and leaps out. His hat is flung after him by Pounce "with great violence".

The last Book opens with the arrival of Lady Booby at her country house, where she works hard to get Fanny sent to Bridewell to prevent her marrying Joseph. Her agent, Lawyer Scout, is worthy of Fielding's satire, for he is of the opinion that we have too many of the poor about; "we ought to have an act to hang or transport half of them". But Adams calls the banns for Joseph and Fanny in defiance of the lady, even though she has called in Justice Frolick to help her. This Justice, we are told, takes a real pleasure in sending men to Bridewell.

Great play is made by Fielding of the charge brought before this magistrate against Joseph and Fanny. This "depusition", written by the Justice himself, affirms that a witness "zede Joseph Andrews with a nife cut one hassel twig, of the value, as he believes, of three half-pence, or thereabouts" . . . and that Fanny did "receive and karry in her hand the said twig".

For this fell deed the lovers were to be sent to Bridewell, through Lady Booby's influence. But they are saved when Lady Booby's nephew, the Mr. B—— of Richardson's *Pamela*, appears on the scene, with his famous wife.

All is suddenly wound up, and we have the English happy ending in its most complete form: Joseph is found to be Mr. Wilson's lost son, and Fanny is Pamela's sister, all this being the work of the gypsies, who carried away the babe Fanny and substituted for her the boy Joseph, so that Gammer Andrews accepted the strange boy in place of her girl baby.

The stealing of babies by gypsies in order to sell them, as Fanny had been sold to Sir Thomas Booby, seems to have been a common crime at this period. Test Fielding's story where you will, and you come on real life.

The identity of Joseph, as Mr. Wilson's son, is proved by a strawberry mark on his breast, " as fine a strawberry as ever grew in a garden ". And at her wedding Fanny wore " one of her own short round-ear'd caps ", a reminiscence of the famous cap in *Pamela*, with over it, a little straw hat, lined with cherry-coloured silk, and tied with cherry coloured ribbon.

Nor is the Parson left out of this happy picture : he is presented by Mr. B—— with a living worth £130 a year, and allowed to retain his old curacy, so becoming an innocent pluralist.

Parson Young, the original of Parson Adams, was in fact idealised to a certain extent by Fielding. It is said of him that he was in every tradesman's debt in his parish. Perhaps not to be wondered at if, like Adams, his curacy was worth no more than £23 a year. It was in Major-General Lascelles' regiment of foot that he acted as chaplain. With Fielding he went to London in 1742, perhaps travelling ' ride and tie ' with the novelist, to earn his living as a translator among the writers of Grub Street. It is said that when acting as a tutor at £70 a year he one day wanted a holiday, and thereupon fabricated a letter to be shewn to his employer as a proof that he must have leave of absence. Young died in Chelsea Hospital three years after his friend Fielding.

It has been questioned whether Fielding had read *Le Paysan Parvenu* of Marivaux, where a country boy fights against seduction, and where the strawberry mark, near the heroine's right eye, also makes its appearance. But it appears now that the strawberry mark was only inserted in Marivaux's novel after the publication of *Joseph Andrews*.

The book was published in two volumes, on Feb. 22nd 1742, at the price of six shillings.

According to tradition Fielding was advised to offer the manuscript to Millar, the publisher, whose wife after reading it told him that he must not let the book slip through his fingers. In a tavern the two men met, and after the second bottle of port, so the story goes, Millar said to Fielding : " I don't think I can afford to give you more than £200 ".

" £200 ; are you serious ? " cried Fielding.

" Never more so ! "

" Then, give me your hand. The book is yours ".

The agreement survives. It is written in Fielding's own hand, and signed by William Young as one of the witnesses. The date is April 13th 1742.

As a matter of fact £183 11. was the sum paid for the novel, with ten guineas for the play *Miss Lucy in Town*, and five guineas for *The Full Vindication of the Duchess of Marlborough*. The first edition seems to have been fifteen hundred copies.

Among the books in Fielding's library was Bishop Burnet's *History of His Own Times*, and in the list of subscribers to that book there are to be found the names Joseph Andrews and Abraham Adams. To his young countryman Joseph Fielding gave much of his own physique.

It was not until the third edition that Fielding's name appeared on the title page of *Joseph Andrews*, and this only after several attempts had been made to claim the authorship. It reached France in 1743, the translator, actually the Abbé Desfontaines, calling himself " Une Dame Anglaise ". On the shelves of the Petit Trianon Marie Antoinette kept a copy of this. But the novel was not nearly as popular as *Pamela*, of which six editions appeared in the first year of publication.

The scenes in the country, the merry bustle of the inns, the whole atmosphere of *Joseph Andrews* is as gay as a May morning, as merry as Chaucer's Prologue, and as full of typical English figures. Yet at the time of writing, Fielding's circumstances were as dark as they could possibly be ; in the Preface to his *Miscellanies* he describes the scenes in his own life when the novel was being written, " with a favourite child dying in one bed and a wife desperately ill in another ". We get here one of very few glimpses of Charlotte as a wife. " I remember ", her husband writes, " the most excellent of women, and tenderest of mothers, when, after a painful and dangerous delivery, she was told she had a daughter, answering : ' Good God ! have I produced a creature who is to undergo what I have suffered ? ' Some years afterwards, I heard the same woman, on the death of that very child, then one of the loveliest creatures ever seen, comforting herself with reflecting, that her child could never know what it was to feel such a loss, as she then lamented ".

The gaiety of *Joseph*, written in the midst of such sorrow, is matched by the serenity with which Fielding faced the approach of his own death in that scrap of autobiography, *The Voyage to Lisbon*.

Few there were at first to appreciate the power of this new way of painting common life, yet the book crept slowly into favour. Gray wrote disparagingly : " the incidents are ill-laid ", he says, " and without invention ; but the characters have a great deal of nature, which always pleases even in her lowest shapes. Parson Adams is perfectly well, so is Mrs. Slipslop, and the story of Wilson ; and throughout he shows himself well-read in stage-coaches, Inns and Inns of Court ". Gray prefers the romances of Marivaux and Crébillon.

" Well-read " is hardly the phrase for Fielding's knowledge of stage-coaches and inns. But Fielding's robust humour and freedom of mind would naturally find no echo in the perfect propriety of Gray's nature.

But the women were more acute critics. Seven years after the publication of *Joseph Andrews*, a box of books arrived from England for Lady Mary Wortley Montagu, then living in Italy. In it was a copy of *Joseph*. And, although it was then ten o'clock at night, she says, " I could not deny myself the pleasure of opening it, and falling upon Fielding's works was fool enough to sit up all night reading. I think *Joseph Andrews* better than his Foundling ". That is, than *Tom Jones*.

Where everyone rushed to acclaim the beauties of *Pamela*, few dared at first to speak well of *Joseph*, and especially not before Richardson. All honour therefore to Miss Carter, actually one of his circle of adoring ladies, whose description is cordial indeed.

" *Joseph Andrews* ", she writes, " contains such a surprising variety of nature, wit, morality, and good sense, as is scarcely to be met with in any one composition, and there is such a spirit of benevolence runs through the whole, as I think renders it peculiarly charming ".

This is royal praise, but even this gallant lady, though she remained a staunch defender of Fielding's genius, dared not express her opinion publicly ; only in private letters.

Yet *Joseph* was making its way, slowly and surely. The

surest test of popularity is—piracy. And we find Sir Dudley Rider writing in a letter of his attempt to rescue Joseph Andrews and Parson Adams out of the hands of the literary pirates. Especially was the Parson becoming popular and well-known, so that in his *Miscellanies* Fielding writes that he had communicated the manuscript of *The Journey from this World to the Next* to his friend Parson Adams, who, " after a long and careful perusal, returned it to me with this opinion that there was more in it than at first appeared ".

It seems too that the round-ear'd cap which Fanny wore at her wedding had become fashionable. And nothing in the world can be a surer mark of popularity than fashion. But possibly, since Pamela also wore the same sort of headgear, the new fashion may rather have been derived from her than from Fanny. The honour of appearing in a wax-work exhibition, like that " young Politician " of Richardson's, never fell to Parson Adams.

But Fielding lost a great opportunity in refusing to give us Parson Adams' comments after a reading of *Pamela*. His opinion would have been worth having, if indeed he could have been induced to read a novel at all.

CHAPTER XV

The Heart of Henry Fielding

WITHIN a few weeks of the publication of *Joseph Andrews* there appeared an entry in the registers of St. Martin's in the Fields recording the burial of that beloved child, Charlotte Fielding. In his *Journey from this World to the Next* her father tells us how he meets his lost little one in Elysium. " Great Gods ! " he cries, " what words can describe the Raptures, the melting passionate Tenderness with which we kissed each other, continuing in our Embrace, with the most exstatic Joy, a Space, which, if Time had been measured as here on Earth, could not have been less than half a Year ". She was seen close to old Homer, this baby who had put on immortality in her father's dreams.

After the summer Assizes of 1742 Fielding and his wife were in Bath, probably for the benefit of the waters, since gout was now adding to the many distresses endured by him.

In the Pump Room that autumn we catch a momentary glimpse of Fielding's " elastic gaiety of spirit ". For here he met one Jane Husband, a girl of exquisite beauty, who, after an illness, had for a time to be carried about in a bath-chair. But by the help of the waters and the skill of Dr. Brewster she recovered, finally hanging up her crutches as an offering to the " nymph of the spring ".

Fielding addressed her in verse :—

> " Soon shall these bounteous springs thy wish bestow,
> Soon in each feature sprightly health shall glow,
> Thy eyes regain their fire, thy limbs their grace,
> And roses join the lilies in thy face.
> But say, sweet maid, what waters can remove
> The pangs of cold despair, of hopeless love ?
> The deadly star which lights th' autumnal skies
> Shines not so bright, so fatal as those eyes ".

This " cold despair " was, it appears, endured by Robert Henley, afterwards Lord Chancellor. He saw this Jane when travelling on the Western Circuit and managed to get introduced to her, possibly by Fielding himself. But Henley's sufferings cannot have lasted long, for Jane soon threw her crutches aside and married him.

In 1742 Ralph Allen was Mayor of Bath and its most famous citizen. As post-master he had made himself a very wealthy man by planning a system of cross-posts between towns in the West. Before this all letters had to pass through London. At his beautiful house Prior Park he kept open house for men of letters, entertaining almost every celebrated author of the time. Here was written part of the *Dunciad*, and according to a statement made by the Master of the Ceremonies at the Pump Room, Allen presented Fielding with £200, " after reading something he liked ". This appears to have been just before the publication of *Joseph Andrews* and the *Full Vindication of the Duchess of Marlborough*. For this, a pamphlet written in reply to an abusive attack, the sum of five guineas was paid to Fielding by Millar as has been said.

It gives a vivid picture of the period when Sarah and the great Duke were running the Queen and the country. There was a family connection between the Duchess and the Fielding family, for Henry's first cousin was the wife of General Churchill, the Duke's brother. No doubt in publishing his *Vindication*, Fielding looked for some largesse from the great lady, but apparently without result. For some years later there appeared in his paper *The True Patriot* a satirical notice of " a Man supposed to be a Pensioner of the late Duchess of Marlborough ", with the ironic note, " he is supposed to have been poor ".

Colley Cibber was in love with the Duchess, or so he hints in his *Apology*. That " glorious woman " was one of the idols of his youth. And for years he kept the secret of this adoration to himself ! It is a delightful thought, this passion cherished so long for the great Sarah, who was not at all likely to concern herself with a fribble such as Cibber.

The final apostrophe to the lady is truly Cibber-like. " A peculiar favourite of Providence ! " cries the laureate. " A person so attractive ! A husband so memorably great ! And a great grandmother without grey hairs ! "

Desperately seeking money in any direction as Fielding now was, he took a small share in the production of the farce *Miss Lucy In Town ;* and with William Young brought out a translation of Aristophanes' *Plutus*. Already that curious collection, the *Miscellanies*, was being advertised.

With "a Degree of Heartache" at his wife's continued illhealth, he collected together certain essays, poems, especially those to Walpole and Celia, a few plays, a poetical address to Bubb Dodington, with an unfinished fragment, the *Journey from this World to the Next*, and, tacked on in a third volume, his great satirical masterpiece, *Jonathan Wild*.

When these *Miscellanies* failed to appear after being advertised, he apologises because of "the dangerous Illness of one from whom I draw all the solid Comfort of my Life, during the greatest Part of this Winter".

The Wedding Day, an old play of Fielding's, hastily furbished up but not revised, was produced by Garrick at Drury Lane on February 17th, 1743, but failed completely. The scene where the great actor was hissed was probably the one where Stedfast marries his own daughter by mistake, or possibly the encounter with the bawd, Mrs. Useful. And, as we have seen, all that Fielding found to say, with Garrick in hysterics before him, was " Damn'em, so they *have* found it out, have they ? "

In this incident, at a failure in 1743, there is a desperate note, perhaps because Fielding felt himself driven back to the work he had hoped to leave behind him for ever. Yet here he was, a "Playhouse Bard" once more, and an unsuccessful one to boot.

In a jesting Prologue Macklin advised him to abandon the stage :—

"Ah ! thou foolish follower of the ragged Nine,
You'd better stuck to honest Abram Adams, by half ;
He, in spite of Critics, can make your Readers laugh ".

No wiser advice was ever given to a man. But the words prove that the Parson was now a well-known character. Yet how strange it is to think of the cynicism of *The Wedding Day* following close on the gaiety and goodwill of *Joseph Andrews*.

Garrick and Fielding were intimate friends. And of this friendship there is told a charming story that after a dinner party at the actor's house, when vails were being presented by the departing guests to the footman, Fielding pressed into the man's hand a piece of paper with something folded inside it.

"Something from the poet, bless his merry heart !" exclaimed the eager recipient. But, alas, when he opened the paper, he found therein only—one penny !

The following morning Garrick complained to Fielding of the impropriety of joking in this way with a servant.

" Joking ! " replied Fielding, " so far from it, that I meant to do the fellow a real piece of service, for if I had given him a shilling or half a crown, I knew you would have taken some of it from him ; but by giving him only a penny, he had a chance of calling it his own ".

The actor of course was famous for his parsimony. Once, we are told, he watched in real agony a candle burning away uselessly in his room, while a friend kept him walking up and down outside the house. And when again Peg Woffington was about to put more tea in the pot, Garrick cried out, " the tay is already as red as blood ".

But this was also the man who, after a night at cards, would send back I O U's for big sums owing to him, with the direction: " Do me the favour of burning this at once ".

Perhaps the greatest tribute ever paid to Garrick for his acting came from the First Murderer in *Hamlet* who, when the actor cried, " There's blood upon thy face ! " forgot his part, and answered : " Is there, by God ? "

After the failure of *The Wedding Day* Fielding seems to have again applied himself to the Law, attending at the Assizes, and in Westminster Hall. But his name occurs in no important case, though there is a tradition that he left behind him at his death three volumes on Crown Law. These, however, have never been found ; possibly the manuscript may have been burnt when his brother's house was destroyed in the Gordon Riots.

That he delighted in the legal passages at arms to be heard in Westminster Hall can be seen from his account of a debate between Sergeant Bramble and Sergeant Puzzle : " Now Bramble throws in an argument, and Puzzle's scale strikes the beam ; again Bramble shares the like fate—Here Bramble hits, there Puzzle strikes—till at last all becomes one scene of confusion in the tortured minds of the hearers ". One hearer at least was certainly not tortured. There is every evidence that Fielding's legal studies were a joy to him. For once at any rate in a brain ruled by Apollo, Coke and Littleton found themselves gladly welcomed.

In the autumn of 1744 Mrs. Fielding was again staying in Bath. And here it was that she died in her husband's arms. Her body was brought up to London, and there in the chancel vault of St. Martin's in the Fields she was buried beside her child Charlotte. Four men bore the coffin, the great tenor bell tolled, with lighted candles on the altar, and all the ceremonies customary at the funerals of noble families.

Lady Bute knew Charlotte Fielding well. " That beloved wife ", she writes, " whose picture he drew in his *Amelia,* where —even the glowing language he knew how to employ did not do more than justice to the amiable qualities of the original, or to her beauty. He loved her passionately, and she returned his affection ; yet had no happy life for they were almost always miserably poor, and seldom in a state of quiet and safety. His elastic gaiety of spirit carried him through it all ; but meanwhile, care and anxiety were preying upon her more delicate mind—She gradually declined, caught a fever and died in his arms ".

Fielding's grief approached to frenzy, so that his friends thought him in danger of losing his reason. For a whole year he published nothing except the Preface to his sister's *David Simple.*

But at last the *Miscellanies* were published by subscription and brought the author £700. The list of subscribers, more than half of them belonging to the law, included almost all the distinguished names in literature as well as law. But there was no Johnson and no Pope. Such a list is a certain proof of a man's work, if we may judge it by popularity. And these names should be put against the scurrilous abuse so often poured on Fielding by his many enemies ; according to the principle, by your friends ye shall be known.

The Journey from this World to the Next, mere fragment as it is, shows the real Fielding : his philosophy and his humanity. Yet he soon tired of it, and towards the close, when he started on the story of Julian the Apostate, the orignial impetus had died down, and the book peters out into nothingness ; but not till the writer has written himself down in this half-jesting tale of a dream. And Fielding is always at his best when he is handling a great theme in a half-jesting manner.

The legend here is that in a stationer's attic he had come upon a manuscript left behind by a man gone to the Indies.

You may take it either as a tale sent from the other world, or "the production of some choice inhabitant of New Bethlehem", otherwise Bedlam. The copy is half illegible, but the finder loves to decipher scrawls, "especially from that lovely part of the creation for which I have the tenderest regard".

On Dec. 1st, 1741, at his lodgings in Cheapside, a soul quits his body, and, guided by a tall young gentleman with a wing on his left heel, otherwise Mercury, finds himself in a stage-coach along with several other spirits. One of these had been set on fire by his physician " in the hot regimen for smallpox " ; another had died of a surfeit of mussels, a third in a duel, and one fair spirit—from dancing too much. But it is as difficult to explain how all this came about to anyone who does not understand already, " as it would be to explain Sir Isaac Newton's problems to one who knows no arithmetic ".

The coach passes through the City of Diseases, which is uncommonly like Covent Garden, and beside the Palace of Death with its murmur of winds and roaring waters which, inside, is very much like Blenheim Palace. They meet the souls coming into earth-life : a Duke marching arm-in-arm with a hackney coachman, and a King being pelted, though he fully intends to be the father of his nation. " I wonder not ", observes this spirit, " at the censure which so frequently falls on those of my station, but I wonder that those of my station so frequently deserve it ".

Near the Wheel of Fortune, which allots our earthly destinies, is an apothecary's shop where one can buy the Pathetic Potion to be taken just before birth. In it is a mixture of the passions, its ingredients all haphazard. Another decoction is " an extract from the faculties of the mind—rather unpleasant but wholesome. Some throw it away, some drink double and treble quantities. I observed a beautiful young female, who, tasting it immediately from curiosity, screwed up her face and cast it from her with great disdain, whence advancing presently to the Wheel, she drew a coronet . . . and indeed I observed several of the same sex, after a very small sip, threw the bottles away ".

Such gentle satire, yet so stern in fact ! Fielding's irony at its best.

At the door of Elysium stands Minos. Here Fielding begins to enjoy himself, as the suppliants for admission stand before the guardian of the gate.

One who has been, as he says, liberal to hospitals, is sent back for ostentation. Another claims that he had dis-inherited his son for begetting a bastard. "Have you so? cries Minos, "then pray return to the other world and beget another; for such an unnatural rascal shall never pass this gate".

Here is the Fielding who flung on the stage his ribald scenes in the face of lies and hypocrisy.

A playwright arrives: he has recommended virtue in his works. Says Minos, "the first person who passes these gates by your means shall carry you in. But I think that, to hurry things a little, you had better return and live another life on earth". Only when the fellow confesses that he has given his profits on a benefit night to a friend, is he allowed to pass in.

When a perfect gentleman arrives Minos thinks it a pity to rob the earth of him. But the lad who was hanged for stealing eighteen pence is instantly admitted, with a friendly slap on the back, because he has been a good husband and father, and has given bail for a friend. Just as Fielding himself had done, and with deplorable consequences.

One who had been "slain in the service of his country" claims admission. But he had been an invader of other countries, and had burnt cities.

"Do not call the depopulating of other countries the service of your own!" thunders Minos. "No work for you in Elysium, where there are no cities to be burnt, no people to be destroyed".

A parson who has allowed starvation in his parish is forced back. "No man enters this gate without charity"; so too is a Prude, "for there are no Prudes in Elysium".

Julian the Apostate is too insignificant to be damned, since he has been only acting the wise man all his life. And "Great Gods! could one but see what passes in the closet for wisdom!" Back! Elysium was never meant for those who are too wise to be happy.

As for Anne Boleyn, to her the gate is thrown wide, for "whoever had suffered with being a Queen for four years, and been sensible all that time of the real misery which attends that exalted station, ought to be forgiven whatever she has done to attain it".

The end of the manuscript, we are told, is destroyed. But

people should be more cautious about what they burn—especially when they consider the fate which had likely to have befallen the divine Milton, and that the works of Homer were probably discovered in some chandler's shop in Greece.

He closes with a word on Seraphic Love. " I do not intend by this, that sort of love which men are very properly said to make to women in the lower world, and which seldom lasts longer than while it is making. I mean by Seraphic Love an extreme delicacy and tenderness of friendship ". This is the light which shines round those two portraits of his Charlotte in *Tom Jones* and *Amelia*. It was shewn, too, many times in his care for Mary Daniel, his second wife.

During those happy days of courtship in Salisbury Fielding wrote the verses to ' Celia ' which he now, in the sad days, collected in the *Miscellanies*. He was no poet, but when he was young, he chirped very prettily, and not only to Celia, but to that Great Man, Sir Robert Walpole. It is amusing to compare this witty jesting with the bitterness of the attacks on the Prime Minister in *Jonathan Wild*, where he is symbolised as a mere receiver of stolen goods.

In 1730 he addresses Walpole thus :—

" Forbid it gods, that you should try
What 'tis to be as great as I.

The family that dines the latest
Is in our street esteem'd the greatest ;
But the latest hours must surely fall
Before him who never dines at all.

Your taste in Architect, you know,
Hath been admired by friend and foe :
But can your earthly domes compare
With all my castles—in the air ?

We're often taught it doth behove us
To think those greater who're above us.
Another instance of my glory,
Who live above you twice two story,
And from my garret can look down
On the whole street of Arlington ".

In Arlington Street was Walpole's town house.

" Greatness by poets still is painted
With many followers acquanted ;
This too doth in my favour speak,
Your levee is but twice a week ;
From mine I can exclude but one day,
My door is quiet on a Sunday ".

That is—from duns who pester all the rest of the week.

It is curious to watch the searchlight of social history switched round to different points as the centuries change. In the 17th century we think first of saints and fanatics, of those who felt so poignantly the pull of flesh against spirit : of Fox and Bunyan, Donne and Milton, Cromwell and his Ironsides. By the 18th century the light falls on men of the world, on Chesterfield and Johnson, Fielding and Gay ; on men living in society where clubs and coffee-houses, routs and masquerades fill the scene, and even a Swift goes mad when he views humanity in the mass.

Social life and how to live together : here is the subject, and the coffee-house is its symbol. And here is Fielding, in the three Essays he included in these *Miscellanies*—the Apology for the Clergy, the Essay on Conversation, and on the Characters of Men—laying down rules for the conduct of social life. They are " cautionary " sermons, of course with sudden glints of humour, such as—" with what envy must a swine be surveyed by a glutton ! "

The lavish living, lavish giving Henry Fielding peeps out in his appeal for Charity, " under which head I shall introduce liberality, a necessary qualification of any who would call himself a successor of Christ's disciples ". And there is a superb definition of the virtue which lies at the root of all his ethics : " it weighs ", says he of Charity, " all mankind in the scales of friendship, and sees them with the eyes of love ".

This is the Fielding who is emerging into the daylight ; yet the man who wrote it was the man who in political contest could storm and rail with the worst of the scribblers of his day. It is the human nature of Fielding that, as we go deeper into his life—that " touch of Harry "—which brings out the twisted tangle of his nature, and our love.

As for the clergy, he who painted such a noble clergyman cannot but be horrified to learn that " Clergy convicted of felony are to be delivered over to the Ordinary, (a priest), before whom he was to purge himself ". That is, a priest was not subject to the common law. " A cursed privilege ! " cries Fielding, the future Bow Street magistrate.

The king of vices is, of course, hypocrisy. And good-breeding is vital, but it cannot be bought from a milliner, a tailor, or a periwig-maker ". I should not have scrupled to call Socrates a well-bred man, though I believe he was very little instructed by any of the persons I have above enumerated ".

He condescends to discuss etiquette : guests should be met at the gate with a smile, and when dinner is on the table " and the ladies have taken their places, the gentlemen are to be introduced into the eating-room ". That " large eating-Parlour " which he required in his London house was evidently, in Fielding's eyes, the heart of the place.

One must " give precedence rather to birth than to fortune ". Yet Fielding the aristocrat put highest in the scale an inn-wench, a poor curate, and a postilion who robbed hen-roosts. Always, according to his friend Mrs. Hussey, the mantua-maker in the Strand, he insisted on being treated as a gentleman. More than once he shows how he rebuked rough manners in his voyage to Lisbon.

One must never press food on the guests or be too zealous in showing " the rarities of one's house or garden ", and as to the host who insists on keeping an unwilling guest, he deserves " an action of false imprisonment ". But with a stingy host, " the bottle as surely stops when it comes to him as your chariot at Temple Bar ".

How frank and friendly must have been a greeting from hearty Fielding ! No patience has he with that superciliousness, that looking down on our fellow-creatures, which doth betray the idiot : " the lowest and meanest of our species are the most strongly addicted to this vice—men who are a scandal to their sex, and women who disgrace human nature ".

" I have myself seen a little female thing which they have called " my lady ", of no greater dignity in the order of beings than a cat . . . whose face would cool the loosest libertine, with a mind as empty of ideas as an opera . . . I have seen this Thing express contempt to a woman who was an honour to her sex, and an ornament to the Creation ".

To that " honest, hearty, loud chuckle which shakes the sides of aldermen and squires ", he has no objection, " though it is a symptom ... of a very gentle and inoffensive quality called Dulness, than which nothing is more risible, as Mr. Pope, with exquisite pleasantry, says : " Gentle Dulness ever loves a joke " ; *i.e.* one of her own jokes. These are sometimes performed by the foot, as leaping over heads, or chairs, or tables ..... ; sometimes by the hand, as by slaps in the face, pulling off wigs ".

A man's character is writ by Nature in his face. But especially beware of that " glavering, sneering smile ", of which the greater part of mankind are extremely fond ... generally a compound of malice and fraud.

One kind of generosity is that which relieves a friend in distress by " a draught on Aldgate pump ", which, in Fielding's century, was merchants' slang for a false bank-note.

Against saints he warns us : Sanctified hypocrisy is " the destroyer of the innocent, a protector of the guilty, which hath introduced all manner of evil into the world, and hath almost expelled every grain of good out of it ".

It is this hatred of humbug which led him to savagery of expression, and made him enemies who were always at his heels like a pack of hungry dogs, men to whom his free and careless way of living was like the scent which guides the hounds. Man of the world as he was, he yet in the mean sense, possessed no worldly wisdom, but gave his enemies every possible chance of asking : how is it possible for the devil to cast out Satan ?

The attorneys who probably liked and honoured him were too cautious to give him briefs ; the Grub Street writers whom he satirised ; the rakes whom he put on the stage ; the stage-manager whom he reviled, all these rose against him, using the pricks of defamation to oppose the blows from his cudgel.

Yet among his friends were some of the best men of his time : Garrick and Hogarth, Lyttelton and Ralph Allen. If one judges him by the report of his enemies one sees a certain kind of man ; if by his friends, quite another. Yet both were certainly Harry Fielding.

CHAPTER XVI

The Doves and the Serpents

"THOUGH IRONY," observes Fielding in *The Jacobite's Journal*, "is capable of furnishing the most exquisite Ridicule, yet as there is no kind of humour so liable to be mistaken it is of all others the most dangerous to the Writer. An infinite Number of Readers have not the least Taste or Relish for it, I believe I may say, do not understand it; and all are apt to be tired when it is carried to any Degree of Length".

He might well have been speaking of his masterpiece of irony, *Jonathan Wild*, which makes up the third volume of his *Miscellanies*. It certainly furnishes "the most exquisite Ridicule", but of those who have intelligence enough to understand it, few perhaps have enjoyed it. Nor is this to be wondered at if Professor Saintsbury was right when he wrote that one who loves this satire must possess "a mystical faith; a readiness to laugh at oneself; an extreme tolerance; an immense pessimism". Not many readers possess all these qualifications, and especially not the mystical faith needed if one would plunge into the depths of human depravity. Yet for thirty years, said Saintsbury, he had been in the habit of turning to *Jonathan Wild* for rest and refreshment: to look at life ironically is to find a cure for disappointment on the one hand, and on the other, a corrective of illusion, especially the illusion of one's own greatness. But most people prefer to cling to their illusions.

The book was probably written in 1742, perhaps in the spring, soon after the fall of Walpole. There are jokes about "signs in the heavens", referring to the comet of that year when "wondering mortals" sat up all night to watch for some great disaster.

Wild, the historical character on whose story the book is based, was hanged at Tyburn in 1725, when Fielding was eighteen and about to leave Eton.

Jonathan was a mere receiver of stolen goods, but a genius at his trade. In his "lost property office" those who had been robbed could buy back their possessions. Gangs of thieves, pickpockets, and highwaymen worked for him and received small rewards, while he himself made great profits. Two branch offices were actually opened by him, and goods not easily redeemed were shipped abroad, chiefly to Holland. Jack Sheppard, the famous highwayman, worked for Wild, but at last rebelled, and with Wild's help was finally hanged, to the joy of twenty thousand spectators. Sheppard's colleague, whom Fielding calls " Blueskin ", was actually arrested by Wild himself. When a thief became troublesome he was informed against by his employer, and ended his career on the Tyburn Tree.

After the Act making receivers liable to arrest as accessories, Jonathan still evaded the law and was used by the Government in tracking down criminals. But at last the position became intolerable ; Wild was arrested for selling stolen lace, and met his end at Tyburn on May 24th.

Here then is Fielding's great financial organiser, a type of all the " Great Men " who brings misery to thousands. He is " Jonathan the Great ", one of those whom the foolish world has worshipped down through the ages, the great thieves and the great conquerors. From that shop full of loot Fielding looked out into the great spaces of history and saw the conquerors of ravaged lands who, standing on a holocaust of the slaughtered, look over the desolation they have made, the homes they have ruined, the hearts they have broken, and feel no remorse, but turn to receive the acclamations of fools and the worship of the historians. They are great ; but wretched.

It is curious to see, with such an ancestry as his, how Fielding loathed, not only the chicanery by which men become " great ", but also the conquests by armies and men of war. With Thomas Hardy he would have joined in the prayer for new men which ends the *Dynasts* :—

" Men surfeited of laying heavy hands upon the innocent,
    The mild, the fragile, the obscure content
        Among the myriads of thy family.
    Those, too, who love the true, the excellent,
    And make their daily moves a melody ".

No shadow of Napoleon had fallen across the soul of Fielding, as it did on Hardy. Yet with those " great men ", Charles

XII and Alexander, he had seen from history how men, " earth's jackaclocks ", " can be fugled by one will ", and led towards the hell upon earth that is made by great conquerors.

But Jonathan Wild and all his associates were just the scum of London's night-cellars, and their natural destiny was a cell in Newgate and an end at Tyburn. Their bodies would rest under no marble monument, but either in quicklime, or among the " Atomys of Surgeons' Hall ".

In this lies the supreme irony of *Jonathan Wild*. Newgate and the Palaces of the Great are one in spirit. But with this difference, that in one place the Great are rewarded with honours, and in the other, with shame.

The book is " low " in every sense. The arch villain, whom Fielding slowly builds up into a monster compact of avarice, cowardice, lust, and self-seeking, with never a gleam of light anywhere in his nature, is surrounded by a bestial horde of like wretches—Snap, the keeper of the spunging house, Tishy and Doshy, his daughters, neither with a scrap of womanliness about them, except a taste for stocking-mending in Doshy, who, perhaps because of that, and because she honestly brings forth a baby, is merely transported to Virginia ; Count la Ruse, cheat and cheated ; Bagshot, under-study to Wild, but less of a genius ; Blueskin the butcher, who defies Jonathan and pays the penalty ; Fireblood, the ruffian, and Roger Johnson, Jonathan's rival as an agitator in Newgate : a whole crowd of superb rascals. Jonathan alone is worthy of his title, the Great. He is only second to Iago because, although he can talk grandiloquently, he has not that subtle finish of a gentleman which is Iago's last touch of perfection.

Many another writer has delighted to paint villainy ; notably Balzac, but in him it is isolated, a deadly upas-tree in a forest of more or less honest oaks and beeches. Fielding creates a dense forest of evil. And not everyone is bold enough to venture in. Even the dry wit of the style seems cruel, so Olympian is the calm with which Fielding looks down on his creatures. You have to be bold to enjoy *Jonathan Wild :* it is a masterpiece of the creative intellect, a sustained and perfect Doom Painting, even in the last pages, when turning from avarice to lust, Fielding deals with Mrs. Heartfree wandering among men at sea, and on land.

Fielding's genius is extraordinarily varied : gay and sunny

in *Joseph Andrews*; caustic and critical in *Tom Jones*; tender, when in *Amelia* he paints the beauty and sweetness of a woman; and unflinching in *Jonathan Wild*. And, as he passed from one phase of authorship to another, he was unconsciously preparing to grapple in actual life with the Laocoon of vice in his Court at Bow Street, loosening tentacle after tentacle in what was literally—for him—a death-struggle between him and the serpent.

Yet read with appreciation, *Jonathan Wild* gives courage. Partridge, in *Tom Jones*, is afraid of ghosts, chiefly because he has never seen one. When Fielding drags into the open before our eyes the horror of hell which can live in a human heart, we take courage in the very intelligence with which he paints it. It is irony, pure and perfect; it is true to life. And the two qualities are intellectually satisfying.

Yet the reading of *Jonathan Wild* is " a strain on the nerves "; unless the reader possesses a courage equal to Fielding's, he may shrink from the truth of the vision. And all vast visions, of good or evil, make the spirit quail; even as Pascal shivered before the vast spaces of the starry sky.

The strangest saying of all is Saintsbury's: that in reading *Jonathan Wild* he found " rest and refreshment ". For this book gives the other side of ecstasy; which is wholesome. " To the most poignant individual enjoyments of sense or intellect . . . it contributes that reflex sense of the other side, of the drawback, of the end, which is required to save passion from fatuity, and rapture from cloying ".

You have great moments, in the music of a symphony, or the sight of sunset, or even in the first shock of your own success. Then, lest you should feel yourself a god, remember that you are of the same human race—as Jonathan Wild. " Come down proud spirit ! " is the command given by the judgment of the intellect.

Dostoevsky looked into the well of evil. But this he did in a mood of pity, not of irony; never was he Olympian and calm, since the evil in others he saw also in himself. Since he was one with the reptile, in a communion not of saints, but of blackguardry, he could not quietly watch one reptile kill another.

But Fielding in spirit is the judge; the judge who hopes that once the reptilian habits are plainly shewn, then reptiles may one day cease to exist.

If it takes immense pessimism to enjoy *Jonathan Wild*, it also took a sublime optimism to write the book. But Fielding carried that happy temper of his into almost everything, even into his analysis of human depravity.

In this everyday life of ours which Fielding observed so accurately the goodness of the good is only too often the food on which the wicked batten. The other side of evil is folly, and that, in *Jonathan Wild*, is given in the history of the Heartfrees, husband and wife, who are mere simpletons.

Heartfree is a jeweller who allows himself to be cheated with a trustfulness as foolish as anything shewn by Adam in the Garden of Eden. All the lies told him by Jonathan he takes for gospel, and not till he finds himself landed in gaol does he so much as suspect " his friend ". And Mrs. Heartfree allows herself to be caught in the toils of vice by devices that would never have deceived the shrewdness of a Pamela, or the simplicity of an Amelia. Even Count la Ruse, a gambler and a cheat, allows himself to be robbed of his gains by the master-villain.

The harmlessness of the dove without the wisdom of the serpent is the devil's own chance. The lamb is so innocent : the serpent so subtle. If, as has been said, the Heartfrees and their faithful apprentice are the light of the whole book, then their glimmer is so faint that it only serves to make darkness visible ; which no doubt was Fielding's intention.

Fielding analyses the passion for " greatness ". "Ambition ", he says, " without which no one can be a great man, will immediately instruct him . . . to prefer a hill in Paradise to a dunghill ; nay, even fear, a passion the most repugnant to greatness, will show him how much more safely he may indulge his mighty abilities in the higher than the lower rank ; since experience teaches him that there is a crowd oftener in one year at Tyburn than on Tower Hill in a century ". Therefore the only difference between the great man and the " prig " is that the former is the luckier of the two.

Much talk of " honour " fills the mouths of Jonathan's crew of rogues. But how misused is that word ! " Do not some by honour mean good-nature and humanity ? Must we deny it then to the great, the brave, the noble ; to the sackers of towns, the plunderers of provinces and the conquerors of kingdoms ? Were not these men of honour ? And yet they scorn those pitiful qualities I have mentioned ".

Here we get a glimpse of Fielding himself : it was, so he tells us, when " travelling westward over the hills near Bath ", that he visualised his hero, Jonathan, " passing on from scheme to scheme, and from hill to hill, with noble constancy, resolving still to attain the summit . . . he at length arrives—at some vile inn ". The vile inn being — Newgate, in Wild's case, some hedge tavern in Fielding's.

The great man " is an abject slave to his own greatness ". " When I consider whole nations rooted out only to bring tears into the eyes of a *Great Man*, not indeed because he has extirpated so many, but because he had no more nations to extirpate, then truly I am almost inclined to wish that—no *Great Man* had ever been born into the world ".

But among Wild's tools, his " prigs ", dissension arises in the matter of hats, or principles. Two parties there were, one who wore their hats fiercely cocked, the other, with the brims flapping. The former were called Cavaliers, and the latter Roundheads, or old Nolls. This is Fielding's way of describing the political parties of his time, the difference between them being nothing but Tweedledum and Tweedledee.

The Heartfrees once ruined, Jonathan spirits Mrs. Heartfree to Holland, but he is ship-wrecked and cast adrift in an open boat with half a dozen biscuits to prolong his misery. Fear, not remorse, attacks him, though he tries to deny it. " If there should be another world, it will go hard with me, that is certain . . . No, no, when a man's dead there's an end of him. I wish I was satisfied of it though ".

Of course the devil looks after his own, and Jonathan escapes a watery death, since " Nature having originally intended our *Great Man* for that final exaltation which is the most proper and becoming end of all great men, it were heartily to be wished they might all arrive at, would by no means be diverted from her purpose ".

Murder is not the worst. Fielding demands through the mouth of Wild : " What think you of private persecution, treachery and slander, by which the very souls of men are in a manner torn from their bodies ? . . . Believe me, lad, the tongue of a viper is less harmful than that of a slanderer ".

There is in this the unmistakable note of personal feeling.

The marriage between Jonathan and the fair Laetitia Snap having taken place, Fielding has his joke against matrimony, which is " a state of tranquil felicity ", yet includes " so little variety, that, like Salisbury Plain, it affords only one prospect, a very pleasant one, it must be confessed, but the same ".   The dialogue between the newly-wedded plumbs the very depths of hatred and distrust.

But the final plot against Heartfree is to engage him in a robbery and then to give information against him, so that he may be convicted and hanged. Jonathan however, is unwilling to incite to murder, lest he " should make an additional example in that excellent book called *God's Revenge Against Murder* ", which Fielding was then distributing among those who appeared before him at his Court in Bow Street.

His plots becoming ever more marvellous, Wild determines to charge his victim, Heartfree, with having carried away his most valuable jewels in order to defraud his creditors.

But by now the Great Man is living in hourly fear of his own gang, every man of whom has " a knife for his throat and a pair of scissors for his purse ".   At last, caught out over the trivial matter of a bit of lace, Wild is sent to Newgate, where he plays the virtuous demagogue by trying to incite the wretches of the prison to fight for " the liberties of Newgate ! "   Irony can no further go.

Heartfree is pardoned, his wife returns safely, but the Great Man is to die.   And the Ordinary of Newgate comes to prepare his soul for the ride to Tyburn.   The good man has already preached a sermon in the chapel proving that Wild must expect the *Everlasting Fire* to be his portion. But Wild had, unfortunately, fallen asleep the moment the text was given out.

" D—n me, what is death ? " cries Jonathan.   " It is nothing but to be with Platos and with Caesars—and all the other great heroes of antiquity ".

The Ordinary, now in the cell, proceeds once more to preach, but Wild suggests that they should drink a bottle of wine.

" Why wine ? " asks the parson, " if you must drink, let us have a bowl of punch—a liquor I the rather prefer, as it is nowhere spoken against in Scripture ".

The hanging, or apotheosis of the *Great Man*, gave " our hero an opportunity of facing death and damnation, without any fear in his heart ".   " D—n me, it is only a dance without music ", said he.   And his last act was in keeping, for he " applied his hands to the parson's pocket, and emptied it of his bottle-screw, which he carried out of the world in his hand ".

But " the character which he most valued himself upon, and which he principally honoured in others, was that of hypocrisy ", And this is Fielding's first and last word : that there is " little greatness to be expected in a man who acknowledged his vices, but always much to be hoped from him who professed great virtues."

All through the parallel in the mind of Fielding is between the careers of Walpole and of Wild. What difference was there between the robber's booty and the statesman's taxes ? Jonathan Wild too, in his laced coat with a silver staff played the part of perfect gentleman. No goods were ever handled by him. In the *Champion* newspaper Fielding put Walpole and Wild together, describing Wild's levee as attended by personages of the first rank.

Walpole, like Jonathan, had built up his power by means of a host of ministers who preyed on the nation. He too was relentless when a man failed to serve him. The two demagogues orating in Newgate till the walls echoed with " Wild for ever ", and " Johnson for ever ", and Wild won, is a reference to the Prime Minister's power of speech.

In the account of Wild's ancestry his father is called Robert, and his grandfather Edward. These were the names of Walpole's immediate forebears. And when Jonathan and Tishy Snap arrange that neither shall interfere in the other's love-affairs, Fielding is echoing the current gossip about Walpole and his wife. The Ordinary, so easily diverted from sermonising by punch, is again Walpole, so it is said, for he was not sure whether he was a Christian or an atheist. But in the second edition of his satire Fielding smoothed over these political references.

Coleridge's verdict on *Jonathan Wild* is that it surpasses anything either in *Lilliput* or even in *The Tale of a Tub*, that " dazzling and blinding master-piece " in the words of Professor Saintsbury.

But to say that is to call Jonathan Wild the greatest satire in the English language.

CHAPTER XVII

Fielding and the Forty-five

ROUND Fielding at his house in Old Boswell Court there were now gathered a group of women—his sisters, those friends and admirers of Richardson, Harriet, his Charlotte's surviving child, and Mary Daniol, her maid ; apparently also the two Collier girls, Jane, who wrote *The Cry* in collaboration with Sarah Fielding, and Margaret, who appears, judging by her behaviour in Lisbon later on, to have been a flirtatious damsel.

The friendship between the Fieldings and the Colliers probably dated back to the time of Henry's boyhood in Salisbury. But when, after Fielding had gone bail for £400 on Collier's behalf, he was disgusted to find that this philosophical creditor remained unconcerned by his friend's distress. " Collier, whose very name I hate ", is his comment.

But all England was soon to be roused from its apathy by the second Jacobite Rising, when Charles Edward landed in Scotland and raised his standard at Glen Finnan, where to-day the deer crowd under the trees in a countryside which Scottish tradition connects with the historic Macbeth, who was buried nearby on the hill of Lumphanan.

Marching south with six thousand men, the Prince took Carlisle, and Cope was defeated at Present Pans on September 21st.

Though the country might sing :

" If it isna weel bobbit,
We'll bob it again ",

it was in great danger, since the South at first failed to realise the position.

Fielding thereupon made his appeal in three pamphlets, published anonymously, but undoubtedly his.

The first bore the following title :—

A serious Address
to the
People of Great Britain
in which the
Consequences of the
Present Rebellion
are fully demonstrated.

Necessary to be perused by every Lover of his Country.

In this the author shows himself to be, in Squire Western's phrase, a right " Hanoverian rat ". To Fielding the return of the Stuarts meant the rule of the Pope and the end of all freedom under the sway of the Inquisition. Hogarth too began to pour forth picture after picture painting the arrival of monkish fanatics bringing with them a whole collection of instruments of torture.

" Let us call forth the old English spirit ", says Fielding, " in this truly English cause ; let neither fear, nor indolence prevail on one man to refuse doing his duty in defence of his country, against an invader by whom his property, his family, his liberty, his life and his religion are threatened with immediate destruction ".

A dialogue follows between the Devil, the Pope, and the Pretender. And Fielding's anti-Popish fury makes him write with a pen dipped in gall. " Have I not ", demands the Pope, " unveiled the only religion in the world, which hath ever taught the doctrines of benevolence, peace and charity, to be the foundation of hatred, war and massacre ? "

Did not the writer have in mind that Doom Painting in St. Thomas's Church at Salisbury, where Christ looks down complacently on demons dragging souls to hell ?

The Pope promises the Prince, on condition that he will massacre every heretic in England, a hundred thousand indulgences and two hundred thousand curses for his own use. The dialogue is certainly Fielding's, and first-class propaganda. This man is no longer a gay spark with his fiddling Quidam, and thieving Pillage ; where he once laughed, he now storms. Yet it is still Harry Fielding.

Not content with pamphlets, he starts on November 5th— possibly the date is significant—the paper called *The True Patriot*. His first duty in this is to announce the death of

Swift, " a genius who deserves to be ranked among the first whom the world ever saw ".

This paper will be, according to its editor, of a higher standard than others since it is written by " a gentleman ! " It will also cost one penny more than others, but for the penny " the reader will gain six times the knowledge and amusement ". And of course no man will drink " cider-water " if he can get champagne.

To the tune of *Lillibulero,* his readers are asked to sing a loyal song, of which it will be enough to quote the first verse :—

> " O Brother Sawney, hear you the news,
> Twang 'em, we'll bang 'em and hang 'em up all.
> An army's just coming without any shoes ".

This is " proper to be sung at all merry meetings ". But Fielding had forgotten that *Lillibulero* was a Cavalier song !

He calls for volunteers in every county. And his appeal, or the terrors of the time, as the rebels advanced towards Derby, only a hundred and fifty miles from London, did stir up the spirit of the country. The theatres at any rate played their part. Anti-Papist plays were put on, including Fielding's *Debauchees* or *The Jesuit Caught,* and Peg Woffington spoke an Epilogue cursing all cowards. Profits were given to help the patriots, while the young lawyers of the Temple went daily to be drilled by sergeants.

According to the evidence of Benjamin Victor, the outspoken contemporary critic of Garrick's style of acting " : The stage (at both houses) is the most pious, as well as most loyal place, in the three kingdoms. Twenty men appear at the end of every play, and one stepping forward from the rest, with uplifted hands and eyes, begins singing, to an old anthem tune, the following words :—

> " O Lord our God, arise,
> Confound the enemies
> Of George our king ;
> Send him victorious,
> Happy and glorious,
> Long to reign over us,
> God save the King ",

which are the very words and music of an old anthem, that was sung at St. James's Chapel for King James the second, when the Prince of Orange was landed, to save us from popery and slavery : which God Almighty in His goodness was pleased not to grant ".

In his *True Patriot* Fielding started a curious column which brings us near him in jesting mood. This was headed *We Hears*, or *Apocrypha*, and consisted of quotations taken from other journals, with facetious comments printed in italics.

One paragraph in a rival paper had announced that the Saddles of the Duke of Bedford's Regiment of Horse had " set out ". Fielding observes : " As the Duke of Bedford hath only a Regiment of Foot, it is probable that their Saddles will shortly set out on their way home again ".

When another paper remarked that " the Rebels are much afflicted with the bloody Flux ", the comment is : " A Distemper which may probably increase, if General Hawley should be able to come up with them ".

And after a notice of the death of two rich men, he adds another on " one Nowns, a Labourer, *Most Probably Immensely Poor, and yet as Rich Now as Either of the Two* ".

We get little pictures of him at home in his study " meditating for the good and entertainment of the public, with my two little children . . . playing near me ". His little girl pulls open his eyes in the morning, just as he is suffering a nightmare in which a Jacobite executioner is putting a rope round his neck.

His benevolence peeps out in the advertisement directed in *The True Patriot* to " Any Person who hath enough of real Christianity to preserve a large Family from Destruction, by advancing the sum of Two Hundred Pounds ". The address given is that of Fielding's publisher, " Mr. Millar, opposite Katharine Street in the Strand ".

Probably belonging to this period is the story of the taxcollector who has been pressing for payment. Fielding collects £10 or £12 and is bringing it home to settle the debt. But on the way he meets a friend in distress, and hands the money over to him. At home, when his sister asks for it he answers that a friend has called for the money, and had it. " Let the collector call again ! "

Whatever we may think of the ethics of this, the story is in the true temper of *Tom Jones*.

The danger of the Jacobite rising at last came home to the

Londoners. Bishops preached repentance, and Parson Adams called for " a total amendment of life ". The Parson added— a Fielding touch even at this moment—that all the young men wish to become members of the society of *Bowes* (beaux), a word he cannot find in any dictionary. Apparently it seems to have been forgotten that the Parson was a linguist.

To heighten the drama of the moment, Fielding recounts his dream. In this he declares he was being dragged by Highlanders through streets piled up with dead, and carried before a judge who could only speak broken English.

In that court, presided over by a Papist, a Physician is fined for saying that Bath water is better for the gout than Holy Water. And " as for my little boy Jacky, he was taken ill of the Itch ". He had, it seems, been on parade the day before, " to see the Life Guards and had just touched one of the Plaids ".

The last number of *The True Patriot* appeared on June 17th 1746. There was no reason for its continuance after the victory of Culloden, announced as has been said, by the King at Drury Lane, with the preface " Oh ! " Everyone was now a true patriot.

But Charles Edward became a reader of Fielding's novels : in 1750 he sent for *Joseph Andrews* in English, and *Tom Jones* in French. He must have been greatly amused to read in *Tom Jones* that Sophia Western in it had been taken for his mistress, Jenny Cameron. But the Prince, according to Lady Mary Wortley Montagu, was " really not unlike Mr. Lyttelton " : The good Lyttelton, that is.

We catch sight for a moment of Fielding in his home. That is in the account of a visit paid to him by Joseph Warton, son of the Professor of Poetry at Oxford. " I wish you had been with me ", he writes to his brother ; " last week, when I spent two evenings with Fielding and his sister, who wrote *David Simple*, and you may guess I was very well entertained. The lady indeed retir'd pretty soon, but Russell and I sat up with the Poet till 1 or 2 in the morning, and were inexpressibly diverted. I find he values, as he justly may, his *Joseph Andrews* above all his writings ; he was extremely civil to me, I fancy on my Father's account ".

Joseph Andrews was certainly far above the plays, and *Tom Jones* was not then published. Yet it is simply tantalising to be told that the two young men were " inexpressibly diverted ", and to hear no word of the talk that night.

Sarah Fielding's *Familiar Letters*, in which the characters of her *David Simple* are supposed to carry on a correspondence with one another, was not published until after the Jacobite Rising. Among those who subscribed were Ralph Allen, Richardson, Fox and Lady Mary Wortley Montagu.

These two books, simple and touching in an innocent way, show Fielding's influence everywhere in the stress laid on character. Human Nature is as much the Bill of Fare in them as in *Tom Jones*, but without either the wit or the story-teller's gift. There is a certain amount of observation in all Sarah Fielding's work, but it is like a joint smothered in floods of sauce, the sauce of long-winded moralising. Sarah had all her brother's longing to make the world better, but not a spark of his power. She, however, was learned, and translated Xenophon's *Memorabilia*, a rare achievement for a woman at that time.

Fielding in his Preface to the *Familiar Letters* hopes that " these excellent pictures of virtue and vice . . . will not be thrown away in the world ". But his true apology for his sister's outpourings is expressed in his Preface to *David Simple* : it is that she must be pardoned for this lapse, however unwomanly it may appear, because her real reason was—that she wanted money ! Even Dr. Johnson might have accepted that excuse.

Mary Daniol, or Daniel, Charlotte's maid in the days of Fielding's first marriage, was then twenty-six. Her portrait, by Francis Cotes, which may exist to-day, was described as " a very fine drawing of a very ugly woman ". By all accounts she was a good soul, full of tenderness, faithfulness and courage. Fielding was married to her on November 27th 1747, at the obscure little church of St. Bennet's, Paul's Wharf, which was often used for quiet ceremonies. It was an act of reparation, since in the February following Fielding's son William was born.

In order to make a retreat for his wife, he took a house at Twickenham in what was then Back Lane, now Holly Road. According to Lysons, writing in 1795, it was an old-fashioned wooden building near the river. Now a row of cottages stands on the site. Here Mary would be free of the house in Old Boswell Court. Both Fielding's friends, as well as his wife, had to get accustomed to the new situation.

Horace Walpole writes of this stay in Twickenham, then of course a quiet village :—

> Here " Fielding met his bunter Muse,
> And as they quaffed the fiery juice,
> Droll Nature stamp'd each lucky hit
> With unimaginable wit ".

" Bunter " signifies a woman who picks up rags in the street, and is a term certainly more suitable for a Muse which collected anecdotes from every quarter, as " Horry " did.

This marriage, to " his cook-maid " was of course greeted by Fielding's enemies with an outburst of glee. *Old England* told the tale, apocryphal probably, of how, when Fielding had applied for a box at the theatre for himself and his wife, it was refused on the ground that she was only a woman of the Town. He had in fact done just what Mr. B——, the object of his scorn in *Pamela*, had done : married a servant-maid. But no one seems to have observed the coincidence.

Curiously enough, Lady Mary Wortley Montagu, who had written so sternly of her cousin's ways in the past merely observed quite kindly that " his natural spirits gave him rapture with his cook-maid ".

And Lady Louisa Stuart, her grand-daughter, many years afterwards wrote : " His biographers seem to have been shy of disclosing that after the death of this charming woman (Charlotte) he married her maid. And yet the act was not so discreditable to his character as it may sound. The maid had few personal charms, but was an excellent creature, devotedly attached to her mistress and almost broken-hearted for her loss. In the first agonies of his own grief, which approached to frenzy, he found no relief but from weeping with her ; nor solace, when in a degree calmer, but in talking to her of the angel they mutually regretted . . . . In process of time he began to think he could not give his children a tenderer mother, or secure for himself a more faithful housekeeper and nurse. At least this was what he told his friends ; and it is certain that her conduct as his wife confirmed it, and fully justified his opinion ".

From a reference in Smollett's *Peregrine Pickle*, it appears that Fielding's old friend Lord Lyttelton gave Mary Daniol away at the marriage service.

A month later Fielding started a second patriotic paper,

The Jacobite's Journal at twopence a copy every Saturday. Two thousand copies of each number were bought by the Government for distribution by post to all the inns and alehouses in the country. The editor, calling himself this time by the name John Trott-Plaid Esquire, set out with the intent to give Jacobitism its final kick, by pouring mockery on the whole theory. For Jacobitism, now the danger was over, had become the fashion. In country houses they drank to " the King over the water ", especially when the gentlemen were warmed by wine after dinner. Women took to plaid petticoats, men to waistcoats of the same pattern. Hounds were dressed in the colours, and the fox, as before, wore a red uniform.

Fielding was bent on laughing England, and perhaps even Scotland, out of its fit of romantic folly.

This outbreak Fielding puts down to the heat of summer, or possibly to the mildness of the sentences passed on the rebels. Even the great plenty of good liquor may have had something to do with it, " neither malt nor cyder having been ever cheaper than lately ".

Fielding declared once, and justly, that no one could accuse him of liking cruelty. But, alas, there is no protest from his pen against the terrible sentences passed on the Jacobite leaders, who were taken down, half-hanged, to have their bowels cut out and burnt.

The woodcut in the *Jacobite's Journal*, attributed to Hogarth, shows two Jacobites riding on an ass. The man waves a Highland cap in one hand, the other grips a French sword, while the ass is led by a bare-footed friar. Over it is flung the *London Evening Post*, with a copy of Harrington's *Oceana*; this last as a hit at the Republicans.

The ass, or the Jacobite idea, is a noble animal who never mends his pace, beat it as you will. No argument ever made the slightest impression either on the ass, Neddy, or on the Jacobite.

As to the name, since the party is one of heavy drinkers, it is surely derived from Bacchus or Jaccus. But Parson Adams considers that it stands for Jacob, a supplanter, although certainly, if one must tell the truth, the supplanting had been done, not by the Stuarts, but by the House of Hanover.

But all the Jacobite ways are dark, so that when a Somersetshire Squire writes against the window-tax, Fielding makes him say : " I put out one half of my windows last year, and if there comes another, I'll put out t'other half—Damme, a man may drink in the dark, and mayhap he may then be the buolder in toasting honest healths ", that is, of course, to " the King over the water ", as the full wine-glass was passed across the water in the finger bowl.

But irony is not to the English taste after all. Fielding therefore withdrew the woodcut, in which the friar is the Old Pretender, the man on the ass Charles Edward, and the woman —possibly—Jenny Cameron.

Since the Jacobite principles are " founded on certain absurd, exploded tenets, beneath the lowest degree of a human understanding ", Fielding renounced them for ever. But his support of the Government, after he had been so long in opposition, naturally brought down on his head the scorn of his enemies. He was saluted as " a whirling coxcomb, who had travell'd round the whole Circle of Parties ". And " pensioned scribbler " was the cry from every side.

"A heavier Load of Scandal ", he comments, " hath been cast upon me than I believe ever fell to the Share of a Single Man ... They pursued me into private Life, *even to my boyish years;* where they have given me almost every Vice in Human Nature ".

He certainly hit back. When Horace Walpole entered the lists against him, although not under his own name, Fielding ascribed the authorship of the attack to " a weak-minded woman " of the Jacobite party, so feeble was the writing. It is not hard to understand " Horry's " antipathy to the man who had satirised his father.

As for the *London Evening Post* and *Old England*, both persistent enemies of his, Fielding announces that all the Grub Street writers having gone into the country to do harvest work their places have been taken by one " Anna Maria Supple ", who, for half their pay, is writing in these journals. Fielding is thereupon described as " a madman, found straying in St. James's Park : the outcast of the playhouse ! the refuse of the book-sellers ! the jest of authors ! the contempt of every ingenious reader ".

For fine examples of envy, hatred and malice, the papers of this period are a magnificent repository.

But *The Jacobite's Journal* did not confine itself to political warfare. John Trott-Plaid Esquire started a Court of Criticism in which he established himself as the *Censor of Great Britain in the Republic of Literature.*

His first attack was made on Samuel Foote, the comedian, then drawing great audiences by his mimicry of prominent people. He showed Quin as an actor crying with a resounding voice : " Past two o'clock and a cloudy morning ! " in the guise of a watchman ; Garrick in dy-dy-dying speeches ; and Peg Woffington, with her squeaking voice, calling " Oranges, any Chiney oranges ! "

Foote is condemned by the Court for keeping " a Scandal Shop ", and Mr. Plaid announces that these mimicries are " indecent, immoral, and even illegal ".

In reply Foote put Fielding on the stage as a figure shabbily dressed and in complete black, " except for two or three chasms in his *Galigaskins*, and the flap of his shirt hanging out ". As for the Court of Criticism, its Censor appears " pulling a Chew of Tobacco from his mouth, in Imitation of his Honour who is greatly fond of that Weed ".

The Court responds by passing sentence on Foote as the defacer of God's images. Fielding here seems almost to have lost his sense of humour. It is curious to find him objecting to caricature at a time when most public men liked to see themselves painted by real portraits in Hogarth's pictures.

When the curious story of the affair at Avignon was published, Fielding fell upon it with zest in his paper.

In the first volume of Thomas Carte's *General History of England*, published in December, 1747, there appeared a statement to the effect that one Lovel of Bristol, being in Avignon in 1716, was cured of " a scrofulous humour " on his neck by the touch of the Old Pretender, although the Prince had neither been crowned nor anointed. This cure was regarded as a proof of the divine power possessed by all the Stuarts of touching for the King's evil.

The wits seized upon the story, and made a nine days' wonder of it with the result that the Common Council of London withdrew their subscription of £50 a year for the publication of the History.

Fielding then brought Carte before his Court of Criticism and charged him with having stolen this tale—from an old wife. But Carte's lawyer is made to plead that the legend only got into print when he was asleep. Carte was thereupon declared by the Judge to be an object of compassion rather than of contempt. So the story ended in a burst of laughter.

In July, 1748, Fielding went on Circuit for the last time, and in the same year, again on that famous day, November 5th, there appeared the last number of *The Jacobite's Journal* and the fourth edition of *Joseph Andrews*.

Old England published as an epitaph :—

> " Beneath this stone
> Lies Trotplaid John,
> His length of chin and nose,
> His crazy brain,
> Unhum'rous vein
> In verse and eke in prose ! "

' Unhum'rous ' is a good word, but that chin and nose must have been well-known to all " in the movement " of thought in London.

On October 25th of that year Fielding had taken the oath as Chief Magistrate for Westminster. Six weeks later he was presiding over the court at Bow Street and sending to gaol men and women of the same character that he had satirised in *Jonathan Wild*. The ex-playwright, barrister, novelist and journalist was now entering on the last phase of his changeful life.

His predecessor in this office, the famous Sir Thomas de Veil, gives us in his *Apology* a clear picture of what it meant to preside in Bow Street. But de Veil's ways were not those of Fielding.

But for one man to be J.P. for Westminster, and another for the County of Middlesex was inconvenient. In order therefore that Fielding might hold both offices, his friend and supporter the Duke of Bedford gave him two houses, one valued at £70 a year, and another at £30, together with a lease of twenty-one years for certain smaller properties. This was to satisfy the proviso that a County Magistrate must own real estate worth £100 a year.

On January 11th 1749, Fielding took the Sacrament at St. Paul's, Covent Garden, and signed—with all his heart, no doubt—a declaration against Transubstantiation and the Supremacy of the Pope, at the same time abjuring King James II and all his descendants, including of course Prince Charles Edward.

The author of *Jonathan Wild* was now Justice of the Peace for Middlesex and Westminster.

CHAPTER XVIII

A Labour of Hercules

SO opened up the last five heroic years of Fielding's life. "Whatever he desired, he desired ardently", was said of him. And surely never did he desire anything with more ardour than to put a stop to the robbery and brutality of the time.

Gangs of robbers, well-organised and daring, attacked quiet citizens with cutlasses and bludgeons, often in full daylight. In January 1749 they broke open the Gatehouse prison and carried off one of their fellows, leaving the turnkey desperately wounded. London at night was under mob rule, so that "even with warrants in their pockets, the officers of Justice often dared not make an arrest".

The only force for the suppression of such criminals was first the Watch, " chosen ", as Fielding remarks in *Amelia,* " out of those poor old decrepit people, who are from their want of bodily strength, rendered incapable of getting a livelihood by work ". These Dogberries were helped by constables who were often only to be found in the alehouses, and had in any case to apply to the military when called upon to act. The alleys, courts and lanes were, as Fielding says, " like a vast wood or forest in which a thief may harbour with as great security as wild beasts do in the deserts of Africa or Arabia ".

Very few people dared to give evidence against these wild beasts. And for very good reasons. When two men were caught on the way to give information, the robbers broke every joint in one man's body, and after torture, left him dead. The other, less fortunate, they hung over a dry well, and days later, when he was heard to groan, they cut the rope, let him drop, and covered his body with stones. Highwaymen rode in the Haymarket and Piccadilly, even attending the gambling houses.

" I was sitting in my own dining-room on Sunday night ", wrote Horace Walpole, " the clock had not struck eleven, when I heard a loud cry of ' Stop thief ! ' A highwayman had attacked a post-chaise in Piccadilly ; the fellow was pursued, rode over the Watchman, almost killed him, and escaped ".

With this state of affairs it was that Fielding, a man of broken health, often only able to move about in a wheeled chair, set himself to wrestle with all the strength of his fiery nature.

But there was an evil nearer home ; that was " the trading Justice ", who made his income partly by fees exacted from the accused. De Veil, Fielding's predecessor, frankly described the methods used by these worthies in his *Apology*. It is not surprising that so many prominent people found it desirable to write *Apologies*.

A famous Bow Street runner gave evidence against one Justice whose " plan used to be to issue out warrants, and take up all the poor devils in the streets, and then there was the bailing of them, two and fourpence, which the magistrate had ; and taking up a hundred girls, that would make, at two and fourpence, £11 13 4. They sent none of them to gaol, for the bailing of them was so much better ".

Naturally therefore the post of Justice of the Peace was regarded as a degraded one. Addison, then Secretary of State, declared that he thought he had already provided for Fielding by making him Justice for Westminster. Few meaner speeches have ever been made.

But the author of *Jonathan Wild* refused absolutely to make an income by such pitiful means. As Ambrose Phillips puts it : " though poetry was a trade he (Fielding) could not live by, yet he scorned to owe his subsistence to another that he ought not to live by ".

Fielding's own account of his refusal is a noble worded plea for honesty. He says : " By composing, instead of inflaming, the quarrels of porters and beggars (which I blush when I say hath not been universally practised), and by refusing to take a shilling from a man who most undoubtedly would not have had another left, I had reduced an income of about five hundred pounds a year of the dirtiest money on earth to little more than three hundred pounds ; a considerable portion of which remained with my clerk . . ."

This clerk, Joshua Brogden, who had signed the agreement with Millar for *Tom Jones*, was Fielding's most trustworthy assistant, next to the High Constable of Holborn, Saunders Welch. These three good men and true, afterwards with the help of Fielding's half-brother John, now set themselves to slay the

Hydra of London's iniquity. And all were right good fighters.

But, if the filthy lucre of legal dishonesty was not available, some other means of finding money must be tried. The two Fielding brothers therefore set up a Universal Register Office, suggested by a passage in Montaigne, so it is said. This was managed by John Fielding, and actually puffed in the first edition of *Amelia*. Besides handling exchanges of livings and insurances, it dealt in houses and estates, sold pistols and snuff-boxes, and especially that specific against all diseases—water from the Chalice Well at Glastonbury.

But now for the first time a man of high character reigned at Bow Street in an office that was universally regarded as degrading. Lady Mary Wortley Montagu says: "The highest of his preferment (was) raking in the lowest sinks of vice and misery. I should think it a nobler and less nauseous employment to be one of the staff officers that conduct the nocturnal weddings".

In his youth Fielding felt the same. In *The Covent Garden Tragedy* he had written :—

"Bridewell shall be thy fate ; I'll give a crown
To some poor Justice to commit thee thither".

Now he was "a poor Justice" himself.

Old England of course joined in the chorus of malicious merriment :—

"Now in the ancient shop at Bow
(He advertises it for show).
He signs the missive warrant,
The midnight wh—e and thief to catch
He sends the constable and watch
Expert upon the errand.
From thence he comfortably draws
Subsistence out of every cause
For dinner and a bottle".

Out of such a position Fielding was now to wrest the prize of honour for himself, and before the end to think so straight, to feel so deeply, to plan so wisely, that he not only awoke the conscience of his time, but actually succeeded in getting on the Statute Book several new laws which, it was hoped, would attack evil at its roots.

Novelist as he was, even his art was used to serve the purpose of reform. In his last novel, *Amelia*, produced while he was at Bow Street, the story of the feeble Captain Booth, incessantly gambling and getting into the debtor's prisons, is used to show up the wickedness and folly of the system which dealt with fools such as Booth.

The Court was often open at night, when a fresh case was brought in. The magistrate was liable to be summoned at any hour, and raids were frequent on the gambling houses. We hear of Fielding in person conducting a search in the houses of the Strand.

This clearing-house of vice and misery was on the ground-floor. Above lived Mrs. Fielding with her young family, William born at Twickenham, then Mary Amelia, and a second daughter, Sophia, born in 1750, with of course Charlotte's daughter, Harriet. No doubt at the hospitable table in the " eating-Parlour " an old friend would often be entertained with a meal and a bottle.

And here is Horace Walpole's famous story of Fielding at home. Its ill-natured tone is probably due to the fact, not only that he had always hated the author of *Pasquin*, but more especially because he had just heard that Fielding had been given another hundred pounds by Millar, the publisher of *Tom Jones* and *Joseph Andrews*. Two visitors, Rigby and Bathurst, call one evening at Bow Street and there " find him banqueting with a blind man, three Irishmen, and a whore, on some cold mutton and a bone of ham, both in one dish, and the cursedest dirty cloth ! He never stirred nor asked them to sit. Rigby, who had seen him so often come to beg a guinea of Sir C. Williams, and Bathurst, at whose father's he had lived for victuals, understood that dignity as little, and pulled themselves chairs, on which he civilised ".

The " whore " of course was Mrs. Fielding, and the " blind man " John, afterwards Sir John. Who the Irishmen were we know not, but, since they were Irish, their talk was probably wittier than Rigby's. Quite probably they were " low ", and not at all genteel.

But Fielding was held in honour by his own profession, even though they had refused to brief him. And six months after his appointment to the magistracy, he was called upon to deliver the Charge to the Grand Jury of Westminster.

This Charge which, according to Austin Dobson, " is still regarded by lawyers as a model exposition ", might almost be described as a key to the mind of England : here are the ideals which we may trace through all her history.

First, he gives a *Sursum corda* to those who are loyal to their country. The Jury system itself is " a privilege which distinguishes the liberty of Englishmen ", who are not subjected to any absolute rule. By the method of the Grand Jury, " No Englishman, so far from being convicted, cannot be even tried . . . in any capital case, at the suit of the Crown ". For Grand Juries do not hear lawyers, only witnesses, and have nothing to do except to decide whether there is a case against any man. If they decide not, " they may tear up the Charge ".

Therefore, and this is the point of all Fielding's arguments, the Grand Jury has in its own hands the great duty of bringing forward all cases of evil that come to their notice, offences against the Divine Being ; against the authority of King and Parliament ; against Liberty, (" Lettres de cachet, Bastilles and Inquisitions would give us a livelier sense of our Blessings "); and against individuals. In their hands is the punishment of all lewdness and gambling ; and to ensure the protection of the poor.

Finally, and most furiously, for good reasons on Fielding's part, the Grand Jury should protect against the evil of libel, " this viper, this poisoner, this secret canker in society ". Offenders' hands should be stricken off for a vile book, ballad, letter, or writing.

" Grand Juries, gentlemen, are, in reality, the only censors of this nation. As such the manners of the people are in your hands, and in yours only ".

In Fielding's view the mad craving for pleasure is the root cause of London's criminality. " Our newspapers from the top of the page to the bottom, the corners of the streets up to the very tiles of our houses, present us with nothing but a view of masquerades, balls . . . fairs, wells, gardens, tending to promote idleness, extravagance and immorality ". And—amusing as coming from Fielding—not content with three theatres, they clamour for a fourth.

Two days after the Charge Fielding had to deal with a street riot. On Saturday, July 1st 1749, a mob gathered round the house of Owen in the Strand, where a sailor declared that he had been robbed by a woman. The place was, it seems, a brothel. The house was then broken open, the furniture thrown into the street and fired, so that engines had to be sent for. Not a magistrate could be found. Fielding, who often spent the week-end in the country, was out of town. The mob had been dispersed, but on the following night, a Sunday, a second house was raided and the goods burnt. Saunders Welch got together an officer and forty soldiers, but the mob became still more dangerous. They not only set fire to a third house, but broke into the Beadle's house, and attacked the Watch-house. Till three o'clock that night Welch and the soldiers remained on guard.

By noon on Monday Fielding was back at Bow Street ; the prisoners were brought to him guarded by soldiers through the crowd. Fresh reinforcements were sent for, and Fielding addressed the crowd. But all the next night soldiers patrolled the streets while Fielding and Welch sat up till the morning.

A sailor, one Bosavern Penlez and others were examined in Court and committed to Newgate. Three witnesses swore that they had seen a man with a bundle of linen, who declared that it was his wife's, and then, scrambling the things into his pocket, made off, followed by a watchman. Being seized and borne off to the Watch-house, Penlez there sat down on a bench, but an unknown man came in and cried : " Pull the things out, and don't let the constable find them on you, unless you have a mind to hang yourself ".

Finally Penlez, in liquor but not dead drunk, confessed that, after being robbed of fifteen shillings, he had stolen the linen. Peter Wood's wife swore that the lace caps, bands and ruffles belonged to her. Penlez pleaded that he and his mates had been enraged against bad houses and tried to destroy them.

He was sentenced to death at the Old Bailey, along with one Wilson, for whom Fielding pleaded. But he refused to do so for Penlez, and the man was hanged.

There was such an uproar over the death of Penlez that Fielding took the unusual step of writing a pamphlet on the case, quoting law after law to show that to " throw down enclosed dwellings " has always been regarded as an act of treason. In this case there was great danger of a general fire, and of the robbery of a bank. How can it be cruel to execute for such a serious offence, when death is inflicted on a man who robs you of a farthing on the highway, or who privately picks your pocket of thirteen pence?

But the public was not convinced. And Penlez, said to be the son of " a reverend clergyman of the Church of England ", was buried by public subscription and a monument erected to him in the Church of St. Clement Danes as a hero who had acted " from an honest detestation of public stews ".

Perhaps the most interesting point about this affair is that Fielding here appealed to public opinion to act as judge in the case. Evidently he felt deeply the charge of cruelty that had been made against him. " Sure I am ", he says, " that I greatly deceive myself, if I am not in some little degree partaker of that milk of human kindness which Shakespeare speaks of ". Yet his character had been " barbarously aspersed without regard to truth or decency ". And then with a grim twist of humour, he thinks that surely Penlez might " be permitted to rest quietly in the grave " as an object of compassion.

Certainly Fielding's milk of human kindness had not dried up. We find him now appealing that his clerk, Joshua Brogden, may be made a magistrate. If he had been in receipt of Fielding's own salary, he would have been " but ill-paid for sitting almost sixteen hours in the twenty-four, in the most unwholesome, as well as nauseous air in the universe . . ."

The other appeal, contained in a letter to Lyttelton congratulating him on his marriage, is on behalf of Edward Moore, a young poet, who is " in love with a young creature of the most apparent worth ". And " nothing is wanting to make two very miserable people extremely blessed but a moderate portion of the greatest of human evils. So philosophers call it, and so it is called by divines, whose word is the rather to be taken, as they are, many of them, more conversant with this evil than ever philosophers were ".

The post Fielding suggests for the young man is that of Deputy Licenser to the Stage, since apparently Lyttelton had considered him worthy to wear the Laureate's " withered laurel ". Never, even at this date, could Fielding avoid a jest at Colley Cibber.

But Moore, a linendraper by trade, and the son of a dissenting minister, seems to have been a censorious prig. To his friend, John Ward, a dissenting minister at Taunton, he writes in order to explain why he has been unable to arrange a meeting with Fielding :—" It is not owing to forgetfulness that you have not heard from me before. Fielding continues to be visited for his sins so as to be wheeled about from room to room. When he mends I am sure to see him at my lodgings, and you may depend upon timely notice. What fine things are Wit and Beauty, if a Man could be temperate with one, or a Woman chaste with the other. But he that will confine his acquaintance to the sober and modest will generally find himself among the dull and the ugly. If this remark of mine should be thought to shoulder itself in without an introduction, you will be pleased to note that Fielding is a Wit; that his disorder is the Gout, and Intemperance the cause ".

There were two moralities in this century, that of the middle-class and that of the gentry. Moore professed one, and Fielding another.

The *General Advertiser* of December 28th announces that Justice Fielding " has indeed been very dangerously ill with a Fever and a Fit of the Gout, in which he was attended by Dr. Thompson ". This Thompson, called by Smollett " Dr. Thumpscull ", was a well-known quack. Fielding, in despair of the doctors, was now going from one quack to another, finally to fall back on the famous tar-water.

It was a sad end to the year, for his little daughter, Mary Amelia, only twelve months old, was buried in St. Paul's, Covent Garden, a few days before Christmas. No child could be expected to flourish in the foul air of Bow Street.

By the year 1750, since nothing had been done by the Government, conditions in London were more scandalous than ever. The prisons were so full that they ran short of fetters and two or three felons were often chained together. Within a week Fielding had sentenced no less than forty highwaymen, burglars, vagabonds and thieves.

Soldiers, for fear of a rescue, were forced to bring him prisoners from Newgate for examination. Fielding, in lack of support from those who had been robbed, inserted a notice in the press that all complaints should be brought to him " at his house in Bow Street ". Finally, the person of the Lord Chancellor himself was threatened by the keepers of three gambling-houses closed by his order.

So bad was the situation that the Government actually issued a notice offering a reward of £100 and a free pardon to any accomplice of robbery and murder who would give information, always providing that he had not himself dealt a mortal wound.

This was nothing less than an acknowledgement of social bankruptcy. But in January, 1751, Fielding published *An Enquiry into the Causes of the Late Increase of Robbers*.

This is in many ways one of the most remarkable works produced by him. Several of the remedies suggested by him were incorporated in certain Acts of Parliament. But more than this: in its revelation of the mind of Fielding it shows him to have been in some ways a Herald of the Dawn, the Dawn of the better social conditions which were to follow in the nineteenth century. It is a pamphlet full of his wisdom, knowledge, compassion—and satire, satire which goes laughing out into the world even in a booklet likely to be read only by serious students of social conditions. But Fielding's humour is always so much a part of himself that nothing on earth can dam it back. He was capable of playing the humorist even in an Act of Parliament.

He writes, not so much as a man of his own time, but rather as a man of ours. He bases his arguments on psychology, on the character and traditions of the English people, and even, in his attack on the "Tyburn holiday", on the peculiar atmosphere bred by mob passion. A politician needs " not only knowledge of law, but of the genius, manners and habits of the people ", the very facts which he had been studying all his life.

England, he says, "so jealous of her liberties, "has now allowed " the invasion of her properties by the lowest and vilest ".

But why are they low and vile? Because they are made so by the voluptuousness of the entertainment put before them. " Their eyes are feasted with show and their ears with music, and where gluttony and drunkenness are allured by every kind of dainty ; where the finest women are exposed to view ". And it is all cheap in this Paradise of the Flesh.

Drunkenness used to be punished by the stocks. But now the worst evil is the poison called Gin ; " which I have great reason to think is the principal sustenance ... of more than one hundred thousand people in this metropolis ".

A few weeks after Fielding's pamphlet had appeared, Hogarth published that most terrible of all his prints, Gin Lane.

As to the rich offenders, he would leave them alone in their gaming, since " he is not so ill-bred as to disturb the company at a polite assembly ". The chief evil here is that low sharpers sometimes appear at the gambling table, often joining in the robbery of " an egregious bubble, some thoughtless young heir ".

Yet after all, with the rich the consequence of a gamble is " no other than the exchange of property from the hands of a fool to those of a sharper, who is, perhaps, the more worthy of the two to enjoy it ".

Fielding is never more plainly a man of the eighteenth century than here, when he turns to those leaders of society whom he scourges, but from whom he expects no help, since " to be born for no other purpose than to consume the fruits of the earth is the privilege (if it may really be called a privilege) of the very few ".

" Let the great therefore answer for the employment of their time to themselves, or to their spiritual governors. Society will receive some temporal advantage from their luxury. The more toys which children of all ages consume, the brisker will be the circulation of money, and the greater the increase of trade ".

Fallacy after fallacy of course in the eyes of the modern economist. Fielding had no notion of anything but a closed society, one half of which is ordained by Providence to play, and the other to work.

For those who play he has nothing but contempt, a contempt pleasantly expressed, but none the less real.

" In this restraint (of places of amusement) I confine myself entirely to the lower order of people. Pleasure always has been, and always will be, the principal business of persons of fashion and fortune, and more especially of the ladies, for whom I have infinitely too great an honour and respect to rob them of any of their least amusement. Let them have their plays, operas and oratorios, their masquerades and ridottos ; their assemblies, drums, routs, riots and hurricanes ; their Ranelagh and Vauxhall . . . and let them have their beaus and danglers to attend them at all these ; it is the only use for which such beaus are fit ; and I have seen, in the course of my life, that it is the only one to which, by sensible women, they are applied ".

Here, unwittingly, Fielding is showing up the causes which

made the life of the rich and great in his century so despicable, so coarsely given to that "pleasure", which he cannot help despising in his heart. Unless a rich young man of those days would devote his energies to his estate, there was no career open to him, no ambition for him to serve, except by occasional service in the French wars. Nothing called for effort of mind or body, except gambling, hunting, " wenching " and intrigue. Boredom was the curse for all the men and women of fashion.

Still in the future was the time when careers were to open out before young aristocrats and young nouveaux riches : either in the armies which opposed Napoleon or in the new industrial order where wealth was to be gained, and finally, at long last, by the conquests of the mind, in science, politics, literature and art. Pleasure of course remained, especially for the brainless, but it ceased to be the only occupation of the young male.

But ultimately it was the example of the rich that tempted the poor man in Fielding's days to get pleasure for himself by all manner of crimes, from sneak-thieving up to highway robbery.

Fielding scarcely seems to have grasped this. What he saw was only the Poor rotting in misery while no man regarded their fate. His heart was torn, his anger roused at the sight of Lazarus lying at the rich man's gate. When Saunders Welch took him into the dens of poverty, he did a fine deed. " Much ", says Fielding, " have I learnt of him ". And later on, members of Parliament were taken by Welch into these rookeries that they might see for themselves.

Fielding tells us something of what they saw of the conditions that bred the crime and misery with which he had to deal every day at his Court in Bow Street.

In St. Giles's, where lodgings were let out at twopence a night, a double bed cost threepence, and gin was sold at a penny a quartern. In Shoreditch in two little houses, nearly seventy men and women were found, and amongst them a pretty young girl whose wedding night it was. The money found on all of them together amounted to less than one shilling.

The spirit which moved Charles Dickens had first inspired Henry Fielding, whose name might fittingly be inscribed over the better Common Lodging Houses of to-day.

" If ", he writes in his *Proposal for a New Poor Law*, " we were to make a progress through the outskirts of this town, and look into the habitations of the poor, we should there behold such pictures of human misery as must move the compassion of every heart that deserves the name of human. What, indeed, must be his composition which could see whole families in want of every necessary of life, oppressed with hunger, cold, nakedness and filth, and with diseases the certain consequence of all these ; what, I say, must be his composition which could look into such a scene as this and be affected only in his nostrils ? "

These housing conditions destroy Morality, Decency and Modesty ; if men fall sick, there is nothing but the street, and " it is almost a miracle that Stench, Vermin and Want should ever suffer them to be well . . . . the wonder in fact is . . . that we have not a thousand more Robbers than we have ".

And nothing is done ! " There is no country, I believe ", he cries, " in the world where that vulgar Maxim so generally prevails that what is the Business of every Man is the Business of no Man ".

Wrath against folly possessed his soul when he damned the imbecility of sending offenders to the Bridewells, " there to be kept to hard labour ", as the phrase went. There was no labour in such places for the culprits, since the Bridewells were nothing but schools of vice.

If Fielding's compassion was to be found once more in Dickens, his anger at the prison methods was also behind John Howard and Charles Reade. In his efforts to arouse the social conscience, he is like a man brooding over a stagnant pool, watching in horror what is going on in the depths of it and calling others also to look.

Then too he would end the " Tyburn holiday ", which was no punishment since it produced no shame in the murderer, and nothing but admiration or pity in the spectators, with forgetfulness of the crime for which the man was to die. Executions should be carried out immediately, and in private.

He turns to the stage to explain his reasons. When Garrick played Macbeth the hair of the audience stood on end because the murder of the king took place behind the scenes. " The mind of man is so much more capable of magnifying than his eye, that I question whether every object is not lessened by being looked upon ". A devil unseen is more terrifying than the devil we look at.

Therefore a death within the prison walls, with no crowd to see it, would seem more dreadful to the criminal than a public exit ; there would be no cordial to keep up his spirits, nor any breath of flattery to make him play the hero.

Nothing that Fielding ever wrote shows a deeper knowledge of human nature than this observation. To play a part before a huge audience is to deaden the very fear of death itself.

In fact, there's nothing good or bad but thinking makes it so. And Fielding quotes a passage from Montaigne on this very terror of death, even if it comes in one's own bed.

" I do verily believe, that it is those terrible ceremonies and preparations wherewith we set it out that more terrify us than the thing itself ; a new and contrary way of living, the cries of mothers, wives, and children, the visits of astonished and afflicted friends, the attendance of pale and blubbered servants, a dark room set round with burning tapers, our beds environed with physicians and divines, in fine, nothing but ghastliness and horror round about us, render it so formidable that a man almost fancies himself dead and buried already ".

" If the image of death was to appear thus dreadful to an army, they would be an army of whining milksops ; and where is the difference but in the apparatus ? Thus in the field (I may add at the gallows), what is encountered with gaiety and unconcern, in a sick bed becomes the most dreadful of all objects ".

There should be then at the Old Bailey a gallows erected in the area before the Court house ; Criminals should be executed on it immediately after sentence, and in the presence of the Judges.

Gone would be the sadistic joy of the crowd in a horrible spectacle ; gone too the sense that the man about to die was called upon to play a great part before a mighty audience. No false glamour now either for the criminal or the mob.

Three remedies Fielding sees for crime : first, to put a stop to the luxurious living of the lower people ; then to drive them into industry, while providing for their needs as a reward of industry alone.

All these are forcible means, for a man of the eighteenth century could not look forward to a time when, by a change in ideals through education, a better age would be ushered in.

o

CHAPTER XIX

The Doomsday Book of Human Nature

IN the great invocation to Genius in *Tom Jones*, Fielding asks: " Do thou kindly take me by the hand, and lead me through all the mazes and winding labyrinths of Nature . . . Teach me, what to thee is no difficult task, to know mankind better than they know themselves " ; he prays to know, not only the wise and good, but every kind of character, " from the Minister at his levee, to the bailiff in his spunging-house ; from the duchess at her drum, to the landlady behind her bar ".

His prayer was answered, as *Tom Jones* shows. He had learnt, from his own heart and his own experience, how to find his way through these " winding labyrinths " of human Nature. There is no novel in the English language that shows us so well, as Hazlitt said of Hogarth's paintings, " the common human face ", and the common human character.

Fielding was the better able to do this because in character he belonged to the century which prided itself on its common sense. His world of feeling is the world of all of us in a sense unmeant by Wordsworth ; he walks on the solid earth, he takes his pleasures in the satisfactions and joys of the everyday man. He is, if you like, of the earth, earthy, yet no glutton, no swine, though often as Rabelaisian as—a Rabelais, though it is true that he, rather unaccountably, disapproved of the great Frenchman.

The mystery of life never troubles him ; nor the fantasies and fears which come like fingers out of the darkness to touch the men of more sensitive nature. In his very dreams he is but Minos passing judgment on the selfish, greedy, lustful, or cruel sinners. Of man's strange unknown powers he has no inkling. Yet in his own creative world he is supreme. More, he is a forerunner of the age that was coming.

As a river is fed from springs and rivulets innumerable, so a revolution in thought creeps imperceptibly from many different sources into men's minds long before the new conception is actually formulated. While Richardson was writing *Pamela*, and Fielding *Joseph Andrews* and *Tom Jones*, the rigid barriers of class were being broken down in certain directions till at length it came into the minds of a few that all men have an equal right to " the pursuit of happiness ", as the American Declaration of Independence puts it ; and that there is not one standard of happiness for the rich and another for the poor.

Possibly Fielding, if the idea had been presented to him in so many words, would have disavowed it. Yet he was one of those who prepared the way for this idea which was to usher in the modern world. It is his aim to know, and to paint, " every kind of character ".

But to turn the search light of genius on Everyman, on the whole Field of Folk, is to show that a common Human Nature runs through them all : all rejoice, all suffer, all hate, all love, and die.

The work, which was begun by Richardson in *Pamela*, was recognised as revolutionary, even by the villagers of Slough when they rang the church bells because a maid-servant had married a squire. Unconsciously they were celebrating, not a marriage, but a birth, the birth of a new age.

The aristocrat and the printer, the man of the upper and the man of the middle-class, were carrying the democratic spirit into the hearts of the English people. " Low " as she is, Pamela is an individual soul, so is the uncouth old parson, and Tom Jones, the Foundling and Molly Seagrim, the village prostitute.

Fielding, like Richardson the snob, was a man of his own age, and with the framework of society he has no quarrel at all. Even in the matter of the return of the Stuarts, his anti-Jacobite principles were more due to the feeling that the Hanoverian kingship was convenient than to any theoretical objection to the divine right of kings. The day for such romantic notions was gone by.

But behind this creative work of Fielding's was an instinct which sprang from the depths of his nature ; the sense of the misery and suffering of the human race, in wars, in exactions, in tortures, poverty, ignorance, and the power of tyrants, of those " Great Men " whom he satirises again and again.

Before the eighteenth century, as Leonard Woolf has shewn

in *After the Deluge*, the misery of human existence was accepted, even by men as great as Erasmus and Montaigne, as inevitable. It was accepted as " an animal accepts pain " ; never as the simple result of man's own doings.

By the close of the century this attitude of mind was becoming untenable. Social life began to be looked at with new eyes, and to be judged in the light of reason. At first palliatives were tried, and Carpenter writes " Civilisation, its Cause and Cure " ; this all through the Victorian age, till finally, in despair of palliatives, some few men began to visualise an entire reconstruction of the social state. A few men first, and then multitudes of men.

Fielding could not pierce the mists of the future ; nor did he like Swift feel torn and agonised by the misery of the world. He belonged rather to the school of thought which says, if you want to better society, then make men better, one by one, improve the laws, and see them better carried out.

None the less, he did look at society in a new way ; he did see that the evil he found everywhere sprang from the evil in men's hearts, the folly of men's minds. The wind of the new spirit which says ' Lo, I make all things new ", that was blowing faintly across the Field of Folk, did find its way into Bow Street police court. There a wise mind was to be found, dealing with the affairs of thieves and murderers ; a new kind of magistrate with ideas very different from those of his predecessors.

Tom Jones set the reading world on fire. It was damned for telling too much truth, even in an age that was seldom squeamish. *Joseph Andrews* had been published seven years before, but, although a stage prologue could refer to " honest Abram Adams " as if everybody knew him, no one realised that Fielding, another Cortez, was standing on the shore of a strange new ocean—the great sea of realistic fiction. Although *Tom Jones* shows the manner, and talks in the style, of its author's own times, its knowledge of the springs of the common man's actions is as true to-day as it was in 1749, and will probably be true in the year 2000.

But there is more in it than this : in the novel is enshrined the mind of Henry Fielding, a man greater and more generous than any of his characters. Over and over again, in touches of character and observation, and especially in the familiar talks before each book, we get that "little touch of Harry", most friendly and genial of all human beings.

But how did he acquire this character? We should never have guessed at the mellow warmth he shows in *Tom Jones*, in the comedies, the bitter farces, the rattling verses of his early days, in the savagery of his polemics, or in the cold analytical power of *Jonathan Wild*. For in this "comic-epic" asked for by Lyttelton there is a broad humanity which shines like the sun on good and bad alike, a tempered judgment, a superb vitality.

The style contributes to this. *Tom Jones* is written without any scene-painting. It is stark, bare, human, with little or no background. We do hear of a wood, a hill, and a common, where Partridge is in terror of ghosts, but none of the many inns, or the drawing-rooms is described. The Victorian novelist relies on scene-setting for atmosphere; and very delightful these scenes are—the village life of *Silas Marner*, the pea-soup fogs of Dickens and the heavy dining-rooms of Thackeray.

Fielding, instead of scene-painting, relied on the vitality of his characters. *Tom Jones* with its two hundred characters is like a frieze where one figure after another starts out before one's eyes. That vitality is the key to Fielding's art as a story-teller. As he forgot his troubles before a venison pasty or a bottle of champagne, as he fought his enemies with zest and mourned almost to madness, so he carried over into his novels that same energy and power which bore him through the many phases of his own life.

Look at a runner on the Elgin Marbles, you see no labouring muscles, but the verve and élan of the whole figure. Look in the same way at Tom, at Sophia, at Mistress Western, and the Squire: you see the life of all these men and women as you see the running body of the man in the marble.

Nor are the shades of difference omitted: Fielding draws attention to two inn hostesses, one like the other, and yet different. As he put it, it is easy to distinguish between Sir Epicure Mammon and Sir Fopling Flutter, but not between Sir Fopling Flutter and Sir Courtly Nice. But he shows the difference.

When Fielding had finished those thousands of hours which he spent in writing *Tom Jones*, he was a man of forty-one, who had lived a full life. He took none of his characters at second-hand ; all, so he tells us, come from " the doomsday book of authentic Human Nature ". Vanbrugh and Congreve, he says, copied Nature, but those who copy them draw as unlike the present age as Hogarth would do if he " were to paint a rout or a drum in the dresses of Titian and Vandyke ".

In his plays Fielding sinned against this principle : in these he shows gay life as the Restoration dramatists saw it. His plays are dead ; his novels, taken from " the doomsday book of Nature ", still live. But, as he observes, " in reality true Nature is as difficult to be met with in authors, as the Bayonne ham, or Bologna sausage, is to be found in the shops ".

But in the matter of " originals ", the great question is of course—how much of the character of the hero of *Tom Jones* is Fielding in youth. If, as he tells us, Sophia is Charlotte Cradock, his beloved first wife, is Tom also Charlotte's husband?

In the first place Tom is a country boy, brought up in the squire class, and getting such education as a resident philosopher, and a resident schoolmaster could give him. In complexion sanguine, in looks handsome, almost an Adonis, with an athletic six-foot frame, as a lover of field sports, he might well be Harry Fielding. In character he is like him too : generous, head-strong, kind hearted to the point of folly : certainly Fielding to the life, with an honour of his own, a hatred of cruelty and injustice, and an affectionate heart.

With a fault as natural to a lusty youth as the very blood in his veins, he—as he believes—seduces the village harlot, as Harry himself may possibly have done. In his ignorance of her real character, when he believes she is with child, he is all for repairing his fault and making " an honest woman " of her at whatever cost to himself. After he has found out her real character, and has also learnt to worship Sophia Western, he again yields to his appetite for poor Molly, and that at the very moment when he is about to carve Sophia's name on the bark of a tree after the fashion of 18th century lovers.

There is no doubt that Fielding enjoyed the irony of the situation as between divine and earthly love. But his grim humour in this scene has certainly recoiled on his own head, and for nearly two hundred years Fielding the truth-teller has been looked upon as Fielding the profligate, especially by those who count the sins of the flesh as far more damnable than the sins of the heart. But as Samuel Butler once remarked, every village in England has its Molly Seagrim and its Tom Jones.

More than once, especially in the stories he interpolated in the main narrative, Fielding verged so closely on the autobiographic that it is difficult to tell where autobiography begins and where it ends. Mr. Wilson's tale in *Joseph Andrews* is certainly in part reminiscent of Fielding's own excesses when thrown into the whirlpool of fashionable London. But the gambling story of the Man of the Hill tells us little more of Fielding himself than that he had learnt by experience that " a man may be as easily starved in Leadenhall-market as in the deserts of Arabia ". Fielding may well have had a Molly Seagrim among his memories just as we know that he went the pace in his first days in London.

There is a fine old prayer that " we may so pass through things temporal that we finally lose not the things eternal ". Through things temporal Fielding passed, but held with a sure hand the things eternal. And in him, we may be sure that no cruel act, no shameless indifference to the misery of others, can be laid to his charge. In fact, in the novel, Tom's generous-hearted eagerness to help distress brings him into far more disgrace than his affairs with women.

Fielding, who fought hypocrisy as a man fights the devil himself, yet shows his hero always repentant after his three lapses, and always eager to try the better way. In certain circumstances Tom is a lecherous young rascal ; in others the true lover who finds in real love the awakening of a different self ; at all times he is generous, open-handed, eager to serve others, a perfect contrast to the cunning self-seeker, Blifil. It is a companion picture of two utterly opposite characters, and no one can possibly doubt which Fielding preferred.

Thackeray confessed that he dared not paint the portrait of a man, as Fielding did, and for so doing was damned, even in his own coarse century. His contemporaries indeed were especially shocked at the bold way in which Sophia left her home to avoid a hateful marriage. But that offence would never startle the veriest Puritan to-day.

Fielding's wife had been dead five years when *Tom Jones* was published, but no one can doubt that he was thinking of his own loss when he wrote of Squire Allworthy, the widower, that

" he sometimes said he looked on himself as still married, and considered his wife as only gone a little before him, a journey which he should most certainly, sooner or later, take after her ; and that he had not the least doubt of meeting her again in a place where he should never part with her more ".

Tom Jones was published on February 28th, 1749, in six volumes. Andrew Millar, the publisher of *Joseph Andrews*, had paid Fielding £600 for the manuscript on June 11th 1748. Fielding was then the magistrate for Westminster and Middlesex.

The *London Magazine* of February gave it a leading article, and though the *Gentleman's Magazine* refused a review, it dared not ignore the book, but merely lamented that all the world " is run a-madding after that fool Parson Adams, and that rake Tom Jones ". Lady Bradshaigh, Richardson's admirer, wrote to him saying, " as to *Tom Jones* I am fatigued with the name, having fallen into the company of several young ladies, who each had a Tom Jones in some part of the world, for so they call their favourites . . . In like manner, the gentlemen have their Sophias . . . a friend of mine told me he must show me his Sophia, the sweetest creature in the world, and immediately produced a Dutch mastiff puppy ".

She could not understand Richardson's condemnation of a book he had not read ! But the success of *Tom Jones* was a bitter pill indeed for the jealous little printer to be obliged to swallow. His spirit boiled with rage at every word of appreciation of his rival. Yet Fielding, in the *Jacobite's Journal* had gone out of his way to express his admiration for that great effort of genius, *Clarissa*.

In the spring of 1750 came two earthquakes, one in February and the other in March. Chimneys fell, houses rocked, plates fell off the shelves. Wind and hail showers lashed the earth. An astrologer foretold another earthquake for April 5th. Meteors flashed, and in southern England the Aurora Borealis appeared. From Salisbury this was described as " an extraordinary phenomenon, being a very luminous collection of vapours, that formed an irregular arch like rock-work and extended across the horizon, waving like flames rising from fire ". It suddenly disappeared, leaving a clear, star-lit night.

And all this was just Heaven's condemnation of—*Tom Jones*. Had not Fielding's enemy, the journal *Old England*, declared this book to be " a motley History of Bastardism, Fornication, and Adultery?" On the one side it was full of immorality and irreligion, on the other, " a whipt sillabub of froth and air ". So Fielding caught it both ways.

After the prophecy of the third earthquake great ladies sent out cards, which said : " I invite your ladyship to the earthquake on April 5th next ". Others, less light-minded, went out of London on the night, and sat in their chariots, so that the roads were crowded as far away as Windsor.

The Bishop of London preached repentance, and a Pastoral Letter to the same effect was sent out, forty thousand copies going to the poor. The shocks had affected London and particularly Westminster, because of that notorious Bow Street magistrate. *Old England* called on the Londoners to mend their ways, since the reading of lewd books, particularly *Tom Jones*, had turned the place into a sink of iniquity. Paris, that virtuous city, where the novel, so it was said, had been refused publication, was visited by neither earthquake nor meteor.

Yet there was mercy in the heavens after all, for, after " the streams of dark ruddy fire " there appeared " a mild gleam of light " which meant pardon after judgment. An Act should at once be passed, in order to appease God, forbidding the publication of *Tom Jones*, and " other works of cool and diabolical malice ".

Here Fielding interposed, he who sat in his court on the ground-floor of his house in Bow Street. It was near the public house, the Bunch of Grapes, of later days.

One of the wise men who foretold the arrival of the third earthquake was " a crazy life-guardsman ", John Misavan, who had received " intelligence from an angel " to the effect that the Thames would wash away London Bridge, and the earth would open and swallow Westminster Abbey. The astronomer, Mr. Whiston, was consulted as to whether it was possible to foretell an earthquake. He was of the opinion that without divine inspiration no one could, though in countries where earthquakes occurred, a third usually followed.

Fielding proceeded to tackle the matter. He summoned John Misavan to his court on the very night before the earthquake was to happen, and sent him to Newgate " with strict orders to chain him down in one of the cells ". This was done as " a warning to all Persons how they are guilty of such wicked and blasphemous crimes as terrifying the King's lieges ".

Seldom has an author been able to deal in such a high-handed manner with what Fielding calls in *Tom Jones* " a little reptile of a critic ".

The many traditions which have survived as to the place where Fielding wrote his novel prove how well-known the book must have been ; among them is the Manor House, at the bottom of Milford Hill, in that summer-house where one may still read, cut with a diamond on the window-pane, the words in praise of the divine Clarissa. Another is Fielding's Lodge at Twerton, a mile and a half from Bath. The contemporary vicar of Claverton, the Rev. Richard Graves, tells us that this was where Fielding lived while writing *Tom Jones*, in " the first house on the right hand with a spread eagle over the door ", and that he dined daily with his friend Ralph Allen at Prior Park. An old building in the Wye Valley, once the house of the Abbot of Tintern, is yet another claimant.

But actually Fielding was paying rates for his house in Old Boswell Court from the last quarter of 1744 to the end of the third quarter of 1747, after which he removed to Twickenham. No doubt he was often visiting, or on circuit, in both Bath and Salisbury, and there continuing to spend those " many thousand of hours " in the composition of his masterpiece.

To his friend, George, Lord Lyttelton, known as " the Good ", his book is dedicated. In this dedication Fielding says frankly : " I partly owe to you my Existence during great Part of the Time which I have employed in composing it ". This book, in its gaiety, its wisdom, and power, was certainly written at a time of poverty and sickness. The law had failed its author, and by journalism he had never made much, so that to Lyttelton, and to Ralph Allen, always generous to men of genius, he probably owed the money on which he lived through this time.

Tradition says that at Radway Grange on the Edge Hills, at the house of Sanderson Miller, Fielding read the manuscript of his novel to Lyttelton and Pitt, with whom he had been at Eton. The Rev. George Miller, great grandson of Fielding's friend, wrote to Miss Godden in 1909 that " Fielding came to Radway to visit my ancestor, when Lord Chatham planted three trees to commemorate the visit, and a stone urn was placed between them. Fielding was also of the party and read *Tom*

Jones in manuscript after dinner for the opinion of his hearers before publishing it ".

It was natural enough that the book should have been attacked by Fielding's enemies. But strange it is that his friends utter not a word of praise : not even Lyttelton or Garrick.

The most genuine criticism came, amusingly enough, from two young girls, daughters of Abraham Hill, whom he had absurdly christened Minerva and Astraea.

Hill and his family were then living in a little Essex village when—an amazing fact if he thought the novel immoral—Richardson asked the girls to read and criticize *Tom Jones*. As little girls they had cried over *Pamela* and now they were to laugh over his rival's work, " being ", as their father says, " of late, grown borrowing customers to an Itinerary Bookseller's shop, that rumbles, once a week, through Plaistow on a wheelbarrow ".

Astraea and Minerva consider the sub-title, the Foundling, coarse, thus paying tribute to convention. Many other people objected to this " Foundling " besides the Misses Hill. Some said that Fielding had made Tom illegitimate because his wife Charlotte had been " A Foundling ". There is not the slightest reason to believe this, but it is true that Ralph Allen, or Mr. Allworthy, had married the illegitimate daughter of General Wade.

But to return to Minerva and Astraea. They find in *Tom Jones* " much masqu'd merit both of head and heart ", mingled with " a bantering levity " in the treatment of solemn matters. In Fielding's mock-heroic style they miss, in fact, the sanctimonious note so loved by Richardson.

But after all, Mr. Richardson might find the book " not unworthy of perusal ". At this delightful tone of patronage Mr. Richardson surely sat up and took notice. But disgust must have seized him when these frank young ladies go on to say : " It is an honest pleasure which we take in adding that . . . all the changeful Windings of the Author's Fancy carry on a course of regular Design ; and end in an extremely moving Close, where Lives that seem'd to wander and run different ways, meet, All, in an instructive Center ".

It is precisely this perfection of plot, in which every single incident in the story, however unrelated it may seem at the time to the main movement, is found at the close to have had its part in the total result, that roused the admiration of Coleridge and Gibbon.

But the Hills can do better than this. " In every part ", they say, " it has Humanity for its Intention : in too many it seems wantoner than it was meant to be. It has bold shocking pictures ; and (I fear) not unresembling ones in high Life, and in Low. And (to include this too adventurous Guess-work, from a Pair of forward Baggages) would, everywhere (we think) deserve to please—if stript of what the Author thought himself most sure to please by ".

Richardson, amazed and annoyed, despairs of these Baggages. " What Reason ", he demands, " had he to make Tom illegitimate, in an Age when keeping is become a Fashion, and a kept Fellow the lowest of all Fellows, yet in Love with a Young Creature who was traping after him a Fugitive from her Father's House ?—Why did he draw his Heroine so fond, so foolish, and so insipid ?—Indeed he has one Excuse—He knows not how to draw a delicate Woman—He had not been accustomed to such Company—and is too prescribing, too impetuous, too immoral, I will venture to say, to take any other Byass than that a perverse and Crooked Nature has given him ; or Evil Habits, at least, have confirm'd in him. Do men expect Grapes of Thorns, or Figs, of Thistles ? But perhaps, I think the worse of the Piece because I know the Writer, and dislike his Principles both Public and Private, tho' I wish well to the Man, and Love Four worthy Sisters of his, with whom I am well acquainted ".

" Both fairly cry'd ", says the father of the Misses Hill, " that you should think it possible they could approve of Anything, in Any work, that had an Evil Tendency. But ", he adds, " they maintain their Point ".

And all this time Richardson has not read the book, or declares that he has not. And when he hears that it has been banned in France, he writes : " *Tom Jones* is a dissolute book. Its run is over even with us ". But Monsieur Defreval, his correspondent, though he has never heard of this banning, is ready to declare his opinion. " I think it is a profligate performance upon your pronouncing it such . . . but it has had a vast run this good while ", which must have been sadly disappointing to Richardson.

But a delightful letter reaches him from the author of " A Critical Spelling Book ". Of *Clarissa* he says : " I do not doubt but that all Europe will ring with it, when a Cracker that was some thousand hours a-composing, will no longer be heard or talkt of ". This letter was folded up by Richardson and inscribed with the good words, " Cracker, T. Jones ".

Fielding was no doubt a happy man when writing *Tom Jones*. We may talk of poverty and illness : but he had in his heart a splendid secret—that the book was a great, a living creation. And to a writer this knowledge is a hidden source of eternal pleasure. And yet what a struggle it was !

" But the author ", he says in *Tom Jones* in that confidential way of his, " whose Muse hath brought forth, will feel the pathetic strain . . . while I mention the uneasiness with which the big Muse bears about her burden, the painful labour with which she produces it, and, lastly the care, the fondness, with which the tender father nourishes his favourite, till it be brought to maturity and produced into the world ".

At last he realises that the thing his Muse has brought forth is good, not for one generation, but in the years to come.

Everything in the novel follows from its foundation in the family circumstances of Squire Allworthy and his sister Bridget, afterwards Mrs. Blifil, the mother of the crafty boy who is to act as a contrast to Tom Jones ; her portrait was painted by Hogarth in his Morning Scene. She, in the West Country phrase, is a " vinegar bottle ", a prude, yet the mother of an illegitimate son.

The first scene, one full of humour and pathos, gives us Allworthy turning down his bed-clothes to discover a baby boy fast asleep against his pillow. As the little creature's fingers close round his hand, he conceives that tender affection which lasts throughout the book. And when the housekeeper arrives, it is to find, to her horror, that the master, clad only in his shirt, is held fast by the baby's hand.

The child is Tom Jones, to be brought up as the adopted son of the Squire. But Mrs. Deborah Wilkins, the housekeeper, is thereupon sent down to the village to spy out who the guilty mother may be. " Not otherwise than when a kite, that tremendous bird, is beheld by the feathered generation soaring aloft . . . the amorous dove, and every innocent little bird, spread wide the alarm : " So the villagers behave when they see Mrs. Deborah advancing on them. Poor Jenny Jones, the schoolmaster's servant, is fixed upon as the guilty wench, though actually the culprit is, not Jenny, but Mistress Bridget.

Everyone expects that Jenny will be condemned to Bridewell. But Allworthy sends her to another parish, and adopts the child, keeping him to be educated with his sister's legitimate boy, young Blifil.

It is a curious fact that, although Allworthy is Ralph Allen whom Fielding knew well, he is not really life-like, but rather a peg upon which Fielding may hang all the benevolent virtues just as young Blifil is a mere incarnation of knavish cunning.

The lads are shewn as being educated by two of Fielding's most extraordinary characters, Thwackum and Square, both taken from men living in Salisbury whom Fielding probably knew in his youth.

Thwackum, the Christian, was Richard Hele, Master of the Cathedral school, and a Prebendary, to whose memory there once hung a mural tablet on the wall of the Cathedral.

According to Fielding, this man regarded the human mind as a mere sink of iniquity, only to be redeemed by grace. He has his profession of faith : " When I mention religion, I mean the Christian religion ; and not only the Christian religion but the Protestant religion ; and not only the Protestant religion, but the Church of England ". And all things he settled according to his formula.

Square is a philosopher for whom Human Nature is perfection. He swears by " the eternal fitness of things ". His real name was Thomas Chubb, born at East Harnham, near Salisbury, and quite a European figure. Voltaire regarded him as the most logical of the Deists.

Originally a glove-maker's apprentice and then a tallow-chandler, he acted at one time as Secretary-Servant to the Master of the Rolls, wrote Essays, and finally returned to Salisbury. Fielding makes him a humbug, and in the disputes between Thwackum and Square we no doubt catch echoes of their debates in the Salisbury Club which encouraged such discussions.

Fielding derides them both, but with an apology : had they not " both utterly discarded all natural goodness of heart they had never been represented as the objects of derisrion in this history ", he says. That goodness of heart is with Fielding always the saving grace that preserves from evil. But as for the tutors, Thwackum would have destroyed half mankind with his principle, and Square the other half with his.

Black George, the gamekeeper, is Tom's friend. The pair of them shoot a partridge which has flown from Allworthy's estate on to Squire Western's land, although the latter has forbidden all trespassing. Black George is guilty, but Tom endures a flogging rather than get the man into trouble. And when the game-keeper is dismissed and his family reduced to want, the lad sells both " the little horse and the Bible " given him by Allworthy so that he may be able to provide for the culprit's wants. Also he risks a drowning to save Sophia Western's pet bird which Blifil, with a smug pretence of giving every creature its liberty, had let loose.

But Sophia must be introduced by Fielding himself. All the high lights of his novel shine on this lady whom he ushers on the scene with the same rhapsody that he would use to greet the sunrise.

Sublimity is his note : " Hushed be every ruder breath. Do thou, sweet Zephirus, rising from thy fragrant bed, mount the western sky, and lead on those delicious gales, the charms of which call forth the lovely Flora from her chamber ". Thus heralded, Sophia comes, a second " lovely Flora ".

Fielding's mind must have been full of memories of New Sarum when he wrote of his days of courtship in *Tom Jones*. There in the story is one Dowdy, or Doughty, playing the ghost with rattling chains in order to terrify everybody in the inn. But Fielding seems to have forgotten the name of the joker, for the *Salisbury Journal* of January 18th, 1762, ascribes this trick to a man named Pearce.

As a memorial of the English age-long fight against all tyranny, besides the tomb of William Longspée in the Cathedral, Salisbury possesses one of the four copies of Magna Carta that are still extant. A right spiritual home was New Sarum for the Author of *Pasquin* and *The Political Register*.

The great humorist is never more at ease than in the scene where Squire Western, listening to the debate between Thwackum and Square, cries out : " Pox of your laws of Nature! I don't know what you mean, either of you, by right or wrong. Let's talk a little of the nation, or some such discourse that we can all understand ".

Western is a Jacobite of the old school, but his sister, a lady who knows the world and talks politics in a lingo incomprehensible to her brother, is " a Hanoverian rat ". The talk between the two, her contempt for his understanding, and his terror of her tongue, makes first-class fooling. We only long for more of it.

The " original " of Squire Western has never been traced : some have found him in Sir John Paulett, others in Squire Mildmay. Probably he is of many squires all compact, the very quintessence of the country gentleman who knows nothing of courts or cities ; whose jests are bawdy, whose talk is all of dogs, horses and wenches. The Squire is a three-bottle man of course and loves his daughter—next to his horses, especially the Chevalier, and his mare, Miss Slouch.

" Politics ! " roars he. " They belong to us. With them petticoats should not meddle ".

But his sister sneers at the judgment of men " which can penetrate into the cabinets of princes ". To him such talk is pure gibberish, and he can only reply : " If thou hadst been a man, I promise thee I had lent thee a flick long ago ".

Finding that Sophia is in love, not with Blifil, but with Tom, he uses the only argument he understands—and locks her up.

Like an offended goddess Madam Western turns on him. " English women, brother, I thank Heaven, are no slaves. We are not to be locked up like the Spanish and Italian wives. We have as good a right to liberty as yourself ".

Having no answer to this, the Squire falls to cursing the " Hanoverian rats ", who will " eat up all our corn and leave us nothing but turnips to feed on ".

When Thwackum and Tom fall to blows over Molly, even to bloody noses, Fielding, in that friendly confidential way of his, drops into soliloquy. " Here we cannot suppress a pious wish, that all quarrels were to be provided by those weapons with which Nature, knowing what is proper for us, hath supplied us ; and that cold iron was to be used in digging no bowels but those of the earth ".

He apologises for Tom's offence with Molly in those words which the King of the Beggars found so immoral. " Now we ", he writes, " who are admitted behind the scenes of this great theatre of Nature (and no author ought to write anything besides dictionaries and spelling books who hath not this

FIELDING LODGE, TWERTON, NEAR BATH

OHIO UNIVERSITY
LIBRARY.

privilege) can censure the action, without conceiving any absolute detestation of the person whom perhaps Nature may not have designed to act an ill part in all her dramas ". And again, " a single bad act no more constitutes a villain in life, than a single bad part on the stage ".

And surely here is Fielding speaking of himself when he says of Tom, " though he did not always act rightly, yet he never did otherwise without feeling and suffering for it ". No passage in all his work shows more clearly the sweet and kindly nature of Tom's creator.

To help the poverty of Black George's family, Sophia sends Molly a gay silk sacque. But this finery being worn in church so inflames the jealousy of the village that a Homeric battle rages in the churchyard. And here we get memories of Fielding's boyhood at East Stour, with Jemmy Tweedle, the fiddler, and the Misses Potter, whose father kept the Red Lion.

Tom breaks his arm in saving Sophia from a fall from her horse and is invited to stay with the Westerns. And here comes Mistress Honor, Sophia's maid, to tell her lady how Tom had been seen kissing that little muff which the Squire had once tossed on the fire because it slipped over her hand as she was playing his favourite song, Old Sir Simon.

When Tom finds Thwackum cowering behind the curtain in Molly's bedroom, he reflects that " though such great beings (as philosophers) think much better and more wisely, they always act exactly like other men ". This reflection occurred to Fielding himself in the affair of his friend Collier and the £400.

Tom is banished by Allworthy, whose ear had been poisoned by Square and Thwackum, and promptly loses the £500 given him by the Squire. This Black George finds and keeps to himself. Sophia, however, sends him £16, and with this he takes to the road. His " naturally violent animal spirits " fail him here. In despair he resolves to make for Bristol and take to the sea.

Now at last we are in full swing, starting on that epic of the road for which Fielding has been preparing us. Tom's first stop is evidently at Wells, five miles from Glastonbury. His guide leads him astray, and he finds himself on the road to Gloucester. At Hambrook he falls in with a company of soldiers on their way to join the Duke of Cumberland's army against the Jacobite rebels.

P

The fun grows fast and furious. Tom fights Ensign Northerton and is left for dead, but rises again in the night and terrifies the sentinel, who takes him for a ghost. Partridge, the schoolmaster who had employed Jenny Jones, Tom's supposed mother, turns up, this time as a barber. He joins Tom for the road, to play Sancho Panza with his proverbs, his fears of ghosts and goblins, his cowardice, his folly, and general likeableness.

Meanwhile Sophia has also taken to the road to escape a marriage with Blifil. Here she horrifies her readers both French and English. To go " trapesing "—it is Richardson's word—after her lover! Though Mrs. Honor is afraid of robbers, thieves, ravishers and murderers, she follows—a female counterpart of the good Partridge. But Sophia sets out on her own feet at midnight, and as gaily as if it were midday.

Jones at the Bell Inn, Gloucester, that lovely relic of mediaeval days, comes upon the brother of Whitefield, the preacher, and his charming capable wife, the very ideal of an inn hostess.

Even though the spirit of the story at this point is haste, post-haste, Fielding cannot resist an attack on the Methodists. Of Mrs. Whitefield he says : " She freely confessed that her brother's documents made at first some impression upon her, and that she had put herself to the expense of a long hood, in order to attend the extraordinary emotions of the Spirit, but having found, during an experiment of three weeks, no emotions, she says, worth a farthing, she very wisely laid by her hood, and abandoned the sect ".

At first friendly to Tom and Partridge, Mrs. Whitefield turns from them after lawyer Dowling has told her tales of Tom's depravity, and therefore he decides to leave the inn that night. The Whitefields' clock struck five " just as Mr. Jones took his leave of Gloucester ", but the moon was up, and to her ladyship Mr. Jones recited some poetry by Milton. The moon's red face reminds him of the tale of the two lovers who, being far apart from each other, agreed to look upon her every evening at the same moment.

Fielding, who is known to have consulted a calendar as a magistrate to test the story told by a witness, must have done the same thing in the case of the Bell Inn clock, for the moon and the hour are right, except that the Whitefields' clock was two minutes fast.

At " Mazard Hill ", conjectured to be a spur of the Malverns, the travellers come to a standstill. Tom nourishing his lover's dream, feels that a hill is the most suitable for him as conducive to melancholy. Partridge, however, considers that " if the top of the hill is the properest to produce melancholy thoughts, I suppose the bottom is the likeliest to produce merry ones, and these I take to be much the better of the two ". Actually he is in terror of witches, and when the old woman at the cottage of the Man of the Hill opens the door, her ugliness convinces him that she is one of those dreaded beings.

In the Tale of the Man of the Hill Fielding takes the opportunity of pinning down for ever my Lord Justice Page of the Western Circuit, who said to a man charged with stealing a horse : " Thou art a lucky fellow, I have travelled the circuit these forty years, and never found a horse in my life ; but I'll tell thee what, friend, thou wast more lucky than thou didst know of, for thou didst not only find a horse, but a halter too ".

This is one of the very few anecdotes of the Western Circuit that have survived from Fielding's time.

A woman's scream calls Tom to the wood, as it had called Parson Adams. Here he finds Ensign Northerton tying a woman to a tree in order that he may rob her. Tom plays the rescuer and carries the lady off to the inn at Upton-on-Severn.

In this beautiful village knot after knot is tied in the skein of the plot ; all to be unravelled when the characters meet in London. Again Fielding has to apologise for Tom, declaring that an author should show no angelic perfection, and no diabolical depravity in his characters, since the former creates despair of ever achieving it ; the latter a horror that the human race should be so degraded.

One guesses what is about to happen : Mrs. Waters, the woman Tom has rescued, " gets him " just as Molly Seagrim had done. Sophia and her maid arrive while Tom is with his lady. And so " affable " is Sophia to the inn people that her complaisance reminds Fielding of his friend, the celebrated Mrs. Hussey in the Strand, who is " famous for setting off the shapes of women ".

The story goes that Fielding had promised that he would put all his friends in a novel, with a bracket in a niche for Mrs. Hussey. As the work was passing through the press, he suddenly remembered this, went down to the printers, and was in time to insert this passage.

After the fashion of ladies in Fielding's time, Sophia needs no supper, but Mrs. Honor, demanding fowl, has to content herself with eggs and bacon. Partridge, who has not seen Mrs. Waters, but hears all the gossip, gleefully reveals to the waiting-maid that Tom is in bed with her. And what the maid knows is soon confided to her mistress. Sophia thus learns the worst of her lover.

Next morning Squire Western arrives, and the inn is in an uproar. But his daughter is gone and Tom, in despair, learns that his Sophia has been near him, for he discovers her muff on his pillow, that little muff of many adventures. Sophia, being overtaken by the Squire's niece, Mrs. Fitzpatrick, the two ladies travel towards London in the coach and six which belongs to a certain Peer, in love with Mrs. Fitz.

But all the country is agog with rumours that the Duke of Cumberland has been given the slip and the Highlanders are on the way to London. His imagination fired by all this, the landlord of the inn at Meriden, is persuaded that Sophia is none other than Jenny Cameron, the mistress of Charles Stuart. The Jacobite Rising thus forms the vivid framework of the story.

Tom comes up with a puppet-show and from the Merry Andrew of the company learns where Sophia was last seen. With fresh hope he presses forward till a storm of rain drives him into a barn where gypsies are celebrating a wedding. Here we probably have a reminiscence of Fielding's own adventures when riding on the Western Circuit. But Partridge misconducts himself with one of the gypsy women, and her husband demands blackmail. The King of the gypsies condemns the man, and bids him wear the horns.

Here Fielding turns aside to discuss the question of absolute monarchy. This principle, he says, comes straight from the Prince of Darkness, because no man is fit to be trusted with such power. All absolute dictatorship is anathema to this true Englishman.

It was the story of Partridge and the gypsies which so enraged Bampfielde Moore Carew that in the second edition of his *Apology* he poured scorn on the author of *Tom Jones*, and all his works.

The Peer's coach heading for London through Coventry, Daventry, Dunstable and St. Albans is followed closely by Tom, who now has in his pocket the hundred-pound bill given to

Sophia by her father. It fell out of her pocket in a dark lane when her horse threw her and was picked up by Tom. Sophia evidently was a poor horse-woman, though she hunted to please her father.

At Barnet Tom is confronted by a highwayman, a poor sort of fellow whose pistol is even without ammunition. Hearing that the man has taken to the road to save his family from starvation, Tom gives him two guineas. This, like all the other incidents, will play a part in the final marvellous " revolution and discovery " at the end of the novel. Never was the century's sense of form more perfectly expressed than it is in *Tom Jones*.

As for its morality, Fielding refuses to whitewash his hero, of whom he remarks " perhaps the fair Adonis was not a lovelier figure ". And this Adonis was unfortunately—it is Fielding's own expression—ready to eat every woman he saw. Yet he can still honestly say : " I have been guilty with women, I own it, but I am not conscious that I have ever injured any ". And in fact this Tom is a man whom every light woman desires at sight. That is the truth of the matter.

Tom is no Don Quixote, though Partridge is an English Sancho, a man with whom we must all sympathise when he says : " What matters the cause to me, or who gets the victory, if I am killed ? . . . What are all the ringing of bells and bonfires to one that is six feet underground ? And then there are cannons which certainly it must be thought the highest presumption to get in the way of—A man shall never persuade me he is a good Christian while he sheds Christian blood ".

In London Tom is dazed by the whirl in which he finds himself ; he is penniless in the society of the rich. But he is a lure for all the lascivious women, and falls a prey to the ageing Lady Bellaston. The very thundering rat-tat of the footman at the door of her house shakes his nerves. But Adonis can play the gigolo to the old woman, and does—for a fee. Tom has reached the lowest point of his degradation. Yet all this time he is helping his landlady, Mrs. Nightingale, in her distress ; he is giving money for the support of the poor family of the highwayman he met at Barnet. And that is Tom Jones !

Coleridge said of this incident of Lady Bellaston : " I cannot but think, after frequent reflection on it, that an additional paragraph more fully and forcibly unfolding Tom Jones's sense of self-degradation on the discovery of the true character of the relation in which he had stood to Lady Bellaston—would have removed in great measure any fresh objections . . ."

In a wonderful scene of extreme beauty, and all the more beautiful for the darkness behind it, Sophia comes into the drawing-room at Lady Bellaston's and sees Tom in a mirror standing like a statue. He learns then that she loves him, even with all his faults.

But the net tightens round him. Lady Bellaston's lust turns to contempt and hatred and she tries to get him taken by the press-gang ; he is thrown into the Gate-house prison, the very gaol to which Fielding was then consigning evil-doers, and awaits sentence for having, as he thinks, killed Fitzpatrick in a duel. Worst, most horrible of all, he is told by Partridge, who, it will be remembered had not seen her at the inn, that Mrs. Waters is his own mother.

Suddenly the skies clear : Squire Allworthy learns that Tom is the son of his sister Bridget. The whole of those early chapters is, as it were, turned upside down. And Blifil is shewn to have been the devil of the piece throughout. Fitzpatrick recovers, Tom is released, and Squire Western is delighted that his Sophy should marry Allworthy's nephew. He is for having the wedding the very next day.

Fielding had prayed to Genius in the great names of Aristophanes, Lucian, Cervantes, Rabelais, Molière, Shakespeare, Swift, and in queer company, Marivaux. Not in vain !

And his lesson ? " To learn the good nature to laugh at the follies of others and the humility to grieve at one's own ".

We come very close to Fielding and his ambition in *Tom Jones*. In it he holds out his hands to his readers, and speaks with his own voice. He would have us know him, and we do.

We know too the hearts of his characters. Here is Mistress Western, Sophy's aunt, remembering her own youth as she looks at her niece. " I was called the cruel Parthenissa. I have broken many a window that had verses to the cruel Parthenissa in it. Sophy, I was never as handsome as you are, and yet I had something of you formerly. I am a little altered. Kingdoms and estates, as Tully Cicero says in his Epistles, undergo alterations, and so must the human form ".

Did ever an elderly woman's regrets for lost youth find more tender and yet more humorous expression than this ?

But Fielding certainly reached no higher point in humour than in the scene at the playhouse where Jones and Partridge watch Garrick playing Hamlet.

" It was a wonder ", cried the English Sancho Panza at the sight of the stage, " how many fiddlers could play at one time without putting one another out ". And here Poverty speaks, when he remarks with a sigh that candles were burnt here in one night enough " to keep an honest family for a whole twelvemonth ".

Old England comes to life when he exclaims : " Look, look, Madam, the very picture of the man in the end of the Common Prayer Book before the Gunpowder Treason service ".

At the entrance of the ghost in " a strange dress " Partridge's idea is that the figure is wearing armour. " Though I can't say I ever saw a ghost in my life, yet I am certain I should know one, if I saw him, better than that comes to ".

The Age of Reason in which Dr. Johnson sat up to see the Cock Lane ghost, did actually shiver at the idea of apparitions.

Suddenly Jones observes that Partridge is trembling, with his knees knocking together. This trembling is a tribute to Garrick's acting. " Nay, you may call me coward if you will ; but if that little man there upon the stage is not frightened, I never saw any man frightened in my life ".

And the great actor's fright pulses in every nerve of Partridge's body till he cries as Hamlet follows the ghost : " Lud have mercy upon such fool-hardiness !—No farther !—Farther than I'd have gone for all the King's dominions ".

" And dost thou imagine, then, Partridge ", asks Jones, " that he was really frightened ? "

" Nay, Sir, did you not yourself observe afterwards, when he found it was his own father's spirit . . . how his fear shook him by degrees, and he was struck dumb with sorrow, as it were, just as I should have been, had it been my own case ".

This is the actual illusion which the simple feel at a stage representation : it is half life, half play. And as soon as that simplicity dies in us, half the glamour of the stage is gone. " Though I know there is nothing at all in it, I am glad I am not down yonder, where those men are."

As to the grave-digger, the expert in grave-digging will have none of him : " I had a sexton, when I was clerk, that should have dug three graves while he was digging one. The fellow handles a spade as though it was the first time he had ever had one in his hand ".

But for judgment, what can beat this? Asked by Tom which of the players he liked best, Partridge answers, " The King without doubt ".

" But what about the man who played Hamlet ? "

" He the best player ! Why, I could act as well as he myself. I am sure, if I had seen a ghost, I should have looked in the very same manner, and done just as he did . . . And in that scene . . . between him and his mother, where you told me he acted so fine, why, Lord help me, any man, that is, any good man, that had such a mother, would have done exactly the same . . . The King for my money ; he speaks all his words distinctly, half as loud again as the other—anybody may see he is an actor ".

But all that night the simpleton dared not go to bed for fear of the ghost ; and for many nights afterwards he " sweated two or three hours before he went to sleep ", and then he awoke with the horrors on him.

That others beside the simple Partridge were terrified by Garrick's acting in the scene with his father's ghost can be seen from Lichtenberg's account. He says : " At these words Garrick turns suddenly round, and at the same moment staggers back two or three paces with trembling knees, his hat falls to the ground, both arms—especially the left—are nearly extended to the full—the fingers spread out and the mouth open.—— His features express such horror that I felt a repeated shudder pass over me before he began to speak. The almost appalling silence of the assembly, which preceded the scene and made one feel scarcely safe in one's seat, probably contributed not a little to the effect ".

In *Tom Jones* the curtain goes down with old Squire Western playing in the nursery with his Sophia's two children ; " first a boy and then a girl " according to the old song. And there he finds " the tattling of his little grand-daughter—sweeter music than the finest cry of dogs in England ".

Speaking of Falstaff and William Shakespeare in *The Return*, Mr. de la Mare makes a character say : " a mere Elizabethan scribbler comes along with a gift of expression and an observant eye, lifts the bloated old tippler clean out of life, and swims down the ages as the greatest genius the world has ever seen ". So was it with Fielding. He too " lifted his characters clean out of life ", as Shakespeare did with his fat knight, Sir John. But according to the carefully planned time scheme of the novel, on the evening when Tom and Partridge saw *Hamlet* in London, Garrick was actually playing in Dublin. Fielding had forgotten to use his calendar.

CHAPTER XX

The Fool and the Lady

MILLAR paid £1,000 for the copyright of *Amelia*, and then advertised the book as being in such great demand that he was obliged to print it at four separate presses. According to Scott, he also informed his fellow-booksellers that every copy was " already bespoke ". With appetite thus whetted, they were forced to wait until a new edition was forthcoming. And by this device every copy published on the morning of December 18th 1751, was sold before nightfall at twelve shillings the set of volumes. It would seem that eighteenth-century publishers had but little to learn from their successors of to-day.

Tom Jones, by calling forth portents in the heavens and earthquakes on the planet, had been of course a capital advertisement for its author. Then too the book was the work of the famous magistrate who was already a terror to evil-doers. The excitement over the execution of Bosavern Penlez must have reached high and low, in the tenements of Shoreditch as well as in the coffee-houses of Pall-Mall.

But when the new novel came out, no one had ever read a book like it. The background was " low ", lower than Fielding had ever gone before. To follow Captain William Booth one had to penetrate into the magistrate's court, the sponging house, the debtors' prison. In the background moved no romantic highwaymen, but Blear-eyed Moll, hideous and repulsive, with all the riff-raff of the London slums. Worst of all, the writer was bent on showing how these poor wretches had been made what they were. On the other hand, among the rich and great, here were men and women whose main occupation was the pursuit of innocent women, the fighting of duels, and the ruin of great estates at the gambling tables, with a " trading Justice " on the very first pages, a man who had no knowledge whatever of the law, and no decency in sentencing the poor and helpless, and letting the rich go free. The whole was an indictment, neither savage nor cynical, but quiet and deadly.

Here then is human nature in its vilest form, but here too is the radiance of love, honour, and forgiveness in the person of Amelia, that most beautiful of all the heroines of English fiction. She is love made manifest, the love that nothing can kill. To say this makes her seem a sort of martyr with a halo. But—and here is the power of the characterisation—Amelia is no unearthly saint, no El Greco figure with an emaciated body and a wry neck. She is a beautiful woman, with a sense of humour, and the keenest of keen eyes for the ridiculous. Tough she is, too, and ready to face up to circumstances in a way that poor Amelia Sedley could never have done. When Booth has run up a gambling debt of £50, it is she who goes off to the pawn-shop with her few trinkets, and even at last with her clothes.

Mrs. Delany, who wrote of *Amelia*, " I don't like it at all ", may have been a poor critic, but her mood over the novel was, at first, the mood of most of Fielding's contemporaries. Not a word came from the *Gentleman's Magazine*. And the Rev. Richard Hurd described its author as " a poor emaciated worn-out rake, whose gout and infirmities have got the better even of his buffoonery ".

It seems to have been the general feeling, for the gay spirits which enlivened the first two novels, were gone for ever, banished in Fielding's nature by the deepening current of his genius, as he looked on the world around him. *Amelia* is a novel of domestic life, seen against a background of London vice, crime and folly. Unless you feel the beauty of Amelia's nature, you see nothing except the terrible picture in which Fielding wrote down his condemnation of the eighteenth century. After nearly forty-five years of crowded life he now passes judgment as he sits in that parlour over his court-room and contemplates in review what he has seen.

Captain Billy Booth is an inveterate gambler, a man too who is born to be the prey of every loose woman. In the sponging-house, out of which he has to be bailed, he cannot resist the attraction of Miss Matthews, the demi-mondaine, whom he has known in the past. In gaming-houses and taverns he throws away the money he does not possess. Each temptation knocks him down, and almost before he is set on his feet again, over he goes once more.

But his wife Amelia holds on. The man has one single good

quality—his love for his wife and children. Never was there a roué with a kinder heart. But that is all.

How it was ever possible to conceive of this poor fellow as a self-portrait of Fielding himself, it is hard to imagine. Booth is an idle ne'er-do-well who has failed as a farmer because he persisted in playing the gentleman with a ' chariot ' and finer manners than his neighbours. Probably Fielding had in mind at this point those " yellow liveries " which did so affront the ponderous Murphy. But there the likeness ends. Booth is for ever hanging about rich men's houses, in hopes of a loan, or another commission, although the only chance of getting the latter is by the sale of his wife's honour. And this fact he is too great a fool to realise.

Surely in this spineless being there is nothing whatever of Fielding, who worked at every conceivable trade within his grasp, who scorched and burnt in his rage at hypocrisy, who planned better laws for his country, and who in his last journey could not eat a whiting or a John Dory without thinking of how fish should be cheapened for the benefit of the poor, instead of being merely a rich man's luxury. If Fielding was worn out, it was by incessant labour as well as by eating and drinking too much in a gluttonous and drinking age.

But what Fielding's critics missed in *Amelia* was his genius for farce. The zest of his portrait of Parson Adams rests partly on this power. To set against him, in *Amelia* we have only the eccentricities of Colonel Bath, a monster of a man, nearly seven feet high, with a huge wig stretching across his shoulders. One word is for ever issuing from his lips—the word " honour ". He is the perfect type of the fellow who is ruled by one idea. For Bath the whole duty of man consists in challenging to a duel every male who opposes him, or even contradicts his opinions. He is a dotard, with a kind heart, whose sole idea of argument is a sword-thrust or a pistol-shot. Much play does Fielding make over a scene where Bath is longing to challenge the good Dr. Harrison to a duel, but cannot do so because the Doctor is a cleric. The two men seriously discuss whether the *Iliad* is not full of duellists from Hector downwards, Harrison maintaining that they only fight in their nations' wars.

This was a subject much in Fielding's mind : the contest between the authority of Christianity which condemns killing and the fashionable principle that a man is bound to protect his " honour ". One cannot but feel how in our days he would have been torn between the *Thou Shalt Not* of the New Testament and the *Thou Shalt* of this world's principles in the question of war.

But that is what we feel all through his storm-tossed, strenuous life : he is one of us. There is no bar between our mind and his, as there is between us and the men of the Elizabethan age, or the seventeenth century. His remedies for social evil are not ours, yet he was one of the first thinkers to feel a sense of responsibility for the state of the people and to impress on the great and powerful their duty towards the helpless.

And, most significant of all, he never looked to the next life to cure the wrongs of this one. " Here and now " is his motto as it is ours. Saint Theresa's view that this life is just " a night in a bad inn " was never Harry Fielding's. He turned most definitely to the question of how to run the inn. He is a modern.

Dr. Harrison, the good parson who stands like a guardian angel behind his " children ", Amelia and Booth, is far more of a preacher and far less of a man than Abraham Adams, and by so much the less life-like. He is rather an image of piety than a living human being. And when he writes a letter condemning adultery which is read, amid roars of laughter, to the assembled revellers at a masquerade, we feel that the farce is merely absurd.

But Fielding, like Richardson, seems to have been haunted by a spectre, the vision of a completely perfect man. The idea was in the air of the day, and from it came Sir Charles Grandison. In Fielding's case he had before him in actual life the figure of Ralph Allen, who, although he was an acute man of business, yet spent most of his ten thousand a year on works of benevolence.

In all Fielding's character-drawing there recurs a kind of plan that is almost an obsession : on the one side he shows recklessness and goodwill ; on the other, knavery with a bad will. Honesty, simplicity and faithfulness shewn up against pure cunning. This division is very plain in *Amelia*. Throughout the novel we meet pairs of opposites : Sergeant Atkinson, the faithful worshipper of Amelia, over against the pestilent crew of rascals who would ruin her for their own pleasure. Harrison is opposed to Colonel Bath, the former a sensible man and the latter a pompous ass with his head full of madcap theories; with Mrs. Bennet the blue-stocking as a companion picture to Mrs. Ellison, my lord's procuress.

The moral purpose of the whole is plainer than in Fielding's first novels, for Parson Adams and Tom Jones came out of no theory, but from the heart of life itself, as did Amelia, from whom we learn the secrets of Fielding's heart towards the woman he loved.

Behind the incidents of this story there are many suggestions of his own past experiences. The farm belonging to Dr. Harrison was surely near Salisbury, where there were two sisters, called in actual life Charlotte and Catherine, but in the novel Amelia and Betty. And " Betty ", after she had cheated her sister, left for France from Poole, where once there lived that adoring harbour-master, Harry Price. We do not know, of course, but it is even possible that Kitty Cradock, the " original " of Betty in the novel, may in fact have vanished in this way.

In prison Miss Matthews tells Booth the story of her seduction by Cornet Hebbers, and we suspect that when Booth knew her in the old days she was one of the nymphs of Salisbury. Possibly, too, Dr. Harrison got some of his goodness from Fielding's grandfather, that Canon of Salisbury who was also Vicar of Puddletown in what is now known as the Hardy Country. Or does he owe any of his characteristics to Dr. Hoadley, who was Bishop of Salisbury when Fielding was courting Charlotte?

The officers, Bath, James, Trent and Company were surely friends of Fielding's father, the gambler who lost that £700 when playing faro at White's.

The plot opens in the court of Justice Thrasher who is shewn in all his infamy. First he runs in as a prostitute a poor girl found in the street, although she was merely fetching a doctor for her mistress. At the same time, after a bribe, he dismisses the charge against a " genteel " man and girl.

But here too is Booth before the Justice, on a charge of assaulting the Watch. He had tried to defend a man who was being set upon by two rascals, but since he has no money—his usual condition—he too is sentenced to gaol.

The prison scene was obviously written in indignation from what Fielding actually knew. On Booth's entry, the keeper at once demands " garnish ", the very extortion that set

Howard investigating prison conditions in later years. Here we find a man wounded at the siege of Gibraltar who has been acquitted of the crime of stealing three herrings, but cannot pay the gaoler's fees, and is therefore left in prison to rot. With his head on a girl's lap, an old man lies dying. She had stolen a loaf because they were both starving. And Blear-eyed Moll, a figure of horror after a life-time of vice, tries to coax money out of Booth. It was a strange, disgusting scene to present to the view of the exquisites of the time.

Miss Matthews is in the comfortable, hotel-like part of the prison, since she has money, on a charge of having killed her seducer. She tells Booth her life-story and he, on his part, confides in her the whole tale of how he courted his Amelia.

The pair, Amelia and Booth, like Sophia and Tom, and probably like Fielding himself, had made a runaway match. But a long drawn-out agony parts the newly-married couple when Booth's regiment is ordered abroad. With him goes his faithful batman, Atkinson, Amelia's foster-brother and worshipper, who is in his humility the spiritual father of Thackeray's Colonel Dobbin.

When Booth falls ill, Amelia goes out to join him, and here in France they join forces with Colonel Bath and his sister, the four living together almost like one family.

Fielding is never more at home with his subject than when he is dealing with a simple kindly theme that brings out his tenderness and humour. Such is the opening scene in *Tom Jones*, where Allworthy feels the little foundling's tiny fingers close on his as the baby nestles against the pillows of his bed. And here, between Booth and Colonel Bath, is a similar touch.

Amelia has been brought to bed of a daughter just at the moment when Bath's sister is taken ill of a surfeit. And both men therefore are obliged to betake themselves to their " several nurseries ".

But one morning, when Booth calls to enquire for Colonel Bath's patient, he comes upon that seven-foot figure dressed only in a woman's bed-gown and a very dirty flannel night-cap. The gallant gentleman is also handling a saucepan.

The poor Colonel is horrified at being caught in such a degrading condition, for, as he always says, " no man can be more conscious of his own dignity than myself ". He passes a sleepless night in consequence, since Booth had—most unfortunately—remarked that his friend could not have appeared in a garb " more becoming to his character ! " Surely an old bed-gown and a dirty night-cap could not possibly be " becoming " to a gallant man of honour ? Booth despised him, and a challenge must be sent to avenge such an insult

He is only to be soothed when reminded that even the great King of Sweden refused to see anyone after the death of his favourite sister. The fire-eater calms down. " Damn me ! " he cries, " Nature will get the better of dignity ".

The whole scene is an exquisite picture of pride, folly and tenderness.

But these events were past. And now Booth is in a London prison with Miss Matthews, who promptly catches him, so that for a whole week the keeper, very well paid, " locks up double ". Yet Booth is in agony when he remembers to think of his wife left alone in their lodgings at Spring Gardens.

At length he is bailed out by Miss Matthews, and his friend, Colonel James, takes the lady on as his mistress, though he is already married in a cat-and-dog union with Colonel Bath's sister, whom this rise in life has turned—most amusingly—into a great lady with all the follies proper to such a being. James's principle is a simple one : he never thinks that women's minds are worth considering, only their bodies.

But Booth, happy man, has always behind him " one friend whom no inconstancy of her own, nor any change of his fortune, nor any accident can ever alter ". This is his wife, and Fielding shows his power in characterisation by making us willing to believe it with all our hearts.

Once out of prison, Booth starts bombarding his rich friends to get that commission, or, when he has been gambling again, to pay his card-debts. Both Colonel James and that worse villain, " my lord ", are perfectly willing to pack him off abroad, preferably to the West Indies. At first neither Amelia nor Booth can see the reason for this, though at long last Amelia comes to understand it. Yet, lest he should send a challenge, she dares not whisper a word to her beloved Billy. The position is both absurd and pitiful and Fielding makes the most of it.

The house where the Booths are lodging is kept by a woman in the lord's pay, who takes Amelia to hear one of Handel's oratorios. Surely an innocent amusement ? But in the theatre they happen to sit next to a gentleman in rough clothes who is polite enough to hold a candle all the evening so that Amelia may follow the score. This man is of course the wicked lord.

The next step in the plot is to induce the innocent lady to attend a masquerade. Mrs. Ellison, my lord's tool, tries her hardest to bring this about, but the learned Mrs. Bennet sends a warning missive to Amelia :—

> " Beware, beware, beware,
> For I apprehend a dreadful snare
> Is laid for virtuous innocence,
> Under a friend's false pretence ".

Upon this Amelia learns what " my lord " really is ; how in the masquerade he catches his victims by the help of this woman Ellison.

In her innocence Amelia has been spending hours at the villain's house where he plays the child-lover and loads her babies with rich presents. At first she was completely deceived by him. " Never ", cried she after a visit of this kind, " never were any creatures so happy as the little things have been the whole morning ! "

But now she stands on the edge of a precipice, and sees the gulf opening below her feet. Worst of all is the thought of her children's helplessness, thus caught in the toils of sin and folly.

These babies, as Fielding paints them, are truly childlike. Their chatter is an echo, quaint and touching, of their mother's precepts ; or, as Dr. Harrison calls it, of Amelia's " divinity ". Sometimes even Mrs. Booth's courage fails her, pursued as she is, with her husband playing the fool, and often, the knave as well.

One evening, when he is supping with Miss Matthews, though Amelia knows nothing about that, the faithful lady cooks his favourite dish for him, a fowl with egg-sauce, even adding a bottle of wine to the feast. All is ready, but it grows late, and still he does not come. At a knock at the front door, she hurries down, eyes bright, heart thudding with delight—he is come ! But no, it is not he ! Sadly she goes back to her lonely room. But of course Billy must have been detained by business.

The tale of the hashed mutton, on another evening, is one of the highlights of English fiction. This time it is a homely dish that awaits his return, and Amelia is longing for a glass of white wine. Yet, in order to save the expense, she will not let the maid run out to fetch it, for she must save the sixpence it would have cost.

And all this time " her husband was paying a debt of several guineas, incurred by the ace of trumps being in the hands of his adversary ".

So, she waited, wine-less, and the mutton grew cold, while she read a comedy of Farquhar's, and " twice heard the dismal clock that night and twice the more dismal watchman ". Yet when at last her Billy came to bed, Amelia flung her white arms round his neck, not uttering a reproachful word. And next morning there must be a visit to the pawnbroker where she pledged her diamond ring, her watch, and the child's—to pay for that ace of trumps.

Meanwhile Mrs. Bennet, now the wife of Sergeant Atkinson, has made good use of the ticket for the masquerade which Amelia had refused, and by playing the part of Booth's wife in a mask, has tricked my lord into giving her a commission for her husband : that is, of course, for the good Sergeant, and not for Booth.

A magnificently humorous scene follows, for, when she hears this, Amelia drops all her saintliness, and rages at Mrs. Bennet for this piece of treachery. And while the two women hurl insults at each other, Booth and Atkinson look on in horror and amazement, not daring to utter a word even of protest.

But the god from the machine is at hand. Dr. Harrison arrives in town, and although Booth has been arrested at his suit, Amelia persuades him to release her husband. They even enjoy a little jollification, and after attending church, go to Vauxhall by boat. Here Amelia, naïve and happy, feels herself almost " in those blissful mansions which we hope to enjoy hereafter ". The simple lady exclaims as she listens to the music : " I could not have, indeed, imagined there had been anything like this in this world.

But—it is a frightful comment on the manners of the time— while the Doctor and his friends are eating their ham and chicken, and the children feasting on cheesecakes, up comes a party of beaux. One of these gentry sits down in front of Amelia, crying : " Damn me, my lord, if she is not an angel ! " and follows it up with, " Damn me, if I have not a kiss ! " Of course Amelia's evening is spoilt, but chiefly by the fear that when Booth joins the party, he may fight a duel with the fellow who had insulted her. For ever is she haunted with the horror of those inevitable challenges.

Booth's simplicity is that of a fool, Amelia's that of an innocent lost among worldlings, where even Mrs. Ellison, shameless as she is, knows how to assume a virtue though she have it not. " A sergeant of the Guards is a gentleman, " she declares, " and I would rather give such a man as you describe a dish of tea, than any beau fribble of them all ". Yet mightily is she displeased when the Booths assume that she is going to marry this sergeant ; she, a cousin of my lord's !

But Amelia and her Billy are thoroughly " low ". And Fielding never spares us, but shows the pair, after a scrag of mutton and broth, actually drinking my lord's health in—a pot of porter. That is, of course before they have found him out. Never was Fielding happier than when flaunting the lowness of his genius before the fine gentry of his time. Even his own careless dress suggests a kind of defiance in the wearer of that old grey coat.

Every subordinate character in Amelia is alive : Mrs. James, now a lady of fashion, who complains of the hardship of climbing up two pairs of stairs to visit Amelia ; her husband, cold as ice in heart who soon finds that his mistress, Miss Matthews, puts on fat and develops the temper of a tigress ; and Atkinson, the idealist, who stole Amelia's portrait, and kept it till he thought he was dying.

Here Fielding's farcical humour leaps up once more, and he leaves the poor man drenched in the cherry brandy which his wife had mistakenly poured over him when he fainted.

But happiness comes in the end. Dr. Harrison pays Booth's debts and hustles him off to the country, where he is to farm a part of the parsonage glebe. And as to that affair with Miss Matthews ; when Booth confesses it, Amelia says simply : " I cannot forgive you—for I have forgiven you long ago ".

Actually, perhaps, Sergeant Atkinson's wife had more cause to be jealous than Amelia, since the sergeant's adoration of his lady, Mrs. Booth, had lasted all his life, and wife or no wife, would continue to the end of his days. There she reigned in his heart like a star. But Miss Matthews was soon forgotten, or if remembered, only with shame.

Nevertheless one doubt haunts the reader's mind as he closes the book. Is it possible that Billy can be reformed by his love for his wife, and for those " little things ", his children ? He is as weak as a reed, and what woman can turn a reed into a tree ?

When Fielding published his novel, he was flinging the book into the middle of a nest of vipers. All his enemies raised up their heads and hissed : not only was the subject low, but this domestic story was not what had been expected after the gaiety of *Joseph Andrews* and the varied scenes of *Tom Jones*. The reviews must have reminded Fielding of the hisses and cat-calls in the theatre when his social satires were being played.

Two special points aroused the scorn of his critics, Amelia's nose, and the references, meant to be facetious, to the Univesal Register office, managed by John Fielding. As for the scar on the heroine's nose, Dr. Johnson who, twenty-five years later, was to call *Amelia* " the most pleasing of all the romances ", would have it that this " vile broken nose . . . ruined the sale of the book ". And to the disgusting mind of Smollett it seemed that Amelia was no better than " a wench who had lost her nose in the service of Venus ". He actually published a sixpenny pamphlet, describing Fielding as a Justice, a Dealer, and a Chapman, adding he " now lies at his house in Covent Garden in a deplorable State of Lunacy ".

It appears that ten years earlier, a comedy of Fielding's had been put on the stage instead of Smollett's play, *The Regicide*. Also, the man was a Scot, and a Jacobite. Fielding accordingly is shown in the pamphlet as a drunken madman, at the head of a rout of vagabonds, followed by Amelia without a nose, a sheep-stealer, to signify the Man of the Hill, and blind John Fielding, the proprietor of a " twelve-penny office ". This hideous crowd takes to its heels as soon as Mr. Smollett's characters emerge from his novels.

Absurd as all this is, it must have been injurious to the reputation of the book. But in his journey through this world Fielding had been learning forbearance. " I can ", he says, " with great truth, declare that I do not at this instant, wish ill to any man living ".

Smollett, in fact, as soon as his jealousy had died down, was later on to confess that " the genius of Cervantes was transfused into the novels of Fielding ".

But Richardson never withdrew from his position of enmity.

He adopts a pitying attitude in his letter to Sarah Fielding.
" Had your brother ", he says, " been born in a stable, or been
a runner at a sponging-house, we should have thought him a
genius, and wished he had had the advantage of a liberal
education . . . but it is beyond my conception that a man of
family, who had some learning, and who really is a writer,
should descend so excessively low in all his pieces. Who can
care for any of his people ? "

Fielding set himself thereupon to the correction of his book,
explaining Amelia's nose as showing only a slight scar that
seemed to add to her beauty, and cutting out in the next
edition all the passages referring to the Universal Register
office.

That was a pity, since Fielding's humour had played very
prettily about the venture. Thus, Mrs. Bennet's first husband,
the curate, was offered at the office " choice of above a hundred
curacies " ; Amelia got the name of a good pawnbroker from
it ; and one of the clerks told several spicy anecdotes of Miss
Matthews' past.

All this was to Fielding's mind, merely a sidelight on real
contemporary life which would serve to show up the fiction
more clearly, just as in *Tom Jones* he had used the Jacobite
Rising as a framework to his tale. Besides, such references to
the Register Office served as a capital advertisement to would-be
customers. He was by no means averse to killing two birds
with one stone, and though a man of good family, saw no
objection to making a living by trade. A realist through and
through was the author of *Amelia*.

And *Amelia's* enemies did the work good service after all,
since they drew from him more examples of his wit.

In his last journalistic venture, *The Covent Garden Journal*,
he set up an imaginary court before which contemporary books
were summoned to reply to the charges brought against them.
The challenge to *Amelia* is that " the Book now at the bar is
very sad stuff; that Amelia herself is a *low* Character, a Fool
and a Milksop ". The Judge is then called upon to " pass
such a sentence as may be a dreadful Example to all future
Books, how they dare stand up in Opposition to the Humour
of the Age ".

The Father of *Amelia* confesses frankly that " of all my
offsprings She is my favourite Child ". He pleads for her in a

way which shows his generosity, even though he may be smarting at the bites of the gadflies.

" I do not think my Child ", he says, " is entirely free from Faults. I know nothing human that is so ; but surely she does not deserve the Rancour with which she has been treated . . . I do, therefore, solemnly declare . . . that I will trouble the World no more with any Children of mine ". And this pledge is greeted with a loud huzza from the Court.

But Fielding could still sting. In that same *Journal*, he lays down the rule that " a critic should first learn the art of reading ", nor should he pass sentence on a book unless he has read " at least ten pages of it ".

And as to that nose, " it is currently reported that a famous surgeon who absolutely cured one Mrs. Amelia Booth, of a violent Hurt in her Nose, insomuch that she had scarce a scar left on it, intends to bring Actions against several ill-meaning and Slanderous People, who have reported that the said Lady had no nose, merely because the Author of her History, in a Hurry, forgot to inform his Readers of that Particular ".

The famous surgeon was Dr. Ranby, who lived in Bond Street, attended Fielding himself and in the novel was summoned to Colonel Bath after his duel in Hyde Park.

Soon the tide turned and critics were found to defend *Amelia*. *The Gentleman's Magazine*, under the name *Criticulus*, protested against Mr. Fielding's decision that " he would never trouble the public with any more writings of the kind ". And *The London Magazine* gave nine columns to a résumé of the plot with much amusing patronage of the story.

At this time the caricaturists were busy drawing Fielding with his long nose, and dressed in that long grey coat which went so well with legs swathed in cloth because of his gout, with his crutches and nut-cracker jaws that seem to have lost all their front teeth. He is shewn telling stories with the face of an actor, and making great play with his eyes. That " breaker of God's images ", Foote was also mimicking the Bow Street Justice on the stage, much to Fielding's indignation.

How far Amelia is actually Charlotte Cradock we cannot be sure. It was, however, Lady Mary Montagu's opinion that " Henry Fielding has given a true picture of himself and his first wife in the characters of Mr. and Mrs. Booth . . . and I am persuaded, several of the incidents he mentions are real matters of fact. I wonder he does not perceive that Tom Jones and Mr. Booth are sorry scoundrels . . ."

No doubt he knew very well what to think of both characters. But Booth is not Fielding, whatever Tom Jones may have been. Though he was reckless with money, not one of his traducers ever charged him with the fault of gambling, or the vice of idleness. " All the world knows ", wrote Lady Bute, " what was his imprudence ; and if ever he possessed a score of pounds, nothing could keep him from lavishing it idly, or make him think of to-morrow ".

Here, and here only, is the likeness between Henry Fielding, and Captain Billy Booth.

CHAPTER XXI

The Last Fight

WITH *Amelia* now in the hands of the public, Fielding's activities became volcanic as if he realised that his day was closing in. January 4th, 1752, saw the first number of the *Covent Garden Journal*, which only ran for eleven months, but is more packed with wit and wisdom than any other of his journalistic ventures. Nothing in the daily life of the time was too small, or too great, for his pen.

As Sir Alexander Drawcansir, Censor of Great Britain, he attacks scandal, bad books, the miser, the seducer, the hypocrite, and mocks the folly of a fine lady with her monkey and her black boy, and the insolence of a beau. From that time satirists were often referred to as " Drawcansirs of the goose quill ".

Nowhere, so he declares, can he find signs of " a Religion some time professed in this Country, and, if my Memory fails not, was called Christian ". The youth of the nation are being trained in the evil of the Town, and finished by a foreign tour. Literary taste is vanishing, and politics are now purely party. It sounds like the wail of a Jeremiah, but the jests come thick and fast. The paper was a spicy chronicle of day to day, a critique of men, morals, and books, apparently with help from his brother, as Z.Z., and by Sarah, as E.R. Poets too were invited to send in their verses.

Perhaps the " Modern Glossary " is as amusing as any part. In this Angel is the name of a woman, " commonly a very bad one ". Author is a laughing-stock, likewise " a poor Fellow, and in general an Object of Contempt ". Honour is Duelling. Humour, scandalous Lies. A Patriot is a Candidate for a Place at Court ; Religion a Word of no Meaning, but which serves as a bugbear to frighten Children with ; and a Promise is— Nothing ". As to the word " fine ", it is " an Adjective of a very peculiar kind, destroying, or, at least lessening the Force of the Substantive to which it is joined ; as fine Gentleman, fine Lady, fine House, fine Cloathes, fine Taste ;——in all which

248

Fine is to be understood in a sense somewhat synonymous with useless ".

So does he sum up the age in which he lived as far as the rich were concerned. On the other hand, since he was a man of his time, he objects to too much thinking for the workers. The Robin Hood Society was a debating club for tradesmen and mechanics which met every Monday evening. Burke and Goldsmith sometimes attended it, but Fielding considers it absurd that weavers, tailors and barbers should discuss subjects which have puzzled philosophers since the dawn of time.

During all these months, while the *Journal* came out twice a week, he was sitting at Bow Street, acting as legal adviser, judge and friend to the poorest of the poor. We find him one day confronted with three wives, all claiming the same husband. There had been a fight over the affair, but since there was no evidence of any marriage at all, Fielding, as Solomon, decided that Elizabeth Macculloch had the best right because she knew him first and was therefore the woman in possession. The second and third " wives " were persuaded to consent to this arrangement and so escaped the fate of being committed to that sink of iniquity, the Bridewell.

Another day, when a gambling house in the Strand was raided, the soldiers were summoned, and the Justice dealt with the case till two o'clock in the morning, with the result that forty-five gamblers were roped in. Captain Booth's adventures as a gambler were certainly drawn from the life.

After four men had been charged with begging, there followed a girl from Wapping, her face all blubbered with tears. Her pocket had been cut off and with it the fourteen shillings with which she had planned to buy a ticket for the Playhouse ; she so much wanted to see the Harlequin and all the other famous shows that the Justice loathed. But what do principles matter when the heart is touched ? The fatherly magistrate sent out for a pass to the gallery, and off the girl went rejoicing.

Another day there arrived a " Set of Barbers' Apprentices, Journeymen Staymakers, Maid-servants, etc ", who " had taken a large Room at the Black Horse in the Strand, to act the Tragedy of the *Orphan*, the Price of Admittance one shilling ". And all this had been done without any licence. But the author of *Pasquin* and the *Historical Register*, remembering no doubt his own trouble, " out of Compassion for their

Youth ", did nothing more than bind them over. And " they were all conducted through the Streets in their Tragedy Dresses to the no small Diversion of the Populace ".

Sterner work however was the general rule. Eight and twenty hours were spent in investigating a brutal murder ; and during the last ten days of January the constables brought in no less than ten disorderly men and women, a receiver of three brilliant diamonds, and an Italian assassin all covered with blood.

But at last Fielding's pressure on the government bore fruit : an Act was passed for " The Better Preventing of Thefts and Robberies ". This dealt with the four abuses which Fielding had discussed in his *Enquiry.* A draft by him is lost, but from it the Bill seems to have been framed. This was followed by an Act for " Preventing the Horrid Crime of Murder ". Fielding justly felt that he had conferred " a great and lasting Benefit on his Country ".

Not content with this effort, he proceeded to issue a curious pamphlet with the title " Examples of the Interposition of Providence in the Detection and Punishment of Murder ". The work, dated Bow Street, April 8th, 1752, shows a belief in omens and ghosts sent from Heaven by the miraculous Act of God. It is, in fact, a chap book, copied from a collection of anecdotes collected by a seventeenth century merchant of Exeter, with the additional instances of Mary Blandy and Elizabeth Jeffries, both hanged for murder in Fielding's own time.

The whole is an appeal to the fear of death and the Judgment. In it the Justice declares his belief in the immediate intervention of the divine Providence in the detection of murder. " Who can bear ", he asks, " the dreadful thought of being confronted with the Spirit of one whom we have murdered, in the Presence of all the Host of Heaven ? "

The pamphlet cost but sixpence, and an allowance was made for anyone who bought several copies. Fielding himself distributed it, and an army colonel bought a large consignment for the good of his regiment. The *Covent Garden Journal*, by way of advertisement, declared that " no Family ought to be without this Book, and it is most particularly calculated for the Use of those Schools in which Children are taught to read ".

When a man in court threatened to kill his wife, Fielding

put the little book into his hands, bidding him read it before he slept. And another wretch, then awaiting death in Newgate for murder, begged for a copy with tears, and only wished he had read it before. It must have been but a poor consolation to him.

All this time Fielding was struggling against illness, trying at last the Duke of Portland's powder, made of gentian, germander, ground pine and centaury, and said to be from a recipe by Galen. His health actually improved for a time, and the slightest turn for the better brought back " that Cheerfulness which was always natural to me ".

Now the classical scholar in him awoke and in his *Journal* he advertised a New Translation into English of the Works of Lucian. It was to be written from the original Greek by Fielding and the Reverend William Young. But this plan was never carried out. The notice is mainly interesting because Fielding confesses in it that his style was formed from Lucian, though certainly the vigorous power of his lusty English is all his own.

By 1753 it was evident that but a " short remainder of life " was likely to be his. The body was getting worn out by incessant work, though the restless, indefatigable mind was as active as ever.

Yet suddenly—it is as surprising as anything in his life—he comes forward with a detailed plan of Poor Law Reform for the whole country. If adopted, it would have meant the repeal of the Act of Elizabeth and the reconstruction of the whole system. Behind the scheme were months of thought and study. But nothing was nearer to Fielding's heart than this subject. He dared not neglect the misery and degradation which he saw round him every day of his life. His address to the Chancellor of the Exchequer was meant as a call to the leaders of the nation.

" They starve and freeze and rot ", he says, speaking of the poor in the great city which spent its wealth so lavishly on foolish and vulgar pleasures. It was arranged that a party of members of Parliament should go down into the under-world and see for themselves the hunger, cold, nakedness and filth which their fellow-countrymen endured.

The scheme itself is curious. In each county a vast Workhouse should be built that was capable of sheltering five thousand destitute people, and with it a house of correction for six hundred more. Here trades were to be taught, and every tool required was to be supplied, with instructors. All persons found wandering, or in ale-houses after ten o'clock at night, were to be brought before a magistrate, and by him consigned to the County House, there to remain until the next Assizes. Instruction and training was the main point, with subsistence, and when trained, employment. The sick were to have hospital treatment and two chaplains were to labour to reform the minds of the inmates. An elaborate diagram of the institution was supplied which showed the position of the workshops, the men's quarters and the women's, the provision shops, and, alas, the whipping-post.

And, so Fielding concludes, let no man imagine that he hopes to benefit by any such position as that of Master in a County House. To do so in his state of health would be, in the words of Horace, " struere domos immemor sepulchri ". He believed that his death was not far off.

Two shillings a week were to be paid to each inmate of the House until the sales began of the man's own work, but only one shilling to those in the house of correction. The kindly Justice then discusses the question of whether they should be allowed to buy their own food. " But the refusal of this power ", he says, " savours too much of the treatment of children ", and therefore the plan includes a place for food shops. No paltering with idleness is to be allowed ; those who refuse to work must be sent on to the county gaol, and if they remain persistently idle, they shall be transported.

Nothing was ever done to carry out this scheme, but at last the government took steps in order to grapple with London crime. The Privy Council made a grant to Fielding of £600 to be spent by him in breaking up the gangs of robbers and murderers. And thereupon he collected a band of " thief-takers of fidelity and intrepidity", well-known and respectable householders who went armed, but in private clothes.

This was the first detective force in England and so successful was it that in the two darkest months in the year, November and December, 1753, not a murder was committed in London or Westminster. The first case brought before the Justice by these thief-takers was a gang of no less than fourteen cut-throats.

Fielding had inserted in his *Journal* an invitation to anyone who could give him information of a robbery or a burglary to come to his house. It was all in vain, for no-one dared to inform. The humorist thereupon tried a jest, inserting this notice : " There are now several Dangerous Mad People confined by the Justice who must shortly be let loose ; of which timely Notice will be given in this Paper, THAT HIS MAJESTY'S SOBER SUBJECTS MAY SHUT THEM-SELVES UP IN THEIR HOUSES ".

In 1752 Fielding had taken the farm of Fordhook in Ealing, then of course a country village, six miles from Hyde Park Corner, on the Uxbridge Road, The soil there was dry and the house lay open to the south. It was hoped that this country retreat would benefit his health and that of his family after the foul air of Bow Street.

It is clear that his work was not without danger of personal violence. Thus we find that two men charged with stealing silk handkerchiefs threatened one Sunday to blow out the Justice's brains. A party of soldiers was thereupon summoned to remove the men to Newgate.

It was the strange affair of Elizabeth Canning which gained so much attention that it divided the Town into two factions, the Canningites and the Egyptians. Even in our days it would have interested a psychologist.

On Monday, January 1st, 1753, this Betty Canning, a servant girl of eighteen, living in Aldermanbury, after visiting her uncle and aunt, parted from them in Moorfields, opposite the Bethlehem Gate, about nine o'clock in the evening. According to her story, she was then attacked by two men, who robbed her of half a guinea and three shillings in silver, and afterwards dragged her along a walk towards the gates of the hospital. They struck her several blows, and she fell in a " fit ", but they managed, while she was unconscious, to carry her off to a house where she found an old gypsy woman and two young girls. The gypsy offered her fine clothes " if she would go their way ". When she refused, her stays were cut from her with a knife, and she was forced upstairs into a sort of loft, and there left, with threats that her throat would be cut if she uttered a sound.

And there she remained, with no provision but a jug of water, some mouldy pieces of bread, and a piece of mince-pie which she had been carrying home for her little brother. It was not until half-past four on January 29th that she at last contrived to free herself by breaking a window and stealing away unseen. It took her six hours to get home, where she arrived in the last stages of exhaustion, terribly emaciated and with her skin blackened by starvation.

So ran the tale she told, first to her mother and the neighbours and afterwards at the trial of the two women, Mary Squires, the gypsy, and Susannah Wells, the keeper of the house. Both at the subsequent trial were charged with assault and felony, for striking the girl and for the robbery of the stays, valued at ten shillings.

The case turned mainly on two points, the house itself and the girl's description of the room, and the question of an alibi for the old gypsy woman.

After a collection had been made for her, Betty was taken in a chaise, accompanied by friends and sympathisers, along the Hertford Road in order that she might find the house where she had been confined. She had seen from her prison window the Hertford coach going along the road. At Enfield Wash the house was found, and, after she had been set up on the dresser, the inmates were made to pass before her. She thereupon declared that she recognised both Wells and the gypsy crone, Mary Squires, as well as the two girls, one of whom rejoiced in the name of Virgin Hall. All swore that never before had they seen Betty.

But it was in the description of the place of imprisonment that she went astray. It was a small darkish sort of place according to her account, with a grate and a picture over it. And on the outside was a penthouse down which she had climbed. As a matter of fact, it was on the contrary a large light room, with neither grate, picture nor penthouse. According to her story, she had seen no-one at all during all the days of her imprisonment, yet actually the room stood over the kitchen, with a hole through which ran a jack-line on a pulley. Anyone who bent over this could see into the room below. The place had been used as a store-room for hay, but Canning swore she had slept on nothing but bare boards.

Not only were there these discrepancies, but four witnesses, one the licensee of the Old Ship Inn at Abbotsbury in Dorset, testified that Mary Squires could not possibly have been at Enfield Wash in January, since they had seen her going from village to village in Dorset, selling smuggled goods.

Notwithstanding all this, both Squires and Wells were declared guilty and sentenced to death. But the evidence appeared so doubtful that, after the case had been submitted to the attorney-general and the solicitor-general, Squires received a free pardon.

The affair had now become a party question, and feeling ran higher still when Elizabeth Canning was tried for Wilful and Corrupt Perjury at the Old Bailey. The Trial lasted no less than seven days.

This time forty-one witnesses bore evidence that they had seen the gypsy in Dorset in January. Betty, moreover, had made no mention of a chest of drawers, which must have stood in the room for years according to the evidence of the cobwebs that covered the back of it when it was pulled out. Providence was here called upon by the prosecuting barrister who demanded: " had they not marks of antiquity—marks which could not be made, but by Providence itself, or by the creatures He formed for the purpose ? "

When the girl's uncle was cross-examined as to what meals Betty had eaten on the day when she vanished, Willes, a barrister with a thin, strident voice, asked the question. " Does your wife generally have bread and butter, or toast with her tea ? "

At once the ribald mimic, Foote, put this Willes on his stage, giving voice to the demand : " Pray, now let me ask you, was—the toast buttered on both sides ? "

Incredible as it may seem, the shorthand report of the trial shows that Willes actually did ask this question. Everybody, witnesses and barristers alike, was playing up to the spectators. Mrs. Colley, the girl's aunt, established the date on which she saw her niece after her return by saying that it was " on King Charles' Martyrdom, never till then." For dates usually proved to be stumbling-blocks for all the illiterate witnesses.

For the defence several persons declared that they had seen on the night of the 29th a girl in dire distress making her way painfully towards London.

At last, after being out of court for two hours, the jury returned a verdict of guilty of perjury, but not " Wilful and Corrupt Perjury." Two members in fact believed that Canning had been seduced and afterwards was ordered to tell this story of imprisonment.

A new trial was judged necessary. At this the poor girl

pleaded in a low voice, saying that " she hoped they would be favourable to her, that she had no intent of swearing the gypsy's life away ; and that what had been done, was only defending herself ; and desired to be considered as unfortunate ".

Surely there is something very pitiful in that pleading ? And indeed, from the crude medical evidence there does seem to have been something abnormal about the girl, although those who knew her loudly declared that she had always been a good, honest maid.

Of course the Counsel for the Crown thundered away at her for having tried to " take away the life of one (though the most abject) of the human species ". Of course, too, since by English law perjury was not then punishable by death, there followed a eulogy of legal practices in " a country where severe and sanguinary laws are not so familiar ". It is curious to find how gaily men were then accustomed to praise our English clemency even under the very shadow of the gallows.

The sentence finally passed on Betty was that she should be imprisoned in Newgate for one month, and then transported for seven years to one of His Majesty's colonies—actually to New England " at the request of her friends ". If she returned to England within that time she would be liable to " death as a felon without benefit of clergy ". The jury had recommended her to mercy, but in vain. And on June 24th a notice appeared in the press in her name, declaring that she remained " fully persuaded, and well assured, that Mary Squires was the person who robbed me ; and that the house of Susannah Wells was the place in which I was confined twenty-eight days ". But the sentence was duly carried out.

After Squires and Wells had been committed by a magistrate on a charge of stealing the stays and keeping a disorderly house, Fielding was approached by the attorney employed for Betty Canning's defence to give counsel's opinion. And here we get a glimpse of the magistrate at his home in Bow Street.

" Upon the Receipt of this Case ", he writes, " I bid my Clerk give my Service to Mr. Salt and tell him, that I would take the Case with me into the Country, whither I intended to go the next day, and desired he would call for it the Friday Morning afterwards, after which, without looking into it, I delivered it to my Wife, who was then drinking Tea with us, and who laid it by".

But Brogden, the clerk, brought up the solicitor and begged Fielding to study the evidence at once, and afterwards to examine the accused and the witnesses in the case. To this, although he was " almost fatigued to death ", he consented, and the following day Betty Canning was carried into his court in a chair. Warrants having been issued, several " noble Lords " came down to Bow Street in order to hear the investigation.

Some charge of browbeating a witness appears to have been made against Fielding, who writes indignantly : " I can truly say, that my memory does not charge me with having ever insulted the lowest Wretch that hath been brought before me ".

While the witnesses were being questioned the answers of the girl Virgin Hall were so suspicious that Fielding prepared to commit her for perjury. On seeing this, she suddenly altered her tone, and having been sent out of the room with Salt, then told a story which agreed in almost every particular with the account given by Canning herself. But the suspicious point about this was that her deposition was only made after a private interview, which had lasted two hours, with Betty's lawyer.

By now the girl had become a public figure. She was taken the round of the fashionable coffee-houses and at White's thirty guineas were collected for her. Fielding was so moved by the excitement that, as in the case of Bosavern Penlez, he published a pamphlet explaining his views on the matter.

This pamphlet shows his kind heart and his courage. " There is something ", he remarks, " within myself which rouses me to the protection of injured innocence—without this motive I should scarce have taken up my pen in the defence of a poor little girl whom the many have already condemned ". His indignation was aroused by the cynicism of the world. It is, he says, " too much inclined to think that the credulous is the only Fool ; whereas, in truth, there is another Fool of a quite opposite Character, who is much more difficult to deal with ". In his opinion Betty Canning was not " witty " enough to invent such a tale as she had told. At this period of course exhibitionism was not recognised.

The publishers now rose to the occasion and brought out a picture of an awful gypsy hag which cost one shilling and sixpence. And when the Lord Mayor, Sir Crisp Gascoyne,

R

took the side of the gypsy, they followed this by a caricature which contains the only portrait of Fielding known to have been drawn during his life-time. The title given to this print was *The Conjurors*. In it the Justice is shewn, his legs bandaged for gout, with the sword of justice in his hand and her scales hanging out of his pocket, while behind him stands the trembling figure of the girl whom he is defending. The Lord Mayor presides, and Dr. Hill, a rascal who had once been kicked out of Ranelagh, defends Mary Squires.

Before the end of the affair Fielding seems to have suspected that he may have failed in sagacity. " To be placed above the Reach of Deceit ", he says, " is to be placed above the Rank of a human Being ; sure I am that I make no Pretension to be of that Rank ".

Very few of his letters have survived, but two have been found that are addressed to the Duke of Newcastle from Ealing : the affidavits in the case of the gypsy's trial should have been delivered by the attorney, but for some unknown reason had not been sent. Fielding suspects that something underhand is going on, for he calls Canning's defenders " a Set of the most obstinate Fools I ever saw ; and who seem to me rather to act from a Spleen against my Lord Mayor, than from any motive of protecting Innocence, though that was certainly their motive at first ".

Certainly Fielding himself had but one aim in the Canning affair—to see justice done, and the man in court who once called him " the father of goodness " was in the right. His steady policy was always to give mild punishments where possible, lest the culprit be turned into an actual criminal. Canning may have deceived him, but when he protected her it was with the noblest intention.

Yet in many ways he was immersed in the conceptions of his age : there came from him no protest against those rows of heads on Temple Bar after the Forty-five ; and when he said of the English law that its penalties were " in so eminent a manner mild and gentle ", a man could still be hanged for any one of a hundred and sixty " crimes ", including damage to a rabbit warren.

But his public work was now drawing to a close. Health was gone, life was passing and he knew it. One anxiety there was which weighed on him above all others : that provision should be made for his wife and children when he was gone. And in this attempt he literally sacrificed his life.

In August Dr. Ranby, the famous Court physician referred to in *Amelia*, advised him to go at once to Bath for the benefit of the waters, and Fielding says : " I accordingly writ that very night to Mrs. Bowden, who, by the next post, informed me she had taken me a lodging for a month certain ".

At this moment, when almost worn out with investigating five different murders, he was summoned by the Duke of Newcastle to come to him in order that further steps should be taken to clear the streets of London of the rascals who infested them. At the Duke's house in Lincoln's Inn Fields, although ill and in great pain, Fielding was kept waiting in an ante-room until at last the Duke condescended to send a secretary to speak to him. But this was to be the last time that he waited in vain for an audience in a great man's reception room.

By now he was trying every well-known quack in London for his health, including the " pill and drop " of " Spot Ward ", so called from the claret-mark on the man's left cheek. He even seems for a time to have benefited from the famous tar water of the American Indians, Yet " so ghastly was my countenance, that timorous women with child—abstained from my house, for fear of the ill consequences of looking at me ".

Made much worse by his visit to the Duke's house, he yet within five days had prepared his plan for using those " thief-takers " who had worked so well.

But it was too late for the journey to Bath, since a ride of only six miles left him exhausted. Now, suffering from jaundice, asthma and gout, he had " lost all his muscular flesh ". But after being tapped, and fourteen ounces taken from him, he was relieved, and the laudanum which followed the operation " first gave me the most delicious flow of spirits ", and afterwards " as comfortable a nap ".

But if he was to live, it was clear that he must seek a warmer climate. At first Aix in Provence was suggested, but no ship could be heard of that was going to Marseilles, and Fielding was too weak for a long overland journey, which would also have been very expensive. That year England had no summer. " In the whole month of May the sun scarce appeared three times ".

But ships went to and fro in the Portugal trade, and on June

12th John Fielding found a ship that was sailing to Lisbon in three days. This was the *Queen of Portugal*, the Master being one Richard Veale, and the boat billed to leave Rotherhithe on Saturday, June 15th. Fielding decided to sail on her, and to recover his strength in the sunshine of the South.

His will was already made, though no date is given. Ralph Allen was appointed executor, and annuities were left for " my dear Wife Mary and my daughters Harriet and Sophia ", and when they had reached the age of three and twenty, for William and Allen.

Harriet, his daughter by his first marriage, was then sixteen or seventeen, William, Mary's first-born, was six, Sophia five, and Allen, a baby, baptised April 6th, 1754. The little daughter Louisa had been buried at Hammersmith.

During the voyage all the children, except Harriet, were to be left in the charge of Mrs. Daniol, probably their grandmother, and one Richard Boor was to act as bailiff of the farm at Fordhook. The party accompanying Fielding on the *Queen of Portugal* was a large one : his wife, his wife's maid, Isabella Ash, Margaret Collier, and a footman, always known as William. The fee paid for the whole company was the extremely moderate one of £30.

To blind John Fielding, now living in the Strand as proprietor of the Universal Register Office, was resigned the office of principal Justice of the Peace for Westminster, " and the farther Execution of my plan ". It is said that this " dear Jack " could recognise by their voices the criminals who appeared before him more than once. But as late as early April Fielding was in person committing offenders to Newgate, since a sort of half-recovery seemed to bring new hope. " I began " he says, " slowly, as it were, to draw my feet out of the grave ".

His brain, even during these many months of illness, had been taking no rest. First he revised the *Miscellanies* for a new edition, and then, when Bolingbroke had scared the thinking part of the nation by an attack on the Christian faith, he undertook the work of exposing his fallacies. This attempt meant the reading of no less than five folio volumes. But for the first time in Fielding's life the very idea of such a work gained him the applause of all the reading world. " He devotes ", said the *Evening Advertiser*, " the full strength of his faculties to the honour of God, and the virtue and happiness of the human soul ".

It was popularly believed that for this atheist Bolingbroke torments were waiting both in this world and the next. And when the poor man died of cancer in the face, this was of course regarded as a judgment on him. Fielding's method of refuting his arguments was by proving that the authorities quoted by Bolingbroke had said exactly the opposite of what this blasphemer had made them say. But the work was never finished, and nothing but a fragment of it remains.

Dates were by no means arbitrary points with the Master of the *Queen of Portugal*, and a full week after his ship should have sailed from Rotherhithe, he was to be found dining with Fielding at Fordhook. Little did the good man realise that he was then sitting for a portrait which was to make him immortal. But at last the day for embarking was settled for Wednesday, June 26th.

Behind Fielding when he left England was work well done. In the Statute Book were now several measures for better government inspired by his zeal and wisdom. And the special service money from the Privy Council had been so well spent that an additional £200 a year was granted to the magistrates whom Fielding left in charge at Bow Street. These therefore were the first stipendiary magistrates.

In a despised and once degrading office he had now set up a new tradition of honesty and efficiency. More important still, he had done something to arouse in others that sense of responsibility of each for all which has been working like leaven from his days down to ours, a sense that promises one day to change the face of the civilised world.

CHAPTER XXII

The Journey's End

ON Wednesday, June 26th, Fielding awoke at Fordhook at four o'clock in the morning to face the most melancholy sun he had ever beheld. He had learnt to "bear pains and despise death", yet when he had to take leave of "those creatures on whom he doted with a mother-like fondness", he felt that no philosophy could harden him to such a fate.

The company of his little ones for the next eight hours of waiting was worse than his illness to bear. But at noon the coach was at the door; at once, kissing the children, he went out to it "with some little resolution". His wife, "who behaved more like a heroine and philosopher, though at the same time the tenderest mother in the world", followed with Harriot.

At Rotherhithe, where the *Queen of Portugal* lay, the problem was how to get him on board from the boat. Since he had no use of his limbs, he had to be carried, and with the help of Saunders Welch was hoisted on deck in a chair. Worst of all to bear was the rough laughter of the sailors and fishermen at the queer figure he cut in his helpless condition. "It was", he says, "a lively picture of that cruelty and inhumanity in the nature of men which—leads the mind into a train of very melancholy thoughts".

The *Journal of the Voyage to Lisbon*, regarded merely as the work of a sick man by most of his contemporaries, is a delightful revelation of Fielding in undress, as his everyday associates knew him. Like *Joseph Andrews*, it is a new form of writing, an intimate, chatty travel book, with all the absurd, sad, or awkward incidents of a voyage. The character of the Master of the ship is a masterpiece : Veale is made up of absurdity, he is a mad man, and yet loveable, though exasperating. He is life itself.

So too is Fielding himself. Here is the natural man, with his courage, his serene good humour in the face of approaching death, his concern for his wife and children, his anxiety always to help his fellow-creatures even in the matter of the watermen's charges or the price of fish. Very keen he is about food and drink, and often irascible, especially about good manners before women ; a Henry Fielding whose goodwill shines like the sun on good and bad alike, even on an exorbitant landlady whom he regards with a twinkle in his eyes whatever she may charge for candles, but still the observer who records the damning facts about her bills.

Three days they lay at anchor in London River, enjoying the " delicious air " from Wapping and Rotherhithe with the shouts and oaths of the watermen and fish-wives. The noise reminded him of Hogarth's print, the Enraged Musician, which was " enough to make a man deaf to look at ".

Philosophical thoughts occur to him on the subject of transport and travelling. With a characteristic turn of humour he reflects that " the first man was a traveller, and that he and his family were scarce settled in Paradise before they disliked their own home and became passengers to another place ", so that " the humour of travelling is as old as the human race, and was their curse from the beginning ".

In England is not the stage coachman a tyrant as absolute as a Turkish bashaw ? " You have nothing to eat or to drink, but what, and when, and where he pleases. Nay, you cannot sleep unless he pleases you should ; for he will order you a sometimes out of bed at midnight and hurry you away at a moment's warning ". No wonder is it that the Liturgy numbers travellers among prisoners and captives.

And here is Captain Veale aboard, another bashaw, with his cockade and a long sword by his side. He thought himself a fine gentleman, " which seemed to insinuate that he had never seen one ". And deaf as he was, he had a voice capable of deafening everyone else. Yet he had a tender heart and suffered greatly when a kitten, " one of the feline inhabitants of the cabin ", fell out of a port-hole. Sails were instantly slackened and the boatswain stripped and leapt into the sea, returning with the little creature in his mouth. They laid it down on deck, but " its life was despaired of by all ", and the Captain, declaring that " he had rather have lost a cask of rum or brandy ", betook himself for consolation to a game of backgammon with the Portuguese friar.

The kitten, however, recovered from its swoon to the great joy of the Master, but to the disappointment of the sailors, " who asserted that the drowning a cat was the surest way of raising a favourable wind ". But the creature must certainly have been bewitched, for a few days later it was found suffocated between two mattresses.

This tale of a kitten was the only part of the book which Lady Mary Montagu enjoyed, and that simply because she had once found a similar feline castaway in an Italian orange-grove. All the character-drawing, the courage, gaiety and humour of the *Voyage to Lisbon* were lost on this witty lady.

The wind, being " long nested in the south-west ", constantly blew hurricanes. And Fielding, being again troubled by his dropsy, sent for Dr. Hunter, the famous surgeon of Covent Garden, who used the trocar on him once more.

On Sunday the thirtieth they fell down to Gravesend, and there a new trouble awaited the party, for Mrs. Fielding was enduring torments from tooth-ache. They sent to Wapping for a tooth-drawer, but when the woman, " an eminent practitioner ", at last reached the waterside the ship was gone and she refused to follow it.

The shipyards of Deptford and Woolwich, where they saw the *Royal Anne* on the stocks, the largest ship ever built, filled Fielding with joy as he thought of " the figure which we may always make in Europe among the other maritime powers ", however second-rate our land forces may be in comparison with those of Germany and France.

Still that tooth-ache persisted since it was " secured by a large, fine, firm tooth ", which even an eminent surgeon despaired of being able to extract. But opium and blisters were applied.

When the bowsprit of a cod smack crashed into the cabin of the *Queen of Portugal*, Fielding's ears were saluted with a volley of sea language from both sides. Surely, he suggests, seamen's oaths would be a fine debating subject for the Robin Hood Society.

But that custom-house officer who entered the cabin with his hat on his head was sternly told to remove it since there were ladies present. Fielding thereupon quotes Plato to the effect that in " all states which are under the government of mere man, without any divine assistance, there is nothing but labour

RYDE—1795.

[Drawn and Engraved by C. Tomkins.

From an engraving of a drawing by Chas. Tomkins.
Home of "Mr. and Mrs. Francis," in *Voyage to Lisbon*.

LISBON—1793
From a mezzotint of a drawing by Noel.

and misery to be found ". Not philosophy from stones but from custom-house officers !

On July 1st, at Gravesend, Saunders Welch and Jane Collier left the ship to return to London. Fielding had seen to the victualling question, for wine, hams, tongues, several sheep and live chicken were brought aboard at his expense, so that the party was not dependent on the ship's rusty bacon. Indeed before the end he seems to have been feeding the whole ship's company, though the Master often grumbled at the mere £30 of passage money.

Veale had been in the past an English privateer. This he called the King's service, which qualified him to wear a cockade. After being wrecked on the Barbary Coast, he was set to building up walls and pulling them down again, and fed on bread and water as a slave of the Emperor of Morocco. Finally, after being redeemed, he was carried back to Portsmouth on a man of war. As Master now of the *Queen of Portugal,* he often carried specie for the London merchants to the tune of 30,000 Spanish dollars. An important man, a man of note, this Veale.

Off Deal another surgeon was fetched for Mrs. Fielding, but after giving her intolerable agony, departed, leaving the tooth where it was.

One of Fielding's worst trials seems to have been that when an agreeable hour did come, he had no companion with him to enjoy it. The Captain was so deaf that in order to make him hear one had to shout. But that would have disturbed poor Mrs. Fielding whenever she tried to get a nap. The other women, whenever the ship rolled, were lost in the depths of sea-sickness.

Twice they tried to leave Deal, but each time the wind blew them back. And Fielding was aghast at the fares demanded by the watermen. The gale continuing, they were forced to anchor off Ryde. Here the ladies went ashore and enjoyed a great treat—tea with fresh cream. And in this pleasant place, since the wind still remained in the wrong quarter, it was decided that the family should be put ashore till a change came. He himself was carried across the mud from a small hoy which had luckily come alongside.

When they reached the inn they found, instead of the dinner they were expecting, that the landlady was scrubbing the house. But Mary Fielding would not have her invalid sitting in a damp room, and after looking round, most luckily discovered a dry, oak-floored barn lined with wheat straw and facing a fine view. Amid the lamentations of Mrs. Francis they settled down here in comfort. But why, why, should gentlefolks choose to live in such a place ? It was a problem beyond the landlady's comprehension.

At last a meal of beans and bacon was put on the board, but with neither meat nor fish, although there actually lived next door a fisherman who had soles, whiting and lobsters " far superior to those which adorn a city feast ".

The inn itself was built out of wreckwood, and " probably dedicated to Neptune in honour of the *Blessing* sent by him to the inhabitants ", the blessing of wrecks and visitors.

Next morning the bill came in for thirteen shillings and tenpence, but for this they had been given nothing except bread, small beer, a teacupful of milk and one bottle of " wind "—A remonstrance brought the reply from Mrs. Francis that " her house had always been frequented by the very best gentry of the island ; and she had never had a bill found fault with in her life ". Fielding, observing the way in which they lived at the inn, remarks, " it is inconceivable what sums may be collected by starving only—Rusty bacon and worse cheese was their fare ".

As for Farmer Francis, he was of a round stature, with a plump round face, and a kind of smile on it. " He wished not for anything, thought not of anything ; indeed he scarce did anything, or said anything—so composed, so serene, so placid a countenance I never saw ; and he satisfied himself by answering to every question he was asked : " I don't know anything about it, sir ; I leave all that to my wife ". He was in fact oil to his wife's vinegar. " And as it was impossible to displease him, so it was impossible to please her ".

The lady of the manor offered the party every civility, sending them fruit from her own garden. But now they faced a calamity : their chest of tea had been mislaid and they had before them now the prospect of a long voyage without " the use of that sovereign remedy ", tea. In vain they searched high and low. There was nothing to be done in their distress but to apply to the hospitable lady. Instantly she responded, sending a large canister of China tea, and then, at the very last moment, when they were about to leave, William came running back with the missing chest in his hand. It had been left in the hoy.

Mrs Francis laid on her taxes for the last time : lodging price raised, sixpence extra for firing, and candles charged for with " wantonness " under the term of " oversight ".

When a lieutenant from a regiment just back from Gibraltar came to visit his uncle, Captain Veale, Fielding found him a pretty pup and so merry that " he laughed at everything he said, and always before he spoke ". We have all met that kind of young man. He despised his uncle, because he himself " was a member of that profession which makes every man a gentleman ".

Beyond the Isle of Portland the wind rose to a gale, and Fielding saw from Veale's face that the ship was in danger. " Can I say that I had no fear ? Indeed I cannot. Reader, I was afraid for thee, lest thou shouldst have been deprived of that pleasure thou art now enjoying—"

And here is his tenderness : " My dear wife and child must pardon me, if what I did not conceive to be any great evil to myself I was not much terrified with the thoughts of happening to them ; in truth I have often thought they are both too good and too gentle to be trusted to the power of any man I know ". Yet to Ralph Allen and John Fielding they had to be so trusted, for after Henry's death there was only just enough money to pay his debts.

The wind fell and soon they were near Berry Head, lying at anchor in Torbay. A cheerful breakfast followed, with clotted cream and fresh bread and butter from the shore. Here Fielding bought the famous three hogsheads of Devon cider for £5-10. One hogshead of this *Vinum Pomonae* was to be taken on to Lisbon, and the others sent to London to be shared by Saunders Welch, Andrew Millar and Dr. Hunter. " I wish you all merry over it ", writes Fielding. " It will be fit for drinking and bottling a Month after it hath lain in your Vault ". Some of it was rough cider, and some of the " sweeter Taste ".

These details of his purchase come, not from the *Voyage*, but from Henry's letter to his brother. One of these was written off Ryde, and directed c/o the Postmaster of Portsmouth, July 12th, 1754. It runs :

" Dear Jack,
On the Back of the Isle of Wight, where we had last Night in Safety the Pleasure of hearing the Winds roar over our Heads

in as violent a Tempest as I have known, and where my only consideration were the Fears which must possess any Friend of ours (if there is happily any such), who really makes our Wellbeing the Object of his Concern especially if such Friend should be totally inexperienced in Sea Affairs. I therefore beg that on the Day you receive this Mrs. Daniel may know that we are just risen from Breakfast in Health and Spirits this twelfth Instant at 9 in the Morning ".

But he was racked by anxiety about affairs at Fordhook and the character of his bailiff. " If BOOR BE TRUSTY ", he writes, " Pray let me know any Shadow of a Doubt ; for the very Supposition gives me much Uneasiness. If he is not trusty he is a Fool, but that is very possible for him to be ". Like any farmer he enquires about the price of wheat at Uxbridge market. And still his mind runs on food. " I got half a Buck from the New Forest, while we lay at the Isle of Wight, and the Pasty sticks by us ". That pasty was made by Mrs Fielding at Ryde, and the baking of it may possibly explain the extra fee charged for firing by Mrs. Francis.

In this Paradise of the West that flows with cider, "much more delicious than that which is the growth of Herefordshire ", he finds the explanation of the tale of Circe and the swine. For Ulysses must have been " the captain of a merchant ship, and Circe some good ale-wife, who made his crew drunk with the spirituous liquors of those days. For now, and then, every ship's master dreads sending his crew ashore—lest they be all transformed into swine and made useless ".

Now Fielding had the pleasure of discovering the excellence of the fish from the Devon seas. Particularly did he enjoy the John Dorée, or Dory, which resembles a turbot, but is finer and sweeter. Quin the actor, so it appears, did full justice to the Dorée when he stayed in Plymouth. And Fielding was now able to buy one of four pounds for four shillings.

But unfortunately for the fishmongers of London, the Dorée resides only in these Seas ; for, " could any of this Company but convey one to the Temple of Luxury under the Piazza, where Macklin the High-Priest duly serves up his rich Offering to that Goddess (of Food) great would be his Merit ".

The actor Macklin was then running a famous eating-house under the Piazza of Covent Garden.

But the Dory was an expensive fish, even in Fielding's time, since in Torbay he was able to buy large soles at fourpence a pair and whiting at ninepence a score.

But why is it, he asks, that with our rivers and seas swarming with fish, in London, except for sprats, " there is not one poor palate in a hundred that knows the taste of fish ? " And " if only the starving of the poor was declared to be felony—the fishmongers would be hanged before the end of the session ".

There were lively scenes at times with the Master of the *Queen of Portugal*, when Fielding's sense of propriety was shocked. One day the Captain's man rushed into the cabin and began without a word to fill bottles with small beer from a hogshead. Fielding ordered him to desist since he was disturbing the company. This producing no effect, he threatened the fellow with an empty bottle, for gout makes one irascible. But when Veale heard all about it, he too began to rage, crying : " Did you think I sold you the command of my ship for that pitiful thirty pounds ? "

That was too much for Fielding. Instantly he gave orders for a hoy to be summoned to carry the party to Dartmouth, and, worst of all, threatened Veale with the law, " that which, he afterwards said, he feared more than any rock or quicksand ". And when the hoy appeared alongside, the poor man fell on his knees and prayed for mercy.

" I did not suffer a brave man and an old man to remain a moment in this posture, but I immediately forgave him ", says Fielding.

By this time, for all their wordy battles, he had got a certain liking for the old privateer, who did in fact " love his ship as his wife, and his boats as children ". " Truth to tell ", adds Fielding " he acted the part of a father to his sailors—and never suffered the least work of supererogation to go unrewarded by a glass of gin. He even extended his humanity—to animals, and even his cats and kittens had large shares in his affections ". Indeed his lamentations when the kitten was suffocated " seemed to have some mixture of the Irish howl in them ". In short, " he was one of the best-natured fellows alive ".

But all the while, as we discover later, the old man was carrying on an affair with Mrs. Fielding's maid, Isabella Ash.

No sooner had they left Torbay than the wind shifted again. Veale was convinced that his ship was bewitched, and that no other than Mrs. Francis had laid a spell on it. And all the

Brixham people would no doubt have agreed with him. As late as forty years ago the white witch of Brixham made her living by reading the crystal and selling favourable winds to seamen.

At last on August 5th they lay becalmed in the Bay of Biscay. The calm was soon followed by storm, and once more the women took to their beds with sea-sickness. But again a fair wind returned which carried them past Cape Finisterre and into peaceful waters. There followed a wonderful evening of beauty in sea and sky which Fielding describes in words that show how deeply moved he was.

" We were seated on deck, women and all, in the serenest evening that can be imagined. Not a single cloud presented itself to our view, and the sun himself was the only object which engrossed our attention. He did indeed set with a majesty which is incapable of description, with which while the horizon was yet blazing with glory, our eyes were called off to the opposite part to survey the moon, which was then at full, and which in rising presented us with the second object that this world hath offered to our vision. Compared to these the pageantry of theatres, or splendour of courts, are sights almost below the regard of children ".

It is pleasant to think of that moonlight shining on the southern sea for Fielding, who had so often set his travellers starting out on the road by that same light. But now for him the end of the journey was almost in sight.

The ninth of August was a Sunday, and the old ship's Master read the prayers on deck " with an audible voice, and with but one mistake, of a lion for Elias, in the second lesson for this day ".

They now passed the Rock of Lisbon where there lived like a hermit an old sailor in a monastery hewn out of the stone. Three miles below the city itself they were opposite the royal palace of Belem (Fielding's Bellisle), where Catherine of Braganza lies buried, the wife of Charles II ; not Catherine of Aragon, as Fielding states, for that Catherine rests of course in Peterborough Cathedral.

At last they reached Lisbon, six weeks after leaving Fordhook, and after trouble with the customs officers, drove in a chaise through " the nastiest city in the world ". And here at an inn on the brow of the hill they supped.

The manuscript of the *Voyage* ends abruptly with a strangely apposite line from Horace :

Hic finis chartaeque viaeque.

But the real end of the way was not to come for two months.

Fragments of the letters to John Fielding from Lisbon give us a few glimpses of his brother's last days in Portugal. Many troubles, small indeed, but peculiarly irritating to a sick man, beset him. Yet for a time his health seemed to have so greatly improved that he believed the dropsy was actually cured. After being tapped at Torbay, he writes : " Nine Quarts of Water were taken away, and possibly here I left the Dropsy, for I have heard nothing of it since ".

" In short as we advanced to the South, it is incredible how my Health advanced with it, and I have no doubt but that I should have perfectly recovered—had it not been obstructed by every possible Accident which Fortune can throw in my Way ".

To domestic afflictions were added annoyances caused by Captain Veale. " The Truth is ", says Fielding, " that Captains are all ye greatest Scoundrels in the World, but Veale is the greatest of them all—he is likewise a Madman, which I knew long before I reached Lisbon ".

The family fell ill, all " except myself, Harriot and Bell ". William, too, had made an ass of himself " by drinking too much wine ". And finally, in terror of dying and being buried in a foreign land, " the miserable cowardly driveller " was rushed on board the *Queen of Portugal* to return with Veale to England.

The usual money troubles were pursuing his master, who had discovered that Lisbon was " the dearest City in the World ". Here living cost them two moidores a day, and since the value of the moidore was about twenty-seven shillings, very soon they would be absolutely penniless " a thousand miles from home ". Yet they had one friend at least, " the greatest merchant in the Town ", and, perhaps through him, found a cheap little house at a rental of only nine moidores a year. But, alas ! it was unfurnished, with " not even a Shelf or a Kitchen Grate ". Fielding was now eagerly awaiting a money bill from his brother.

Mrs. Fielding was ill and home-sick, longing for her children. She " cries and sighs all Day ". The fact was that she believed this exile to be unnecessary, and that her husband could just as well have recovered in this country. Margaret Collier, too, was making herself a nuisance. Already, as the Toast of the Town, she was setting her cap at the English Resident. And if Mrs. Fielding returned home, Henry would have been left in sole control of this troublesome young woman.

A most worrying state of affairs ! " By these means ", remarks Fielding, " my Spirits which were at the Top of the House are thrown down into the Cellar ". However, vigour seemed now to be coming back to his limbs, and he had no intention of leaving Lisbon. He sends onions to his friends, with orange trees, lemons and wine. He orders clothes for winter, and these should be cut broader in the shoulder as he is putting on flesh. There is even an order for " a Tye and a new Mazer Perriwig ".

His spirits are now so full of gay courage that he even forgives his enemies, and dispatches a present to Dr. Collier, " who had an Execution taken out against me and whose very Name I hate ". The sentiment is very like the saying of Amelia's little boy, who forgave those who hurt papa, but hated them all the same.

Fielding's constant craving for social life persisted to the last. Jack is requested to send out to him " a conversible Man to be my Companion—who will drink a moderate Glass in an Evening, or will at least sit with me till one when I do ".

Bell Ash was to follow Veale to England, where " he hath promised to marry her ". But she was nothing but a fool who had been deceived by the Captain.

" My Family ", writes Fielding, " now consists of a Black Slave and his Wife, to which I desire you to add a very good perfect Cook ". Not content with the partridges and young fowls he can buy so cheaply, he demands from the farm at Fordhook : " Four Hams, a very fine Hog fatted as soon as may be and being cut into Flitches sent me, likewise a young Hog made into Pork and salted and pickled in a Tub. A vast large Cheshire Cheese and one of Stilton if it be had good and mild ".

This is a strange menu for a sick man, but Fielding remained Fielding to the very end.

He pursues the recreant William, his man, who had cheated him of £3 12. Boor, the bailiff, is to deduct this from the fellow's wages and strip him of his livery.

There were pleasanter subjects however than William. For the chaplain to the British factory in Lisbon had made discoveries in Mathematics and was in every way the cleverest fellow Fielding had met. Miss Collier of course was hunting him, but without success. Toast of the Town as Margaret might have been, she was evidently well-known as a man-chaser. This chaplain survived the great earthquake, and the lady as well, for she returned to England still unmarried.

Fielding's house was at Junqueira, in full view of the " Tajo ", or Tagus. And here he settled down to get his Voyage ready for the press, calling it " a novel without a Plot ", and comparing it facetiously with Anson's *Voyage Round the World*.

Suddenly his health began to fail. His handwriting is now trembling, at times the phrasing almost incoherent.

Just two months and a day after the landing in Lisbon, on October 8th, 1754, there came the end. We know no more. As far as the English world was concerned, Fielding's life was snuffed out like a blown candle.

He was buried in the graveyard of the British factory, in the midst of the cypress avenues, where the tombs are laurel-shaded and the nightingales sing among the geraniums.

In 1772, only eighteen years later, the spot was so neglected that it was difficult to find where his bones lay. But after two unsuccessful attempts to set up a memorial, in 1830 the plot was bought and a monument erected, that " cold tomb " which Borrow tells us that he kissed.

On it are the lines :—

*Luget Britannia gremio non dari
Fovere Natum.*

Britain grieves that she is not permitted to fold her son within her own bosom.

S

EPILOGUE

The Verdict of the Centuries

As the ideals of each century shift and change into another form so does the reaction to Fielding. A challenge to England in his own days, he still remains one in ours. For since he worked in the very stuff of human nature, as long as that endures, so long will he be able to speak to us. He lived zestfully, died bravely and left to those who came after the inheritance of his own fine nature enshrined in his books.

No man ever hated the cold heart and the empty head more than did Henry Fielding; no man fought more vigorously against hypocrisy, lies and sham; no, not even Molière and Voltaire in their greater ways. And as they are immortal, so is he.

His own period was one of formality and convention. To give a frank picture of ordinary life was to run counter to the feeling of the time. The good lady who is said to have objected to his novels " because they dealt with such stuff as passed every day between herself and her maid ", was but voicing the opinion of many of her contemporaries. The man of fashion was the ideal figure of the time, and Fielding laughed at him. For mere elegance he had no use at all. His genteel spirit at the gate of Elysium is refused admission by Minos.

Two things Fielding had against him : his truth-telling and his laughter. And as he went his way as a novelist, he plunged ever deeper and deeper into what actually is, until in *Amelia* his laughter almost failed him. But when he jested about serious things, the world called him buffoon. His books were written at the opening of the romantic age in literature, the period of Richardson, Rousseau and Sterne, when it seemed more enjoyable to weep than to laugh. Few people then believed that wisdom could be hidden behind a joke, or truth be found in a farce.

John Fielding and Sarah might have shown a Fielding of fact instead of legend when they published after his death *The*

Voyage to Lisbon. Instead they adopted a tone of apology both for the book and its author, and Murphy in his Dedication, after remarking that he was " unwilling to disturb the Manes of the dead ", persisted in painting the portrait of a prodigal genius.

Nothing can show more clearly the blindness of contemporary feeling than Edwards's letter to Richardson : " I have lately read over with much indignation Fielding's last piece called his *Voyage to Lisbon.* That a man who had led such a life as he had, should trifle in that manner when immediate death was before his eyes, is amazing—From this book I am confirmed in what his other books had fully persuaded me of, that with all his parade of pretences to virtuous and humane affections, the fellow had no heart. And so—his knell is knolled ".

And this was written of the bravest, tenderest piece of autobiography in the English language !

So it went on, with, in later years, Hannah More writing to a correspondent who had quoted from *Tom Jones :* " I am shocked to hear you quote from so vicious a book ", with Dr. Burney asking, " who would venture to read one of Fielding's novels aloud to modest women ? "

But Madame du Deffand over in Paris was for Fielding, whatever her friend Horace Walpole might say.

Then at last, in 1766, a defence came, not from a man of letters, but a scholar, when Dr Beattie, Professor of Moral Philosophy at Aberdeen, expressed the opinion that Fielding's knowledge of the world might be mentioned in the same breath with Shakespeare's. Gibbon followed in the *Decline and Fall*, speaking of that " great master ", whose *Journey from this World to the Next* " may be considered as the history of human nature ", and of *Tom Jones* as an " exquisite picture of human manners ". But to have one's name mentioned by Gibbon, said Thackeray, was like having it emblazoned on the dome of St. Paul's.

Fielding's day was coming to full dawn in the early years of the nineteenth century. Hazlitt, Lamb, and especially Coleridge, were acute enough to realise the powerful mind which had produced *Jonathan Wild.* This was almost a new discovery that had not been made before, even by those who enjoyed the novels.

What a master of composition Fielding was ! " wrote Coleridge. " Upon my word, I think the *Oedipus Tyrannus*,

The Alchemist and *Tom Jones*, the three most perfect plots ever planned ".

To Coleridge Fielding was " a supreme lover of liberty ", as in his own age he had been " a dangerous leveller ". The same quality looks different in a different light.

Mrs. Barbauld, that " Presbyterian in petticoats ", was convinced that Fielding's mind " had received a taint which spread itself in his works ". Over and over again she dilates on this theme. How shocked she would have been at Charles Lamb's exclamation : " Damn them ! I mean the cursed Barbauld Crew, those Blights and Blasts, of all that is Human in Man and Child ".

Sir Walter Scott was in a peculiar position as a romantic Scottish Jacobite sitting in judgment on Fielding the Hanoverian realist. His plots are shapeless and vague ; Fielding's compact and finished. Nor could the good Sheriff escape from " this eidolon with inked ruffles and towel round his head ", as Saintsbury put it, whom one only thinks of as " reeling home from the Rose ". And accordingly to the author of *Waverley* Fielding was no better in character than a smoking, drinking prodigal and libertine.

Yet the artist in Scott could not but recognise the artist in Fielding. *Tom Jones* he regards as " the first English novel ". It is truth and human nature itself. And as to the morality of the plot : " The follies of Tom Jones are those which the world soon teaches to all who enter on the career of life ". But the satire of *Jonathan Wild* he could not understand. " It is difficult to see what Fielding proposed to himself by a picture of complete vice ". The mind of a pure romantic shrinks instinctively from the analysis of evil.

To Byron Fielding was " the prose Homer of human nature ", but de Quincy found him " disgusting ". It was of this period that Charles Lamb wrote : " My whole heart is faint and my whole head sick—at this damn'd canting unmasculine age ", the age when, to quote Edward Garnett, " Rembrandt's choice of beggars, wrinkled faces and grey hairs—seemed a reprehensible taste in " high art ".

Naturally therefore Thackeray, in some ways so deeply embedded in the spirit of his time, could not " offer or hope to make a hero of Harry Fielding ", while to Ruskin both Fielding and Smollett seemed to be " licking their chops over nastiness ".

But Dickens followed him as a beloved guide and friend. Always it is a case of Fielding the touchstone which tests the nature of every man.

Thackeray's famous portrait of Fielding is an extraordinary instance of what a man may be in himself, and of what his century's influence made him. He knew Fielding to be a great writer, and in essentials a good man, yet, like Scott, he is obsessed by that disreputable " eidolon " handed down from the past. Sound timber was in front of him, but the age demanded veneer. And there is no veneer on Fielding or his work.

Yet here is Thackeray's evidence : " he possessed some of the most splendid human qualities and endowments. He has an admirable natural love of truth, the keenest instinctive antipathy to hypocrisy, the happiest satirical gift of laughing it to scorn. His wit is wonderfully wise and detective ; it flashes upon a rogue and lightens up a rascal like a policeman's lantern. He could not be so brave, generous, and truth-telling as he is, were he not infinitely merciful, pitiful, and tender—"

Magnificent praise of course. Yet it never struck Thackeray to ask how it was that such love and intellect could possibly be found in the castaway he believed Fielding to have been. Do men gather figs of thistles ?

Meredith saw in Fielding that " laughter of the mind " which he valued most among human gifts. To George Eliot he was a Colossus, but in the puritanical eyes of Charlotte Brontë Thackeray resembled Fielding only as an " eagle does a vulture ", and a vulture who, after its kind, loves to stoop on carrion.

Henley's part in the contest is amusing, for he uses Fielding as a stick with which to belabour the Victorianism he so loathed. If the man is as his enemies described him, what difference does it make ? For in Fielding we find " a master of character, a master of style ", who " achieved for us the four great books we have, and, in achieving them, did so nobly by his nation and his mother tongue that he who would praise our splendid, all-comprehending speech aright has said the best he can of it when he says that it is the speech of Shakespeare and Fielding ".

But the specialists were at last getting to work, although it was not till 1918 that Professor Cross produced his full, definitive life of Fielding which shows the plain facts as far as these can be traced at so late a date. And after the discovery of the catalogue of Fielding's library, Austin Dobson's biography in 1883 certainly helped to rescue the body of Fielding from " the swinish hoofs " which had been so long trampling on it. Yet even Dobson shrank from facing his subject's youth. " If any portrait ", he says, " is to be handed down to posterity, let it be the last rather than the first—not the Fielding of the green-room and the tavern—but the energetic magistrate, the tender husband and father, the kindly host of his poorer friends, the practical philanthropist, the patient and magnanimous hero of the *Voyage to Lisbon* ".

As if no young man had ever before fleeted the time carelessly in a by no means golden world ! And after all it was this Fielding of the green-room whose plays had lashed the infamies of his time. No just estimate can ever be formed of the genius and character of Fielding unless one is prepared to look fair and square at his farces and comedies. They are crude indeed, but full of purpose.

Sir Leslie Stephen felt that the bed-rock of Fielding's nature was his pure and generous heart. But he missed, as we all must, any sense of the strange mystery of existence, any feeling of " Oh ! Altitudo ! " in his writings. Harry in fact was so intent on the face of the Sphinx that he forgot the depths of the sky behind it.

Bernard Shaw's tribute is whole-hearted. " Between the Middle Ages ", he says, " and the nineteenth century, when Fielding was by the Licensing Act driven out of the trade of Molière and Aristophanes into that of Cervantes, the English novel has been one of the glories of literature, whilst the English drama has been its disgrace". Both Shaw and Fielding wrote their plays with something of the same critical purpose, Shaw urbanely and Fielding crudely. In the two men there is something of the same temper.

Perhaps the highest appreciation comes from Saintsbury, who puts Fielding among " the four Atlantes of English verse and prose ". Shakespeare, Milton and Swift, with Fielding, carry the world on their shoulders. " There are two moods ", he says, " in which the motto is *Carpe Diem ;* one a mood of simply childish hurry, the other where behind the enjoyment of the moment lurks—that vast ironic consciousness of the before and after which we see everywhere in the background of Fielding's work ".

Fielding indeed grows younger before our eyes as the centuries pass. Many of his qualities are precisely those which we value to-day : the truth, even if it is ugly ; realist pictures of actual life in every class ; wide-reaching thought ; a generous, non-puritanical judgment of most things ; and a toughness of character which can bear pain and hardship and laugh even at the worst moments. None but the " aggressively pure " are likely nowadays to condemn him on either of the two charges, first, that he had a passion for telling the truth, and second, that he was once young and careless.

Taine the Frenchman, in a thoroughly French manner, found Fielding's work " a rough wine which lacked bouquet ". But in our island fashion we rather prefer our wine to be rough —as long as it is the pure juice of the grape. And Fielding's wine came from a fine vintage.

" English in all " runs the inscription they put on his bust at Taunton. " Who loves a man may see his image here ". The century which gave us the title John Bull gave us also one of the most typical Englishmen who ever lived.

BIBLIOGRAPHY

History of Henry Fielding, W. L. CROSS.
Henry Fielding : Novelist and Magistrate, B. M. JONES.
Fielding the Novelist, BLANCHARD.
Essay on Fielding, ARTHUR MURPHY.
Fielding, SCOTT.
Fielding, AUSTIN DOBSON.
Henry Fielding, GODDEN.
Life and Writings of Henry Fielding, KEIGHTLEY.
Fielding, SAINTSBURY.
Memoir of Fielding, LESLIE STEPHEN.
Life of Henry Fielding, WATSON.
Life of Henry Fielding, LAWRENCE.
Beggar's Opera, JOHN GAY.
Trivia, JOHN GAY.
Memoir of Hogarth, AUSTIN DOBSON.
Handel, ABDY WILLIAMS.
Garrick and his Circle, PARSONS.
David Garrick and his French Friends, HEDGCOCK.
Anecdotes, JOHN NICHOLS.
Annals of Covent Garden, H. SAXE WYNDHAM.
Woffington, AUGUSTIN DALY.
Peg Woffington, CHARLES READE.
Social Life in the Reign of Queen Anne, ASHTON.
History of English Thought in the Eighteenth Century, LESLIE STEPHEN.
English Literature and Society in the Eighteenth Century, L. STEPHEN.
English Comic Writers, HAZLITT.
Eighteenth Century Vignettes, AUSTIN DOBSON.
Alexander Pope, EDITH SITWELL.
Pamela, RICHARDSON.
Correspondence of Richardson.
Memoirs, LETITIA PILKINGTON.
Autobiography, MRS. DELANY.
Apology for the Life of Mr. Colley Cibber.
Apology for the Life of Mrs. Shamela Andrews.
Apology for the Life of G. A. Bellamy.
Apology for the Life of Bampfylde-Moore Carew, 2nd Edition.
David Simple, SARAH FIELDING.
Familiar Letters, SARAH FIELDING.
The Glastonbury Script, BLIGH BOND.
Howell's State Trials, Vol. XIX., ELIZABETH CANNING.

INDEX

Acts of Parliament, inspired by Fielding, 250
Adams, Parson (*Joseph Andrews*) 9, 15, 21, 35, 39, 40, 60, 95, 138, 151, 190, 193, 236, 237, 238; epitome of simple goodness, 152ff.
Addison, Joseph, 58, 198
Aeschylus, 21
After the Deluge, 212
Alchemist, The, 276
Allen, Ralph, 91, 92, 168, 177, 191, 218, 219, 222, 237, 260, 267
Allworthy, Bridget (*Tom Jones*) 100, 221, 222, 230
Allworthy, Squire (*Tom Jones*) 9, 105, 215-6, 219, 221-2
Amelia, 9, 20, 83, 94, 105, 116, 171, 174, 197, 199, 200, 274; its background of crime, 234; its moral purpose, 234-8; outline of the plot, 238-42; attacks on its 'lowness', 243-7
Andrew, Sarah, abduction by Fielding, 24-7, 33
Anson, Lord, 273
Apology (Colley Cibber) 30, 75, 134-6, 138, 149, 168
Apology (de Veil) 196, 198
Apology for the Life of Mr. Bampfylde Moore-Carew, 22, 131-2, 228
Arbuthnot, Dr., 63, 69
Arden of Faversham, 125
Aristophanes, 23, 169
Atkinson, Sergeant (*Amelia*) 237, 239, 242, 243
Author's Farce, The, 102, 146; a portrayal of Grub Street, 54 ff.
Avare, L', The Miser, 77

Badger, Squire (*Don Quixote in England*) 38, 39, 97
Balzac, 180
Barbauld, Mrs., 276

Bath, Colonel (*Amelia*) 236, 237, 239, 240, 246
Bath, 10, 11, 89, 90, 92, 167, 168, 171, 259
Beattie, Dr., 275
Bedford, Duke of, 108, 189, 196
Beere, Abbot, 7
Beggar's Opera, The, 41, 42, 44, 48, 50, 68, 109
Bellamy, George Ann, 122
Bellaston, Lady (*Tom Jones*) 229-30
Bennett, Arnold, 83
Bennett, Mrs. (*Amelia*) 238, 241, 242, 245
Blyfil (*Tom Jones*) 215, 221 ,222, 223
Boerhave, Hermann, 37, 38
Boleyn, Anne, 173
Bolingbroke, 260, 261
Booby, Lady (*Joseph Andrews*) 150, 154, 162
Booth, Capt. William (*Amelia*) 96, 200, 234 ff., 249
Borrow, George, 89, 273
Bow Street, Fielding presides at the court at, 196, 197 ff., 212, 217, 249 ff.
Bradshaigh, Lady, 216
Brogden, Joshua, 198, 203, 257
Brontë, Charlotte, 277
Burke, Edmund, 249
Burnet, Bishop, 164
Burney, Dr., 275
Bute, Lady, 171, 247
Butler, Samuel (1612-80) 121, (1835-1902) 215
Byron, 276

Canning, Elizabeth, case of, 254-8
Carew, Bampfylde-Moore-, 22, 131, 132, 228

Carey, Henry, 63, 64
Carte, Thomas, 195
Carter, Miss, 165
Cervantes, 23, 38, 244
Chalice Well, at Glastonbury, 9–10, 199
Champion Journal, 102, 132–3, 136–7, 140, 185
Chancellor, Matthew, 9–10
Charlcombe, Fielding married at, 89, 90
Charles Edward, Prince, 186, 194, 196; a reader of Fielding, 190
Chaucer, 36
Chesterfield, Earl of, 54, 62, 108, 121, 122; opposes Licensing Bill, 122–3
Chronicle, Baker's, 17, 22
Chubb, Thomas, 222
Churchill, General, 168
Churchill, Sarah. *See* Marlborough, Duchess of
Cibber, Colley, 41, 56, 58, 59, 60, 74, 75, 77–8, 79, 111, 119, 122, 145, 146, 149, 168, 203; a coxcomb 30–1; Fielding attacks his *Apology*, 134–6; Cibber's reply 136–7
Cibber, Theophilus, 58, 74, 104
Cicero, 21
Clarissa Harlowe, 91–2, 141, 144 216, 221
Clive, Kitty, 75, 77, 93, 101, 115; Fielding's tribute to, 78
Coffee-House Politician, The, 65, 66, 112
Coffee Houses, 51, 66–8
Coleridge, 185, 220, 229, 275–6
Collier, Jane, 186, 265
Collier, Margaret, 186, 260, 272, 273
Common Sense, 122, 123
Congreve, 34, 38
Cottingham, Mrs., 16, 17
Covent Garden, 51
Covent Garden Journal, 245, 248, 249, 250, 252
Covent Garden Theatre, 123
Covent Garden Tradgedy, 75, 76, 80, 150, 199

Cradock, Catherine, 82, 90, 94
Cradock, Charlotte (wife), 78, 82, 86–8, 92, 95, 115, 160, 164, 219, 238; prototype of Sophia Western, 83, 84–5, 214; marriage with Fielding, 89–90; inherits mother's estate, 94; death of, 171; prototype of Amelia, 246
Cradock, Mrs. 84, 90, 94
Cradock House, Salisbury, 85–6, 87, 95
Craftsman, The, 137
Cross, Professor W. L., 277
Cry, The, 186
Culloden, 190

Dalton, John, 104
Daniol, Mary, 174, 186, 200, 260, 262, 264, 265, 268, 271, 272; marriage with Fielding, 191–2
David Simple, 28, 90, 171, 190, 191
Davies, Tom, 126
de la Mare, Walter, 232
De Quincey, Thos., 276
Death of Alexander the Great, 71
Decline and Fall, 275
De Consolatione, 21
Deffand, Mme. du, 67, 275
Delany, Mrs., 109, 235
Deposing and Death of Queen Gin, 117
Desfontaines, Abbé, 164
Detective force, first, 252
Dickens, Charles, 207, 208, 213, 277
Dobson, Austin, 141, 201, 278
Don Quixote in England, 38–40, 78, 92, 96
Donne, John, 86, 175
Dostoevsky, 153, 181
'Drawcansir, Sir Alexander', 248
Drury Lane Theatre, 29, 77, 78, 93, 120, 123, 136, 169, 190
Dryden, 59, 68, 71
Dunciad, 31, 91, 168
Dynasts, 179

INDEX

Ealing. *See* Fordhook
East Stour. *See* Stour, East
Edgar Chapel, The, 8, 11
Edwards, 275
Election, The (*Pasquin*), 109, 110
Eliot, George, 277
Ellison, Mrs., 238, 241, 243
Enquiry into the Causes of the Late Increase of Robbers, Fielding's diagnosis of crime, 205-7
Erasmus, 212
Eton, Fielding at, 16, 18, 20-23, 178
Eurydice Hiss'd, 120
Evening Advertiser, 260
Examples of the Interposition of Providence 250

Falstaff, 109, 232
Familiar Letters, 139, 191
Fanny (*Joseph Andrews*), 156, 160-6
Fatal Curiosity, The, 124-6
Feilding, earls of Denbigh, 12, 13
Fenton, Lavinia, 49
Fielding, Mrs. Anne (stepmother), 16-19
Fielding, Charlotte (daughter) death of, 167
Fielding, Hon. Edmund (father) marriage with Sarah Gould, 12; a soldier, 12, 13; settles at East Stour, 14; gambling, 15-16, 19, 238; second marriage, 16; Chancery Suit with Lady Gould 17-19; possible prototype of army officers in *Amelia*, 20; death, 138
Fielding, George (uncle) 129
Fielding, Henry, birth 8; his English quality, 9, 38-40, 55; at Eton, 16, 18, 20-23; classical influences, 20-1; abduction of Sarah Andrew, 24-7; as playwright, 29 ff., 55 ff., 65 ff., 93-4, 108 ff., 117 ff.; at Leyden, 37; his attack on crime, 41 ff.; decides on authorship, 53; courtship, 82-88; first marriage, 89; generosity, 96, 175; and Hogarth, 99 ff.; enters Middle Temple, 128, 129; attacks Cibber, 134-6; *Joseph Andrews*, 151 ff.; and Garrick 169-170; greatness of heart, 175-7; *Jonathan Wild*, 178 ff.; and the Jacobites 186 ff.; second marriage, 191-2; chief magistrate for Westminster, 196, 197 ff., 249 ff.; *Tom Jones*, 210 ff.; *Amelia*, 234 ff.; ill health, 251, 253, 258-60; founds first detective force, 252-3; journey to Lisbon, 260, 261, 262 ff.; death at Lisbon, 273; the critics on, 274-9
Fielding, John, Canon of Salisbury (grandfather), 12, 238
Fielding, John (brother) 10, 20, 198, 199, 244, 248, 260, 267, 271, 274
Fielding, Mary Amelia (daughter) death of, 204
Fielding, Sarah (sister) 7, 90, 91, 186, 190, 191, 245, 248, 274
Fielding Lodge, 90
Foote, Samuel, 195, 246, 255
Fordhook, 253, 261, 268, 272
'Forty-Five, The. *See* Jacobites
Fox, 46, 191
Francis, St., 153-4
Full Vindication of the Duchess of Marlborough, 164, 168

Garnett, Edward, 276
Garrick, 32, 58, 61, 74-5, 106, 107, 177, 188, 195, 208, 231-2, 233; friendship with Fielding, 169-170; parsimony and generosity, 170
Gay, John, 41, 43, 44, 47, 52, 62, 175
Gazetteer, The, 138
General Advertiser, 204
General History of England, 195
Gentleman's Magazine, 10, 140, 216, 235, 246
George Barnwell, 124, 126

Gibbon, Edw., 220, 275 ; on *Tom Jones*, 13
Giffard, 122, 123
Gil Blas, 151
Gin Lane, 205
Gin Menace, The, 205
Girard, Father, 76, 77
Glastonbury, 7 ff., 199
Glastonbury Script, 8, 9, 11, 89
God's Dealing with Mr. Whitefield, 148
God's Revenge Against Murder, 184
Goldsmith, 54, 249
Good Natured Man, The, 23
Gould, Davidge, 14, 17, 24
Gould, Sir Henry (grandfather) 8, 14, 15
Gould, Lady (grandmother) 12, 14, 16–19
Gould, Sarah, Mrs. Edmund Fielding (mother) 12, 14, 16
Grandison, Sir Charles, 153, 237
Graves, Rev. Richard, 91, 218
Gray, Thomas, 165
Great Moghul's Company, The, 108, 109
Grub Street, 36, 51, 54, 55, 102, 123, 163, 177, 194
Grub Street Journal, 70, 75, 79–80, 102, 104, 109
Grub Street Opera, The, 68–9, 70, 80
Guzzle, Landlord (*Don Q. in England*) 38–39

Hamlet, 58, 170, 231, 232, 233
Handel, 29, 48, 55, 56, 62, 63, 65, 83
Hapsburg, House of, 13
Hardy, Thomas, 179
Harlots Progress, The, 102, 103–4
Harrison, Dr. (*Amelia*), 236, 237, 238, 241, 242, 243
Hazlitt, 40, 210, 275
Heartfrees, the (*Jonathan Wild*) 180, 182, 183, 184
Hele, Richard, 222

Heidegger, 60, 62
Henley, Orator, 56, 99, 118
Henley, Robert, 167–8
Henley, W. E., 277
Hill, Abraham, 219
Hill, The Misses, 219–20
Historical Register for 1736, 117–20, 121, 124, 127
History of his Own Times, Burnet's, 164
Hogarth, 47, 53, 61, 75, 93, 109, 117, 121, 137, 177, 187, 193, 195, 205, 210, 221, 263 ; contrasted and compared with Fielding, 99 ff.
Holland, 38, 179, 183
Homer, 21, 174
Horace, 21, 252, 271
Howard, John, 208
Howard, Mary, 16
Hudibras, 121
Hunter, Dr., 264, 267
Hurd, Rev. Richard, 235
Hurlothrumbo, 56, 60
Husband, Jane, 167–8
Hussey, Mrs., 13, 176, 227

Iago, 180
Iliad, 236
Intriguing Chambermaid, The, 78

Jacobite's Journal, The, 178, 193, 194, 196, 216
Jacobites, Fielding and the, 85, 186 ff., 211
James, Colonel (*Amelia*) 240, 243
Jesuit Caught. See *Old Debauchees, The*
Jewkes, Mrs. (*Pamela*) 142, 143, 147
Johnson, Dr., 51, 54, 61, 77, 78, 127, 144, 231, 244

INDEX 285

Jonathan Wild, 23, 42, 127, 138, 169, 174, 196, 213, 275, 276; a masterpiece of irony, 178 ff.; Saintsbury's opinion, 178, 181, 185; satirizes Walpole, 185
Joseph Andrews, 15, 35, 36, 92, 107, 129, 151 ff., 169, 181, 190, 196, 212, 215, 244, 262
Journal (Wesley's) 47
Journal of a Voyage to Lisbon. See Voyage to Lisbon
Journey from this World to the Next, 45, 128, 166, 167, 169, 171–4, 275
Justice Caught in His Own Trap (The Coffee-House Politician) 65

Key to Pasquin, A, 109
'Keyber, Conny', 146

Lamb, Charles, 101, 103, 275, 276
Law, Fielding's application to, 128, 129, 170
Lewis, Joseph, 24, 26
Leyden University, Fielding at, 37–8, 128
Licensing Bill 1737, sets up censorship, 122; Chesterfield's opposition, 122–3; silences political satire, 123; ends Fielding's career as playwright, 126
Life and Death of Common Sense, The (Pasquin) 109, 110, 131
Lillibulero, 188
Lillo, George, 124, 125, 126
Lincoln's Inn Theatre, 41
Lisbon, 130, 176, 186; Fielding's journey to and death at, 260, 261, 262 ff.
Little Haymarket Theatre, 55, 70, 74, 108, 109, 117, 121, 123, 124
London, the social scene in Fielding's day, 51–3; the coffee-houses, 51, 66–8; crime and mob rule, 197, 201–3, 204–9; decline of crime in, 252–3

London Advertiser, 10
London Evening Post, The, 193, 194
London Magazine, The, 82, 138, 216, 246
Longspée, William, 85, 223
Lottery, The, 68, 79
Lovat, Lord, 107
Love in Several Masques, 29, 31, 33, 34, 35, 127
Love's Last Shift, 149
Lucian, 231; Fielding plans to translate, 251
Lyme Regis, Fielding at, 24–27
Lyttelton, Lord, 23, 46, 91, 108, 122, 177, 192, 203, 213, 218

Macbeth, 208
Macklin, 268
Magistrate, Fielding as. See Bow Street
Magna Carta, 85, 223
Manon Lescaut, 29
Marforio, 110
Mariage à la Mode, 104
Marie Antoinette, 164
Marivaux, 163, 230
Marlborough, Duchess of, 135, 137, 168
Marlborough, Duke of, 12, 168
Matthews, Miss (Amelia) 235, 238, 239, 240, 241, 243, 245
Médecin Malgré lui, Le, 76
Memorabilia, of Zenophon, 191
Meredith, George, 277
Middle Temple, Fielding at the, 128, 129
Middleton, Dr. Conyers, 146
Milford Manor, 91, 218
Millar, Andrew, 168, 189, 198, 200, 267; agreement with Fielding for Joseph Andrews, 163–4; for Tom Jones, 216; for Amelia, 234
Miller, Sanderson, 218
Milton, John, 118, 174, 278

INDEX

Misavan, John, 217-8
Miscellanies, 27, 83, 130, 164, 166, 169, 171, 174, 175, 178, 260
Miss Lucy in Town, 164, 168
Mitford, Miss, 24
Modern Husband, The, 74, 75, 93, 150
Molière, 76, 77, 274
Monmouth, Duke of, 25
Montagu, Mrs., 67
Montague, Lady Mary Wortley, 23, 28, 29, 35, 74, 165, 190, 191, 192, 199, 246, 264; on Fielding's character, 22, 36-7
Montaigne, 199, 209, 212
Moore, Edward, 203-4
More, Hannah, 275
Murphy, Arthur, 36, 37, 55, 74, 75, 94, 95, 96, 128, 129, 137, 236, 275
Mussett, Alfred de, 144

Newcastle, Duke of, 258, 259
Newgate, 42, 180, 183, 202, 204
Non-Juror, The, 135
Novel, the, comes to life with Pamela, 141; Richardson and the analytical n., 145; Joseph Andrews and picaresque, 151

Oedipus Tyrannus, 275
Old Boswell Court, 92, 186, 191, 218
Old Debauchees, The, 76, 80, 188
Old England, 192, 194, 196, 199, 216, 217
Oldfield, Anne, 28, 29-30, 35
Oliver, Parson, of Motcombe, 15, 157, 158
Orphan, The, 135, 249
Our Village, 24
Overton, 24

Page, Lord Justice, 227
Pamela, 22, 154, 162, 163, 164, 166, 192, 211; a picture of female virtue, 140-5
Pamela's Conduct in High Life, 145
Partridge (Tom Jones) 38, 131, 181, 226 ff.
Pasquin, 118, 133; a satire on folly, 108ff.
Paysan Parvenu, Le, 163
Peacham, Polly, 41, 47, 49
Penlez, Bosavern, 202-3, 234
Pepusch, Dr., 48
Pepys, Samuel, 12, 22, 25
Peregrine Pickle, 192
Phillips, Ambrose, 198
Pilkington, Letitia, 36, 51, 93, 106, 134, 145
Pitt, William, earl of Chatham, 23, 91, 108, 218
Plato, 21, 159, 264
Pleasures of the Town, 57
Plutus (Aristophanes) 169
Polly, 43, 44, 47
Poor Law Reform, Fielding's scheme, 251-2
Pope, 23, 31, 56, 57, 58, 63, 70, 80, 91, 109, 140, 177; on Anne Oldfield, 30
Pounce, Peter (Joseph Andrews) 161, 162
Prévost, Abbé, 29, 140
Price, Harry, 82, 238
Prior, Park, 91, 168
Prompter, The, 115
Proposal for a New Poor Law, 207

Queen of Portugal, 260, 261, 262, 264, 265, 269, 271
Queensbury, Duchess of, 43
Quin, 195

INDEX

Rabelais, 23, 210
Rake's Progress, The, 99, 102, 105
Ralph, James, 108
Ranby, Dr., 246, 259
Rape of the Lock, 63
Rape upon Rape (The Coffee-House Politician) 65
Rapha, or Raza, Anne. See Fielding, Anne
Reade, Charles, 208
Regicide, The, 244
Return, The, 232
Rhodes, Ambrose, 24
Rich, John, 40, 65, 68, 83, 110, 115; satirized in the Author's Farce, 60–2
Richardson, Samuel, 22, 91, 139, 153, 165, 191, 211, 216, 236, 244–5, 274; his Pamela, 140–5; believes Fielding to be author of Shamela, 149, 150; dislikes Tom Jones, 219–221
Rider, Sir Dudley, 166
Roast Beef of Old England, The, 69, 124
Robin Hood Society, 249
Rookes, Mary, 18, 19
Ruskin, John, 276

St. Martin's-in-the-Fields, 171
St. Thomas's Church, 85, 187
Saintsbury, Professor, 276, 278; on Jonathan Wild, 178, 181, 185
Salisbury, 16, 78, 79, 82, 88, 89, 91, 92, 93, 94, 129, 187, 218, 222, 223, 238; etiquette at, 83–5
Sally in our Alley, 63, 64
Sarum. See Salisbury
Scott, Sir Walter, 276
Scudéry, Mlle. de, 140
Seagrim, Molly (Tom Jones) 224, 225, 227
Shakespeare, 8, 58, 60, 63, 109, 115, 119, 153, 203, 230, 232, 275, 277, 278

Shamela, a parody of Pamela, 145–50; question of authorship, 146, 149
Sharpham Park, 7, 10, 11, 25
Shaw, Bernard, 278
Sheppard, Jack, 45, 179
Sheridan, 31
Silas Marner, 213
Smollett, 62, 192, 204, 244, 276
Socrates, 176
Sorrow, 134
Square (Tom Jones) 222, 223
Squeezum, Justice (Coffee-House Politician) 66
Steele, Sir Richard, 36, 58, 67
Stephen, Sir Leslie, 278
Stour, East, 14, 15, 16, 22, 95, 96, 97, 115, 128, 129, 157, 160, 225
Stuart, Lady Louisa, 192
Sublime Society of Beef-Steaks, The 61
Suckling, Sir John, 83
Sunday Chronicle, 10
Swift, 22–3, 42, 54, 107, 175, 188, 212, 278

Taine, 279
Tale of a Tub, 185
Tatler, the, 32
Temple Beau, 65
Thackeray, 66, 152, 213, 215, 239, 275, 276, 277
Theatre, the 18th cent., intimacy between stage and audience, 30–1; conventions, setting, properties, 32; announcements of public events, 32; debasement of, 60; effect of Licensing Bill on, 124; protrayal of humble life in, 125
Thompson, Dr., 204
Thrasher, Justice (Amelia) 238
Thwackum (Tom Jones) 222, 223, 224, 225
Tickletext, Parson (Shamela) 146
Todd, John, 47

INDEX

Tom Jones, 15, 23, 26, 34, 36, 38, 63-4, 83, 85, 93, 94, 100, 105, 131, 165, 174, 181, 190, 191, 234, 238, 239, 244, 245, 275, 276; Gibbon on, 13; traditions regarding place where it was written, 87, 88-9, 90, 91, 218; attacked by the 'King of the Beggars', 131-2; epitome of human nature, 210-214; autobiographic element, 214-6; hostility to, 216-221; the plot outlined 221ff.

Tom Thumb the Great, 54, 100, 112, 150; satirizes Walpole and play-writing of the day, 70-4

Tragedy of Tragedies. See Tom Thumb the Great

Trivia, 52

True Patriot, The, 168, 187, 189, 190

Trulliber, Parson (*Joseph Andrews*) 151, 153, 157, 158

Tucker, Andrew, 24, 25, 26

Tweedle, Jemmy, 15, 225

Twerton-on-Avon, 90, 218

Twickenham, 92, 191, 192, 218

Tyburn, 42, 44, 45, 46-7, 70, 105, 124, 178, 179, 180; Tyburn Holiday, 205, 208

Universal Gallant, The, 93

Universal Register Office, 199, 244, 245, 260

Upton Gray, 24, 27

Veale, Richard, master of the *Queen of Portugal*, 260, 261, 262, 263, 265, 267, 269, 271

Veil, Sir Thomas de, 196, 198

Venus in the Cloister, 148

Vernoniad, 137

Victor, Benjamin, 188

Vinegar, Hercules, Fielding's pseudonyn in the *Champion Journal*, 132, 133, 149

Virgin Unmasked, The, 93

Voltaire, 222, 274

Voyage to Lisbon, 89, 165, 262, 264, 271, 275, 278

Voyage Round the World, 273

Wade, General, 13, 219

Walpole, Horace, 67, 192, 194, 197, 200, 275

Walpole, Sir Robert, 42, 49, 60, 80-1, 108, 117, 119, 122, 123, 132, 137, 138, 174-5; satirized in the *Grub Street Opera*, 68-9; in *Tom Thumb*, 70; in *Jonathan Wild*, 185

Wanton Jesuit, The, 76

Warton, Joseph, 190

Wedding Day, The, 74, 169, 170

Welch, Saunders, 198, 202, 207, 262, 265, 267

Wesley, John, 47

Western, Sophia (*Tom Jones*) 9, 63, 91-2, 190, 223, 224 ff.; portrait of Fielding's first wife, 26, 83, 214

Western, Squire (*Tom Jones*) 9, 34, 35, 38, 223

Westminster, Fielding takes the oath as chief magistrate for, 196

Whitefield, Mrs. (*Tom Jones*) 226

Whole Duty of Man, The, 22, 102, 148, 154

Whyting, Abbot, 10-11

Widcombe Lodge, 91

Wilkes, John, 107

Williams, Charles Hanbury, 23

Williams, Parson, 147, 148

Wilson, Mr. (*Joseph Andrews*) 159-160

Windover House, 87-9, 93

Woffington, Peg, 41, 43, 61, 170, 188, 195

Woolf, Leonard, 211

Worthy, Justice, 66, 101

Wycherley, 34, 38, 151

Xenophon, 191

Young, Rev. William, 97-8, 164, 168, 251; prototype of Parson Adams, 15, 95; death of, 163